AF559880

TEXTBOOK OF MANAGERIAL COMPUTING

TEXTBOOK OF MANAGERIAL COMPUTING

By
Rajib Lochan Panigrahy
M.A. (Economics), PGDCA, MBA

DISCOVERY PUBLISHING HOUSE PVT. LTD.
NEW DELHI-110 002

Published by:
Tilak Wasan

DISCOVERY PUBLISHING HOUSE PVT. LTD.
4831/24, Ansari Road, Prahlad Street
Darya Ganj, New Delhi-110002 (India)
Phone : +91-11-23279245, 43764432
Fax : +91-11-23253475
E-mail : parul.wasan@gmail.com
discoverypublishinghouse@gmail.com
web : www.discoverypublishinggroup.com

First Edition: **2011**
ISBN: 978-81-8356-922-4

Textbook of Managerial Computing

Printed at:
Shree Balaji Art Press
Delhi

Preface

Now-a-days computer is ubiquitous for men in every walks of life. In recent age, the service providers are rendering their service through Information Technology (IT). Today every thing is in information highways consisting of data in database. So, computer is a friendly device to every men. So, no can say I am not to be computer friendly. If anybody is not computer savvy, she/he will be legging behind.

Today education is computer savvy. Education became easier with the help of IT. The IT has helped the students for e-learning. Any type of learning can be available in internet. So, many courses of higher education became on-line. So, except computer, no education is advantageous. Education became vocationalised which needs computer relation with the subject. Many of courses are opening day-by-day and more and more research is going on for the development of IT. Now, every thing is 'e', i.e. electronic which is related to computer and internet. In every sphere of life, the solution is in internet. Internet is assistant, teacher, friend, entertainer, guide and so on for any body. Even government is running through internet called as e-governance. Education became e-education, Business became e-business, banking transactions can be made as e-banking, and so on. So, education of Information Technology became a necessity for all. For the sake of reader, this book has been developed. It also be helpful for the students undergoing courses such as PGDCA, BCA, BBA, BES, BMS, BSc-IT/CS/CA, BA (Econ/Comm.), MCA, MSc-IT/CS/SW Engg., etc., MBA, PGDBM, PGDBA, PGDM, etc. Now, Government of India made IT as a compulsory paper in degree courses, most of the universities are adopting it. In several State governments the college courses are became dual, i.e. technical qualification like e-commerce, IT, electronic and telecommunication, etc. with university certifications.

This book contains chapters from introduction to Computer and its developments up to networking along with the applications of computer in word processing for correspondence and literary works, spread sheet for accounting purposes, power point for presentation of any topic through slide shows in any meeting, conference and seminars. The management students and other students of developmental studies and behaviour science courses barely need the power point presentations in their studies and jobs.

Hope, this book will suit the trainees, IT teachers for reference, so that my effort will be fruitful. And an appeal for any discrepancy, error found in the book may be intimated, which will be rectified in next revised editions. Readers are requested to excuse for any topographic errors. The software used in the chapters are the facilitators of the concerned company and the copyrights are with concerned company. The facilities and provisions are vested with the concerned company who produced it.

Rajib Lochan Panigrahy

Contents

1

Introduction to Computer

Introduction

Computer is generally known as an electronic machine, The word 'Computer' is derived from the word 'compute' which means to calculate. It emphasises that 'computer is a machine which is used for arithmetic calculations at an enormous speed.' But, now-a-days more than 3/4th of the users are using computer for non-mathematical purposes. This computer should be also known as an electronic machine which transforms data into information. Data are just the raw material and information is the finished product. Computer is only the processing machine. The data should be either mathematical or non-mathematical. A computer is very versatile machine which is capable of performing many diversified functions at an unbelievable speed with full of accuracy.

Now-a-days the friendliness of human being is growing in such a way that in the pave of human being computer is there. Thus it is said as 'Computer Age' or 'Computer Era'. In this era, computer is massive in use. In any case computer is helpful as shadow of own is always near.

Computer is ubiquitous in such a manner. Man became mechanical by getting computer as friend. In Railway station ticket counter, bus stand ticket counter, air port, traffic control, diagnosis, in law and justice, weather forecasting, horoscope, translating books one language to another, science and research, satellite, searching words from a book, etc. computer will be mostly helpful. In stead of these in schools, colleges, hospitals computers are mushroom. Today in home also the personal computers are used for funny and playing games. By the use of computer we become free and avail the facilities of time saving, complete accuracy, easy going, easy memory capacity. It is also helpful in office automation, used in banking system, used for inventory control, payroll calculations, etc.

Characteristics of Computer

Why computer is a versatile machine. The versatility of computer as follows :

1. **Abundance calculating speed:** Computer can perform an unbelievable huge work in a fraction of seconds. It can perform a task Millions of times greater than human can. Any body can not imagine the speed of the computer. The speed of the computer should be measured in the fractions of seconds like the terms as Mili-second (10^{-3}) Micro-second (10^{-6}), Nano-second (10^{-9}), Pico-second (10^{-12}). A powerful computer can do 3 to 4 million arithmetic operations per second.
2. **Free from Bug:** The word 'Bug' means error. Computer is free from bug. It gives most accuracy which depends upon its design. But, a particular computer calculates each and every calculation with accuracy. Accuracy is its key advantage. The error occurs not by computer but by human mistake. It will be the mistake done by the user. If the user mis-feed or less knowledge on computer the error may occur.

3. **Diligence:** Computer is free from tiredness, monotony, lack of concentration, etc. and hence can work for hours together without creating any error and without grumbling.

4. **Versatility:** It is used for many purposes. The most wonderful thing is that it does pay roll, after it complete it may prepare electric bill, then mark sheet and so on. There is no tiredness and no lesser intelligence for change of work.

5. **Rememberness:** It is known as storage or memory of a computer. Computer he its own storage capacity, that is known as memory. It is a most significant and worth noting As man forgets there is no such case for computer. If any thing once entered in its memory, there will not be any cases of volatile. It also can store a full house documents. It has its secondary storage capacity which can be recalled from memory in any moment as per our requirement.

6. **No Intelligence Questions:** A computer is not magic box. It cannot have its own thinking power. It only performs the work of human being as the user handle it. Thus it is ask that "Computer is a super servant of human being". Hence, computer cannot take its own decision

7. **No Feeling:** Computer has no feeling. It is devoid of emotions. Computer is mar made, but has no feeling, experience, judgment on life, knowledge in various steps of life. The judgment is required certain instructions will be written in the form of programme by the user which can be executed by the computer and the specific judgment is given by the computer.

In short, we came to the conclusion that *computer* stands for "Commonly Oriented Machine Purposefully Used for Technology, Education and Research".

Limitations of Computer

In spite of several advantages, the computer has certain fallacies as follows:

1. **Particularity:** Computer have to be told exactly what to do. Computer will know only what the programme have stored prepared by the user.
2. **No Judgment Power:** Computer cannot have judgment power. It can only be handled by the user and can be operated through programming techniques. So, if there is any error that is not of computer but of user. Thus it comes to the conclusion that "Computer is a super servant of human being."
3. **Portability:** Programmes and software prepared for one type of computer may not be usable on the other type of computers.
4. **Air-conditioning is mostly required for computer.** Environmental control inside the computer room should be required and uninterrupted power supply needed largely for mini computers and mainframe computers are imposing limitations in computer installation.
5. **Need of a Programmer/Skilled User:** Programming skill must be been used. Application logic must be understood.

EVOLUTION AND DEVELOPMENTS OF COMPUTERS

Necessity is the mother of invention. Invention and discovery is considered as the greatest achievement of mankind. Only in this point of view mankind take effort to develop all kinds of calculating devices. The present computer is an evolution not an invention. Gradually, it is developed. It passes through several stages and thousand years it had taken.

In the Stone Age man used pebbles for calculating people, sheep, quantity of goods, animals, etc. For recurring one they had taken pebbles again and again. In such a way they calculated.

Then the calculations came to earth by replacing pebbles by sticks, scratches, symbols on stones and knots on a role. All these techniques of computing are made by physical efforts from man. The discovery of zero (0) is made by Indian mathematicians who had laid the founder stone for numeric system. The pioneer step in calculating with pebbles is known as 'portable adding machine'.

Abacus - The Pioneering Invention of Computers

The earlier device that qualified as a digital computer is the Abacus which is otherwise known as 'soroban'. Simply, abacus has been use since 350 BC. Abacus was first developed in China. It is still used in the far east. It was the device which introduced the concept of data processing.

As abacus consists of wooden frame with rods carry in ground beads in wires. The frame is divide into two parts. The upper part is known as Heaven and the lower part is know as Earth. The middle wood between Heaven and Earth is known as Divider. In Earth beads close to divider represents the digit one (1) an one in lower parts represents zero (0).

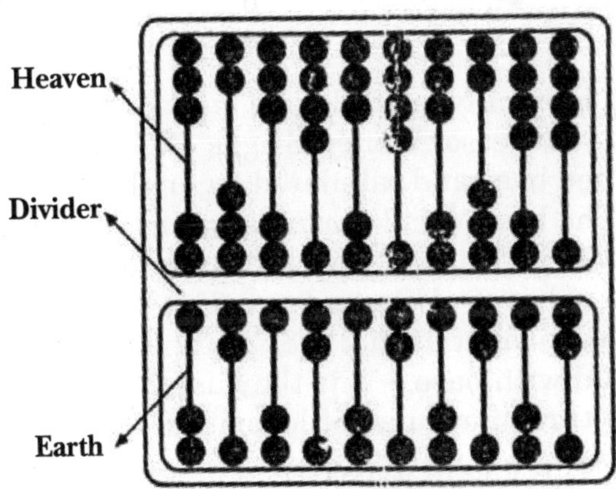

Fig. 1.1: Abacus

Napier's Logs and Bones

John Napier's Bones was the another manual calculating device which was otherwise known as cardboard multiplication calculator. It was designed in the early 17th century. He is a Scottish mathematician invented Algorithm Table. It was published in 1614 with simplified multiplication of large numbers. Formerly the logarithms called as artificial numbers. It is combination of the Greek terms "Logos" which means ratio and "Arithms" which means numbers.

Fig.1.2: **Logs and Bones**

Where Napier invented this he had no idea about base. Later in 1924 Professor Henry Briggs of Gresham College, London defined base and tabulated logarithm to be base as 'e' and '10'. The base 'e' is known as natural logarithm and the base '10' is known as common logarithm. The approximate value of 'e' is equal to 2.711. We may calculate logarithm as exponential. If 2 = 8, 2 will be base and 3 will be exponential with base e. 2 is the base 2 and exponential n. There are three formulae of logarithm as:

Log (M.N) = Log M + Log N;

Log (M/N) = Log M - Log N, Log M^N= N Log M.

Napier also invented a computing device consisting of eleven sticks with numbers carved on them. These sticks are called as 'bones' because they are looked like piece of bones. These bones helped a lot in calculation of multiplication and division involving large numbers.

There are many varieties of slide rules used as calculator performing addition, subtraction, multiplication, division, finding of squares, square root, etc. It is calculated by estimating the actual distance from the starting point of the rule are proportional to the logarithm of the numbers printed on the rule by moving the slide.

Pascal's Adding Machine – An Evolution of Mechanical Calculator

The next attempt on the computing history was made by the great French Mathematician Blais Pascal. In 1642 at the age of 16 he had invented a machine using gears, cog wheels and dials. By rotating cog wheels this machine displays numbers. Cog wheel is the tooth wheels. These tooth wheels are numbered from 0 to 9. This machine was used for addition and subtraction up to 8 digits. It is his pioneering step in the invention of mechanical calculator. It had the important principles as carrying calculation automatically and multiplication of numbers performing by adding repeatedly.

Fig. 1.3: **Blaise Pascal**

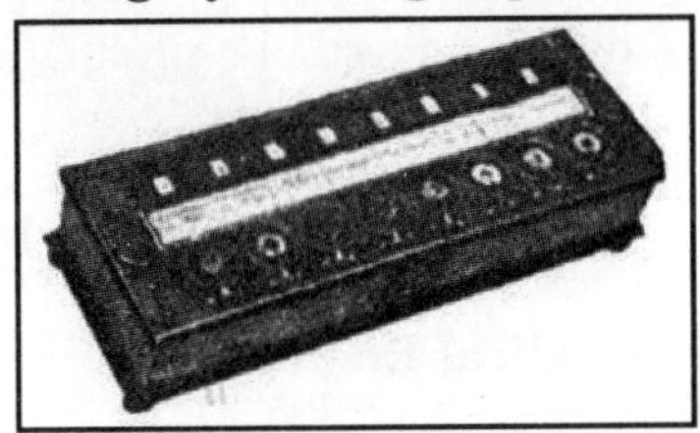

Fig. 1.4: **Pascal's Adding Machine**

Leibnitz's Stepped Reckoner

But in 1673 Gottfried Wilhelm Von Leibnitz invented calculating machine by developing the Pascal's calculator which could add, subtract, multiply and divide. He used stepped cylinders each with nine teeth varying by length instead of wheels used by Pascal. He introduced Binary system in calculating machine with the Binary numbers Os and Is.

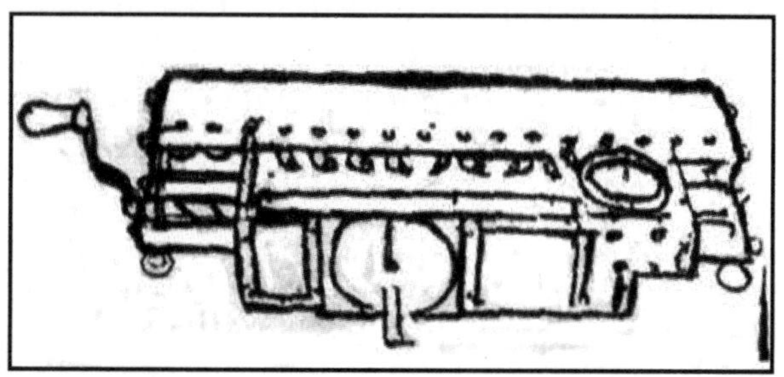

Fig. 1.5: **Leibnitz's Machine**

Jacquard's Loom — 'A Beginning of Punched Card'

At an early nineteenth century Joseph M. Jacquard came up with an ingenious idea which automated a weaving loom. He invented the automated loom in 1804. He used punched cards for automated loom which depends upon the absence or presence of holes on the card. Hence Jacquard's loom paved the way for the modern storage mechanism.

Fig. 1.6: **Jaquard's Loom**

Charls Babbage's Analytical Engine

Charls Babbage, the Professor of Mathematics in British is the founder of modern computer. Thus, he is regarded as "Father of Computers". He had developed a mechanical computer called *Differential Engine* in 1822. It is so called since it was based on the difference tables of the squares of numbers. It was to have hundreds of gears, shafts and counters. In spite of the serious and continuous efforts, Babbage reached at the certain stage of improvement of this machine became constant. Encouraged by the success of Differencial Engine, he planned to design another machine named as Analytical Engine in 1833.

Fig. 1.7: **Charls Babbage**

Analytical machine used the concept of Automated Loom and Difference Engine. It could be capable of performing all the four arithmetic operations - addition, subtraction, multiplication, division and square roots, percentage. It was the significant step in the history of computers. It had the capacity to make decisions, repeated calculation, skip some steps in a calculation, go back to a particular steps. He had developed the mechanism to store numbers. It could be able to store a thousand 80 digit numbers. It has the advantage to input data and getting output. Control unit did the job of supervision of all the units.

Thus it is the pioneer of modern computers. The input materials in the form of programmes was developed by Lady Ada Lovelace. Due to this contribution the language of programme is known as ADA.

Evolution of Calculator

The input step in the growth of electronic machine is evolution of calculators by Frank Baldwin in 1872. This year is the hall mark of beginning of the calculator industry in U.S.A.

Fig.1.8: Analytical Engine

In 1887 D F. Felt constructed a Key-driven adding machine which he called Marconi Box, now known as Comptometer. J. R. Manroe developed a rotary Keyboard Calculator in 1911. This keyboard calculator was commercially very successful. It is extensively used now also.

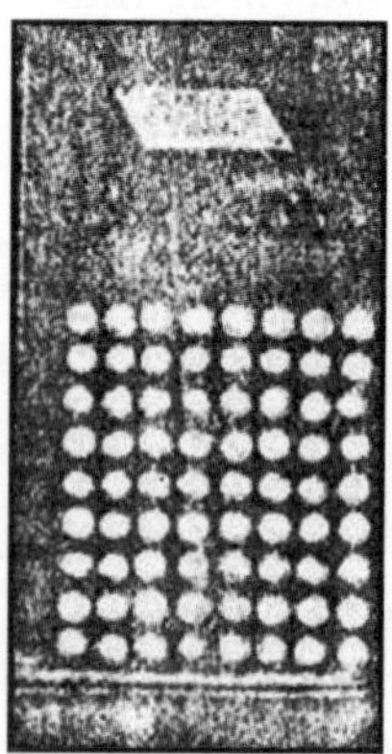

Fig.1.9: Dorr E. Felt's key-driven adding machine

Hollerith's Machine

The first card machine which was electrically activated, used by Dr. Herman Hollerith to compute the statistics of the 1890s U.S. Census Bureau. He invented a machine that punched holes on cards. This machine is called *Tabulator*. In this machine all data to be processed are keyed in a card. This machine processed the cards by detecting holes by electric contacts and also performed the functions of selecting and sorting of the cards. In 1896, he established his own company, named Tabulating Machine Company (TMC). The same company is today popularly known as International Business Machine Corporation in sort IBM.

Fig. 1.10: **Hollerith's Machine**

Havard Mark-1

In 1937 the first automatic computer Havard Mark-I was developed by Hathway Aiken and John H. Nipe which was huge in size. It is used around 3000 electrically activated switches to control its operations. It is approximately 50 feet long and 8 feet high in size. It is capable of five basic arithmetic operations and table reference. A number of 23 decimal digits could be used in this machine.

Fig. 1.11: **Havard Mark-1**

Though it was an electro-mechanical device, both the electronics and mechanical components were used in its architecture. It is also designed for the use of punched papers.

The Atonosoff-Berry Computers (ABC)

This electronic device was developed by Dr. John Atonosoff with his assistant Clifford Berry. It had used 45 Vaccum Tubes for internal logic and capacitors for 300 vaccum tubes to add and subtract.

Fig. 1.12: **John Atonosoff and his ABC computer**

Electronic Numerical Integrator and Calculator (ENIAC)

The Electronic Numerical Integrator and Calculator was the first electronic computer. It is the landmark of generation of computers. It was developed and switched on in 14th Feb., 1964 by Prof. J. Presper Eckert and John Mauchely at Moore School of Electronical Engineering of University of Pensylvenia in U.S.A. It was developed as a result of military needs. It took up the wall space in 20 sq, feet length and 40 sq. feet width room and used 18,000 vacuum tubes. It could add two numbers in 200 Micro (10^{-6}) seconds and multiply in 200 Micro (10^{-6}) seconds.

Although it was much faster than Mark-I computer, having the major drawbacks as its storage capacity is very limited and programmes were wired on boards. These limitations made it difficult to detect the errors and change the programmes.

However, it had the advantages that it was used for ballistic tables, weather predictions, atomic energy calculation and random number studies.

Fig. 1.13: ENIAC

Electronic Discrete Variable Automatic Computer (EDVAC)

Due to the operation of ENIAC was seriously handicapped the wiring board, the problem was later over come by the new concept of 'store programme' by Dr. John Von Neumann a Hungarian Mathematician. He developed Electronic Discrete Variable Automatic Computer (EDVAC) with the concept of stored programme to place the computer instruction in computer's main memory in the form of numbers in the manner that data stored can be processed. He had also introduced the idea of storing both instructions and data in the binary form - 0s and 1s instead of decimal numbers or in readable form. It is the hallmark of modern digital computer. Electronic Delay Storage Automatic Calculator (EDSAC).

Simultaneously, with EDVAC in U.S.A., the Britishers developed the EDSAC. The machine started its operation in 1949. It was developed by a team of scientists headed by Professor Mourice Wilkies at Cambridge University. It takes 50,000 Microseconds and accomplishing arithmetic operations and 4,000 Microsecond for multiplication.

Manchester Mark-1 Computer

It was a small experimental machine based on the stored programme concept, designed by Professor M. H. A. Neumann at Manchester University. Its storage capacity was 32 words, each of 31 binary digits. It is too limited to store data and instructions.

Universal Automatic Computer (UNIVAC-I)

The UNIVersal Automatic Computer (UNIVAC) was the first digital computer. The UNIVAC machines were produced, the first of which was installed in the Census Bureau in 1951 and was used for continuous 10 years. The first business use of a computer a UNIVAC-I which was developed by General Electric Corporation in 1954. The UNIVAC-I was also used for calculation of Presidential

Elections in United States. In 1952 International Business Machine (IBM) Corporation introduced 701 commercial computers. In rapid succession, improved models of the UNIVAC-I and other 700 series machines were introduced. In 1953 IBM produced IBM-650 and sold over 1,000 of these computers.

GENERATIONS OF COMPUTER BY DEVELOPMENTS

After World War II, computers developed at a gigantic rate and have been classified in terms of generations depending upon the technology used by these machines. In computer terminology "generation" means the steps in technological developments. It provides framework for the growth of computer industry. The custom of referring to the computer era in terms of generation came into wide use only after 1964. These are totally five computer generations till today.

First Generation Computers (1942-54)

The ENIAC, EDVAC, EDSAC, etc. are belonging to first generation computers. In these 'vaccum tubes' and 'valves' are used. The ENIAC can be considered as a big house and put light up a small town. These were the advantages that vacuum tubes were only electronic components. It is an advent of electronic digital machine. It was the first calculating machine.

Fig. 1.14: **Vaccum Tube**

The disadvantages were that they were bulky in size, unreliable, very high heat generation, continuous and constant maintenance, require air conditioned, importable, commercial production difficult, costly and has limited use.

The another point of advantage in the invention of input device was Card Reader using Punched Cards. The Output devices was Printer. There was the invention of binary numbers. There was the concept introduced that invention of storage system by binary language.

Second Generation Computers (1955-64)

The machines of the 1st generation were improved. There was the introduction of transistors instead of vacuum tubes and valves. The transistors are introduced by a galaxy of scientists namely J. Bardeen, H.W. Brattain and W. Shockley for which they received Nobel Prize in 1947 at Bell Laboratories. In this generation the vacuum tubes were replaced by transistors and diodes. These transistors made of Germanium Semi Conductor material whose key ingredient is silicon. Since the transistors are highly reliable compared to the vacuum tubes and do not have any filament to burn, occupies less space, require less power for operation, relatively having higher speed, it provides a path breaking contribution to the computer generation. Vacuum tubes were replaced into transistors in 1959. The size of the transistor is l/200th of the size of vacuum tubes. Thus computers using transistors are known as 2nd generation computers.

The Magnetic Core Memory for storage of data and instruction also invented in this generation. This magnetic cores were used to construct large Random Access Memory (RAM). Magnetic Disks Storage were developed during this period.

The computer of this generation which emerged around 1960s using transistors had faster input-output units, better storage capacity, greater programming ability then their processors. The techniques of programming and programming language developed in this generation. The High Level Language (HLL) like Formula Translation (FORTRAN), Common Business Oriented Language

(COBOL), Algorithmic Language (ALGOL), String Oriented Symbolic Language (SNOBOL) and the Assembly Language were developed in this stage. Computer began to be used on a large scale for commercial applications around this time. More than 80% of computers were meant for business and industry purposes.

Despite these developments also there are bottlenecks of the II generation computers as it requires Air Conditioned, frequent maintenance, manual assembly of functional components, costly and difficult nature of commercial and industrial productions through these computers. The example of II generation computer were IBM-7000, NCR-304 (Nation Case Register), IBM-650, ATLAS, etc.

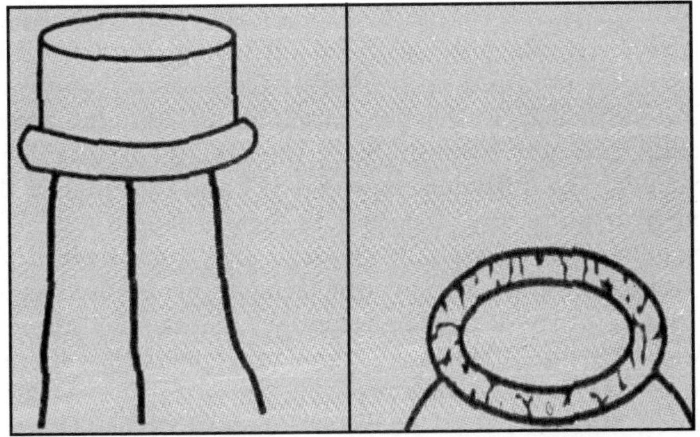

Fig. 1.15: **Transistors** *Fig. 1.16:* **Diode**

Third Generation Computers (1965-76)

The third generation of computers were introduced in 1965. Advances of electronic technology and advent of micro electronics technology made it possible to integrate large number of circuit elements into vary small i.e. 5 m.m. sq. surface of silicon known as *Integrated Circuits* (IC), otherwise known as Chip. The third generation of computer based on IC technology. The IC was invented by Jack Kilby at Taxas Instrument in 1958. There were distinct advancement in the design of Magnetic Core memory. The capacity of magnetic core memory was increased to 4 MB instead of 100 KB in II generation.

The third generation of computers used Printed Circuit Boards (PCBs), each PCB contains a number of ICs, many PCBs are consisting in Mother Board (MB). The Mainframe computers came on earth in this generation. Some of them are IBM-360, ICL-1900, IBM-370/168, Honeywell-316 etc. After development of Microprocessor chips, LSI, VLSI the manufacturer of mini-computers are rapidly increased. The development of SLI, VLSI, Chips mini-computers became small size, decreased its cost, increased the memory capacity and capacity for processing.

The circuits are produced either by Photographic Etching on crystals or by Metal-Oxide-Semiconductor (MOS) technology. In this generation Small Scale Integrated Circuits (SSI) and Medium Scale Integrated Circuits (MSI) were used. The difference between SSI and MSI in only the number of units used together to form a single unit. The third generation of computer were 10,000 times faster than the 1st generation computers. Mass storage devices or auxiliary storage devices or secondary storage devices such as Magnetic Tapes, Disks, etc. came into operation. Different type of I/O devices appeared on the scene i.e. Optical scanner, Magnetic Ink Character Reader (MICR), Graphic Plotter. The processing techniques like batch processing, time-sharing processing came into picture during this period. The other major development in software during this generation was multiprogramming.

The multiprogramming means more than one programme can be present in the memory of the computer simultaneously. Many High Level Languages (HLL) like BASIC, COBOL, FORTRAN IV, PL/I, C & the COBOL compiler were developed.

Fourth Generation Computers (1976 onwards)

The ICs having entire computer circuitry on a single silicon chip are called *Microprocessor*. The development of Microprocessors made the computer possible to place complete CPU of a computer on a single chip. These computers are called as Micro Computers.

Magnetic memories have been replaced by semi-conductor memory in this generation computers. Micro Computers are user friendly and menu driven. Memory size is increased to 16 MB. VLSI packing about 10,000 transistors on a single chip. Disk memory has became very large in size i.e. 100 MB. Secondary storage devices like Floppy Disks and Tapes provide low cost and high capacity peripheral memory.

Network of computers have been developed. The data communication through network communicates the computers electronically and also allow the computers through a terminal located in a remote size. The data communication takes place over telephone lines or other communication methods.

With the development in both Hardware and Software increased the use of another mode of processing data i.e., transaction-oriented mode. In this mode of processing data entered into the computer system at the time of transaction rather than batching the transactions.

The first pocket computer (not the calculator) was a Japanese make sold in 1980. It was called SHARP PC 1211. The APPLE Series of Micro Computers were developed in Steven Wazniak and Steve Jobs in 1976. It was used 8 Bit Micro Processor chip. The chip enabled them to put together complete computer i.e. a Key Board and a screen, few thousand characters in memory, processor, all in a small box This also helped to reduce the cost of computer drastically. The IBM Corporation introduced *Personal Computer* (PC) in 1981. The IBM chose the Intel 8088 Micro Processor as the brains or engine inside the PC. The 8088 is just one memory of a family of Micro Processors, called 8088 family, designed by the pioneering silicon chip marker Intel. In 1983, IBM added to extended Technology (XT) to the PC family that is known as PC-XT. This facility added the higher capacity hard disk storage capacity to the PC. The Advanced Technology (AT) had introduced in 1984 and had been developed over the year which is known as PC-AT. Then the ancestor of 8086 born on as 80286, 80386, 80486, Pentium, Pentium-II respectively known as 286, 386, 486, Pentium and Pentium-II Processors.

All the computer languages introduced in this generation. The development of Programming Languages also became more powerful. One of the powerful language is ADA according to the name of Lady Ada Augustra Lovelace used for defence purposes. The language like C, PASCAL, FORTRAN 77, C+ + , COBOL 85, ANSI COBOL, the Operating System (OS) like DOS, UNIX all are developed during this period. This generation is the most powerful and remarkable period in the computer field.

Fifth Generation Computers

Now we are marching in the era of fifth generation computers. In all the above four generations are only the drawback is that the thinking power or intelligence. But in the Fifth Generation Hardware and Software were developed in such a way that the computer can produce human intelligence. And also with this the computer can speak and understand a simple language. The institute of New Generation Computer Technology in Japan is planning to develop Knowledge Information Processing System (KIPS) based on innovative inference functions and technologies that meet the needs anticipated in the 1990s including intelligent interaction between machine and inference using knowledge bases. Such a machine exhibits what may be called as Artificial Intelligency (AI).

It will dedicate the techniques of automatic programming, computational logic, pattern reorganisation to the computer era. The credit goes to Japan in fifth generation of computers Japan and chosen the PROLOG (Programming in Logic) language as its operating Software and plans to have the final machine talk with human beings, see and deliver pictures and hear the normal and natural languages. In this generation the Software's like JAVA; Oracle and it's version-Developers 2000; Windows 3.1, Windows 95, Windows NT; database-FoxBase,, dBase III+, Foxpro 2.5, Foxpro 2.6; Desk Top Publishing (DTP), communication networking-Internet; operating environment Windows 95, etc. are in mushroom and in most popularity in this computer age.

CLASSIFICATION OF COMPUTERS

The classification of computers is a very significant in going gaining an understanding of the key elements of computer architecture and the key difference among the computers. It is important to realise as per certain characteristics based on the difference of type, size, purpose and design.

Classification of Computers According to Type

The classifications of computers according to type is made into two i.e. Analog and Digital computers.

Analog Computers: Greek word 'analog' means establishing similarities between two qualities. In analog computer the similarities are established in the form of current or voltage signals. These computers operate by measurements and not by counting. In this system an electronic signal is created analogous to the variable of physical.

The automatic speedometer, the water meter, electric meter are some of the examples of analog computers. It has low memory capacity. A major disadvantage of this computer that it cannot represent non-numeric data. And it generally represents continuous varying data.

Thus Prof. D.H. Sanders in his famous book *Computer Today* proposed that "An Analog computer is one that measures physical values such as temperature or pressure that fall along a continuous scale."

Digital Computers: As name shows it operates on quantities represented as digits. They operate on discrete quantities. In digital computer both numeric and non-numeric data can be represented. These computers used binary digits Os and Is through discrete electric pulses. The digital computers only understands basically how to add. By rearranging this the subtraction, multiplication, division can be performed.

Some key examples of digital computers are Desk Calculators, Office Adding Machine etc.

Hybrid Computers: Desirable features of Analog and digital computers are combined to create a hybrid computers. In other words combined features of Analog and Digital computers possesses the features of a hybrid computer. The devices to convert analog signals to digital signals and *vice versa* help a lot to find the result in a desired form, that is known as MODEM, MODEM stands for MODulator and DEModulator. It transforms data analog to digital and digital to analog.

For example, in a hospital intensive-care unit, analog devices measure a patient's heart function, temperature and other vital signs. These measurements are then converted into numbers and supplies to a digit components that monitors the patient's vital signs and signals a nurse's station, if abnormal readings are detected.

Classification of Computers according to Purpose

The computers are classified according to the purpose. They are general-purpose and special-purpose:

1. **General-Purpose Computers:** These machines can deal with a variety of problems and they are able to meet the requirements of different needs. Generally for many purpose they can be used. For example, Payrolls, electric bills, billing counter systems, mark sheets, inventory control account, scientific calculations, etc. they can be used.

2. **Special-Purpose computers:** These computers are designed specially for separate purposes. These can only perform certain tasks. These are pre-designed to handle a particular problem. For example, a computer designed for lending of aircraft, measuring of weather condition, controlling of satellite, etc.

In spite of these most of the computers are digital devices. Digital computers can also be designed to perform one specific function. In special purpose digital computers, the instructions are wired into or permanently stored in the machine. The processors are wired into or permanently stored in the machine. The processors installed in automobiles to control fuel, ignition, instrument and breaking systems are solid examples of such computers. Unlike their special-purpose cousins, general-purpose digital computers can store different programmes and can thus be used in countless applications. By using different instructions such a machine can process a payroll one minute and draw a chart the next. The versatility of these systems is limited only by human imagination.

Classification of Computers by Size

Modern computers vary in physical size from those room size to those with CPUs that can rest on the nail of your little fingers. Generally the longer the system, the greater are its processing speed, storage capacity, cost and ability to handle large number of input and output devices. And also these computer has different characteristics length, main memory size, complexity of the I/O module, complexity of the Operating System (OS), physical size, virtual address space, Secondary memory size and degree of multi-programming. According to these above descriptions of computer by size it is divided into four as Micro, Mini, Mainframe, Super.

1. **Micro Computers:** Systems on the low end of the size scale are called Micro computers. Micro computers are the smallest units. A Micro computer is a processor all the whose components are on a single integer carrying out a single task such as controlling of automobile's ignition and the personal computers (PCs), ranging from Desktop size to present PCs.

Fig 1.17: **Micro Computer**

(a) **Home Computers:** In 3970s the British inventor Clive Sinclair, made home computer first. At that time the memory was 48 KB. These worked with home TVs if it had the VHP band. But at that time in India there were no such TVs in use. Towards 1982 India got colour TV with a VHP band. Thus at 1970s it was not in use in India.

Home computers are hobbyist rather than professional. These consists of Keyboards integrated with CPU on one box type thing and interfaced with ordinary TV and Audio cassettes. They are meant for entertainment and training. It may be used for learning purpose or playing of games as the central theme of entertainment.

Some popular home computers were ZX-80, ZX-81, Tandon's TRS 80, Atari 400, IBM's PC Junior, Commander, BBC Acron, Apple-H, etc. The computer made of Semi conductor Complex Limited known as SCL-Unicron are used largely for computer literacy as Computer Literary and Studies in Schools (CLASS) programme in India.

(b) **Personal Computers:** PCs are designed for personal or small units and small business purposes. They are meant for professionals, small business units and office automation system. PC can be used for variety of applications like computer literacy, computer training programme in BASIC, COBOL, C, Pascal, FORTRAN, FoxPro, etc.; fun and games, business and professional applications, Electronic Spreadsheets, Telecommunications, Data Base Management System (DBMS), Accounting, Word-processing, etc.

The Personal Computers consists of:

(i) Printed Circuit Boards (PCBs)

(a) Mother Board (MB);

(b) Display Board;

(c) I/O Board.

(ii) Key Board (KB)

(iii) Monitor or VDU

(iv) Hard Disk

(v) Floppy Disk

(vi) Memory (RAM)

Portable and transportable type PCs can be classified in size as briefcase or note book. Both types are light enough to be carried and do not need an external power source.

Micro computers used to be 80 KB to 256 KB. These computers are manufactured with 16 bit, 32 bit, 64 bit, 128 bit and 256 bit processors. They are popularly known as 80286, 80386, 80486, Pentium, Pentium-II processors. They have a speed of 100 KPS. The storage capacity has been extended from 640 KB to 64 MB.

PC-XT's (Personal Computer Extended Technology) and PC-AT's (Personal Computer Advanced Technology) can have Secondary or Auxiliary memory storage units. The most commonly used auxiliary memory or storage units are Floppy disks with various sizes i.e. 3.5", 5.25", etc. as well as Winchester Hard Disks. BBC Micro Computers, IBM PCs, Apple, Wipro, PCS, HCL, PCL, Compaq Presario, are some of the popular manufacturing companies widely used as PCs in India. Micro Soft Disk Operating System (MS-DOS), UNIX, Windows 95 are some of the examples of Operating Systems (OS) for Micro Computers.

2. **Mini Computers:** Micro computers are also small general purpose systems but unlike most micros they typically serve multiple users. They are usually more powerful and expensive than micro computers. But the performance of some newer micros surpasses the capabilities of some older minis. In physical size, mini computers vary from desktop models to units the size of small file cabinets. The mini computer was specifically designed for time sharing, It can support a wide range of on line processing activities. The examples of mini computer is BBC 900, Honeywell 1200, POP 11/730, IBM SYS13.

The storage capacities of the mini computers are vary according to the architecture of the computers i.e. from 4 MB to 256 MB. The CPU speed is 5 times more than the micro computers. The word length of mini computers ranges from 16 bits to 32 bits. Digital Equipment Corporation (DEC) of USA, Hawlett Packard (HP), etc. are the some manufacturing companies of the standard mini computers.

Fig. 1.18: **Mini Computer**

A 16-bit computer system with 512 KB memory and 20 MB removable hard disk used in mini computers, adopted 32 bit system with 10 MB main memory. The speed of mini computer is 500 KPS and can support a number of terminals with time sharing mode. Its storage capacity is in the range from 4 MB to 256 MB.

3. **Mainframe Computer:** Continuing the size, scale, mainframe computers are systems that offer processing speeds and greater storage than the typical minis. These computers are capable of solving all types of problems. It is used for significant applications like vast

Fig. 1.19: **Mainframe Computer**

engineering designs, research and development projects, architecture designing, etc. These computers are having huge memory ranging from 16 MB to 2 GB and its CPU speed is 50 to 500 MIPS (million instructions per second). The word length ranging from 32 to 64 bits. These machines uses chain printers as its outputs device, disks having capacity 1000 MB, 32 to 128 terminals as peripherals.

In mainframe computers tasks must pass through a centrally located system which is the focal point of all processing. The CPU acts as a clearing house for all inquires, controlling access to all files.

It is used to solve all type of problems. A few important applications in which these computers are used for large engineering designs, on line applications with large databases. These computers may be found out in universities, research centres, scientific organisations, large business houses, regional computer centres, etc. The key example of mainframe computers are IBM 3000, IBM 360, IBM 370, SYBER 170, Burroughs 7800, VAX 8842.

4. **Super Computer:** The super computers are the fastest computers made to solve a range of voluminous problems which needs abundant numerical calculations, weather predictions, calculation of molecular structure, temperature calculation, movement of satellite, etc. It is the real time system, also supports national defence and vast multinational corporations (MNC). These computers are needed to solve multivariate mathematical problems of real physical process, such as occur in nuclear and plasma physics. These problems need for high precision and programme that repetitively performs floating point arithmetic operations on large array of numbers. Most of these operations fall into the category known as continuous field simulation.

These machines are developed to handle such type of huge problems. These are typically capable of handling hundreds of Millions point Operations Per Second (MFLOPS) and cast in 15 to 20 million dollar range. Although it is capable of general purpose applications found on mainframes. It is optimised for type of numerical calculations with array.

It has the storage capacity ranging from 256 MB to 16 GB. Its CUP speed is more than 500 Megaflops. Its word length is 64 to 128 bits. High speed Laser Printers, Magnetic Disks, Magnetic Tapes, etc. are used as peripheral. The manufacturing companies like CRAY Research Inc. of U.S.A, ETA systems of U.S.A. Fujitsu of Japan, etc. are the producers of standard super computers. These super computers are also called as Hybrid Computers.

Fig.1.20: **Super Computer**

COMPUTER SYSTEMS

Introduction

Computer has a vital role in the field of data processing electronic equipment. The equipment physically required for a computer system is only known as computer. But, there is an invisible part which is most essential for a computer system; otherwise the computer system is meaningless. For example, human being has not only the physical parts like his handsome body but there is the visible part i.e. his memory, intelligence, morale and logic, etc. which activates his physical structure. Without memory or remembering capacity, intelligence, logic a man or woman can not be regarded as human being. Just like, computer system consists of two elements the physical structure called hardware and the internal or logical structure which helps in the activities of hardware called software.

Hardware

The physical components of a computer is known as hardware. They are the electronic, electrical and magnetic equipments which can be visible to the common eye. For example, CPU, VDU, keyboard, mouse, internal circuits, wires, disks, etc. are belongs to hardware. These equipments are the input devices output devices, processing units, etc. used to input, output and control the computer system. When the hardware elements will be equipped to form effective working unit that may be called as computer system. Through software (SW), the hardware elements can activated effectively for specific functioning. As a TV without antenna or disk connection or video connection, TV is futile. Like wise, Computer or hardware is useless without availability of software in the system. Thus, software refers to the kind of programmes that cause the hardware effective purposefully. The hardware alone can not do any job. These programmes or instructions play a vital role in the performance of a computer.

Software

A complete set of instructions written to solve a problem on computer is called as software(SW). SW refers to the set of computer programmes which enhance the capabilities of the hardware. A programme which has a key role which is nothing but a set of sequenced programmes is called as programmer. The programmer has to know the kind of instructions a computer can understand and break up the requirements of a programme into these instructions.

Types of Software

The large variety of programmes, which are required on the computers can be classified into three categories:

1. **Programming Language:** To use a computer there is a need of software (SW). Software is a sequenced set of instructions to be given by the programmer or user

to the computer for solving a required problem. As the instructions given to a servant to get any thing done, so is the case with the computer.

When ever we want to communicate some instructions to other, we need language as the medium of communication that person may understand our views. The language may apply in their daily life to communicate each other, that is the natural languages. And the programmes written with the instructions to communicate it to the computer is called as computer language or programming language. Each language has its several characteristic features suitable for a particular kind of job. So it is important to be in depth in a specific language.

There are several programming languages available on the computers. These languages are classified as

(a) Low Level Language

(i) Machine Level Language

(ii) Assembly Language

(b) High Level Language (HLL)

(i) Problem Oriented Language

(ii) Special Purpose Language

COMPUTERS ARCHITECTURE

Introduction

The physical components of computer refers to the components made it of electric, electronic and mechanical devices. It is known as 'hardware'. But there is one thing software refers to the programmes or programming techniques used to utilise devices of computer(hardware) to perform a specific task. Software activates hardware in a meaningful purpose. Hardware is essential for operation of the computer and the availability of software are required in the computer to utilise hardware for the solving the required solution. In stead of software, hardware is meaningless. Hardware and software altogether form computer system.

The computer is typically equipped with four significant ingredients viz. input, output units or devices, central processing unit (CPU) and memory unit. The CPU consists of Arithmetic Logic Unit (ALU), Control Unit (CU), primary memory and registers. The memory unit envelops primary memory, secondary memory. There is an unit named as I/O device abbreviated for Input and Output which are called as peripherals. The peripherals are the devices connected with CPU instead being a part of CPU. Hence, secondary memory devices can also be called as peripheral devices.

Structure of a Computer System

Every computer system performs five operations as follows:

1. **Input:** The process of entering data and instructions into the computer system. This will be performed by input devices.
2. **Storage**: Storage means saving of data and instructions into the computer system for further processing and future retrieval. It is done through memory device of the CPU of the computer system.
3. **Processing**: Performing required operation like arithmetic and logic on operations on the data to make them useful information. It is performed by the help of output devices or I/O devices.
4. **Output**: After processing data the result for the user should be displayed by the screen or through printer is known as output. It is performed by the help of output devices or I/O devices.
5. **Controlling**: Directing the manner and sequence in which all of the above operations are performed

through the inner components of CPU. It is done through control unit of the CPU.

Units of Computer

The sole aim of the chapter is to familiarise you with the computer system units that performing the functions. And familiarise the components of computer system. The computer system has its few units as:

1. Input unit
2. Central Processing Unit (CPU)
   (a) Control Unit (CU)
   (b) Arithmetic Logic Unit (ALU)
   (c) Register
3. Output unit
   (a) Visual/Video Display Unit (VDU) or Monitor
   (b) Printer
4. Memory Unit
   (a) Primary Memory
      (i) RAM
      (ii) ROM
   (b) Secondary Memory
      (i) Floppy Disk Drive (FDD)
      (ii) Hard Disk Drive (HDD)
      (iii) Compact Disk (CD)
      (iv) Magnetic Disk
5. I/O Devices
   (a) VDU

Flow operations of a computer system.

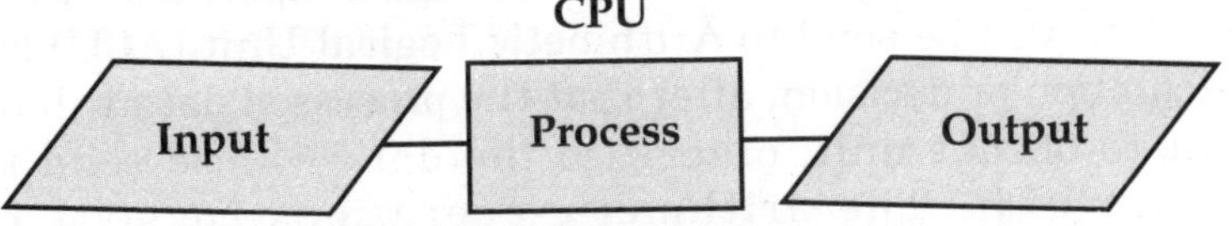

Fig. 1.21: **Computer Structure**

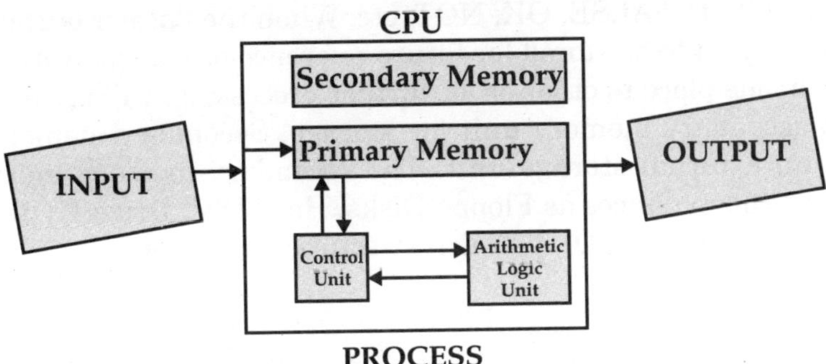

Fig. 1.22: **Computer Structure (Schematic)**

Functions of a Computer

The units of computer are elaborated through the block diagram depicted above. The first figure depicts that data are to be inputted through input units to the processing unit called as CPU(Central Processing Unit). The CPU takes necessary steps to process the data and send the processed things to the output unit(s). The finished things are displayed or printed or stored in the output units as final shape of the data.

The second figure is the schematic or detailed depiction of the units of a computer system how data are converted as output. The input units feed data in the computer. Computer receives data from input units which will immediately received by the primary memory. Primary sends the received data to the Control Unit (CU) to make the data controlled that whether there are any arithmetic (calculations) or logical (decision) operations are there or not. If there are any arithmetic or logical operation, then the data will be send to Arithmetic Logical Unit (ALU) for calculation or decision, after that the processed data will be sent to output unit, otherwise the data will be send to output unit. The arithmetic operations consists of addition(+), subtraction (-), multiplication (*), divisions (/), power, reminder, percentage, etc. and the decisions like YES, NO, TRUE, FALSE, OK, NOT, etc. When the data or output is required to be stored for future reference or transportation from one place to other or for further processing, will be send to secondary memory unit for storage. Secondary memory is an external storage unit. The secondary memory units have the instances as Floppy Disks, Hard Disk Drive(HDD), Compact Disk (CD), pen driver/thumb driver, etc.

Input Unit

Input units are functioning through input devices which transfers data and instructions into computer. These devices translates inputting contents from user language to machine language which the computer can understand. Generally these languages are in special code of language i.e. binary language. This code are known as binary code. The binary form of codes written in computer memory are with the help of 0 and 1.

The inputting data in the form of machine language accepts the primary memory of the computer. The transformation is called input interfaces. Input interfaces are designed to match the unique physical or electrical characteristics of input devices to the requirements of the computer system. The most commonly used input devices are keyboard, mouse, punched card, magnetic disk, floppy disk etc.

Input Devices

1. **Punched Card**: The standard punched card has a size of 9cm   8cm   0.12 cm. It has 80 columns and 12 rows. All the punched cards have left most corner cuts.

The corner cut emphasises that all the cared are facing the same way. Out of 12 rows the top two rows are giving serial number 11 and 12. These two rows are known as zone of numeric punch or numeric zone punch. The rest 10 rows are numbered from 10, 9, . . ., 0 downwards. The rows 1,2, . . ., 9 are called as digit punch. The row 0 is used for both zone punch and digit punch. The numbers are written only to identify the columns and rows. A card can take instructions of maximum of 80 characters. Excess than 80 characters, rest will print on another card. The course developed by Dr. Herman Hollerith. The cards are punched by a machine known as card punching machine. The punching machine is similar to ordinary type writer.

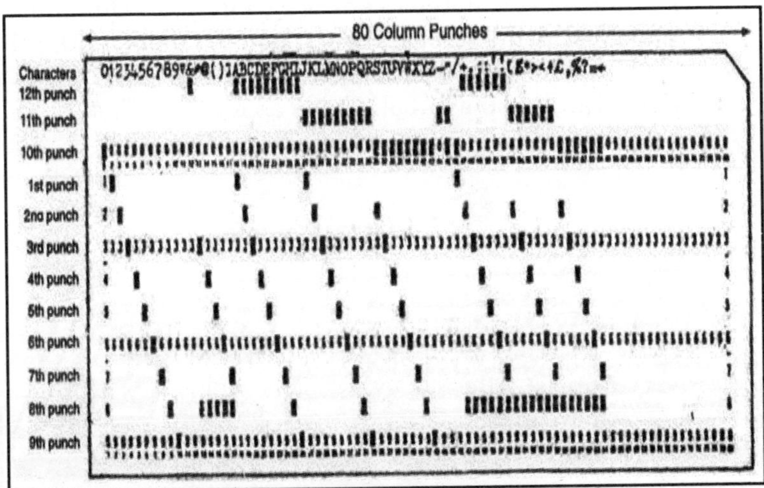

Fig. 1.23: Punched Card

2. **Punched Card Reader**: The punched cards are used for data input. The cards feed into a machine for input that is known as card reader. It is used for transferring a programme or set of instructions into the computer memory. This machine converts holes into electric signals for further processing. Card reader reads the

holes with the help of photocells tests emit rays which pass through the holes punched in the card. It can have a speed ranging for 100 to 2000 per minutes.

3. **Keyboard**: It is a significant and commonly used input device. It is similar to ordinary type writer. It consists of 105 keys in general and more in special keys for internet and audio/video system. There are special keys as function key from F1 to F12 specifying several functions as per the programme. These function keys are called as operational keys or programmable keys. It has another 4 special keys as cursor control keys or edit keys which are the arrow keys. Cursor is the blinking space on the screen on the editing mode (in DOS Mode), insertion point (in Windows/Graphic User Interface mode)The special keys are the special keys as windows key, notepad edit key, PgUp, PgDn, pause, scroll lock, print screen, insert, home, delete, end, tab, caps lock, shift, alt, ctrl, esc, etc. There are numeric keys from 0,1,...,9 and symbolic keys as &, ^, %, $, #, @, !.~, `, *, (,), =, +, |, \, /, <, >, ?, -, etc.

Fig. 1.24: **Keyboard**

The keyboard receives data and it lies in a set of electric contacts and converted into binary numbers. A particular pattern of electric pulses are generated so that computer comes to know which key is pressed. The key comes a set of metal contacts makes the electric signals on when a key is pressed.

Fig. 1.25: **VDU (Visual Display Unit) or Computer Monitor**

4. **Bar Codes:** A bar code is a series of vertical bars that represents numbers and alphabets. It is mostly used by the retail products in USA have the Universal Product Code (UPC) which have been specially accepted by the retailers. These codes are printed on their labels of products. These codes are read by using optical scanning devices. The scanner read the codes identifies the product manufacturer and after this it displays the price of that product.

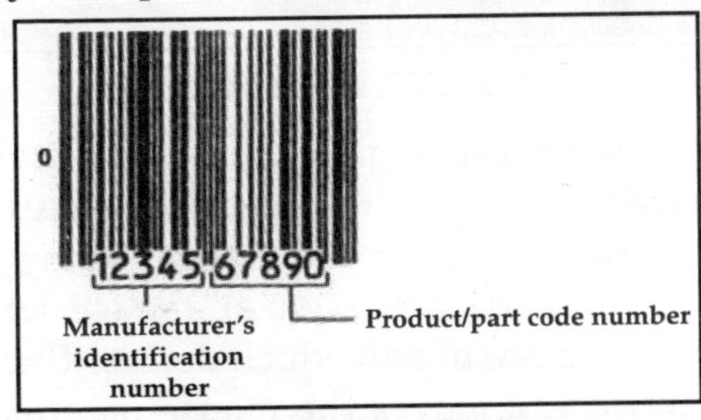

Fig. 1.26: **Bar Codes**

5. **Touch Screen**: Some system allow users to enter limited data simply by touching sensitive areas of the screen.

The touch screen displays many small boxes which on touching, carrying special task for performing like data storage, selecting for modification and deletion of a text, etc. In spite of this its main drawback is that it can not be used in case of large data. Most of the ATM monitors are touch screen enabled devices.

6. **Light Pen**: It is a pointing device. It will point directly at any point of the screen course on electric response at the lighter are where it pointed on. Using the light pen sketches or diagrams can be drawn directly on the screen. The light pen sketches or diagrams can be drawn directly on the screen. The light pen interacts with the screen/VDU of the micro computer.

Fig. 1.27: Light Pen

7. **Mouse:** The mouse is also a pointing device. It is a moving instrument on a pad or plane surface. There is one rolling ball under the mouse. Today the rolling mouse is replaced with sensor mouse which has a sensor in the place of ball which detects the movement of the mouse and moves the mouse pointer (an arrow mark) on the screen/VDU. The movement of cursor on any menu or any where can act accordingly with its direction. There are two or three bottoms on the mouse.

When they are clicked by pointing the mouse on a function, that performed by the machine.

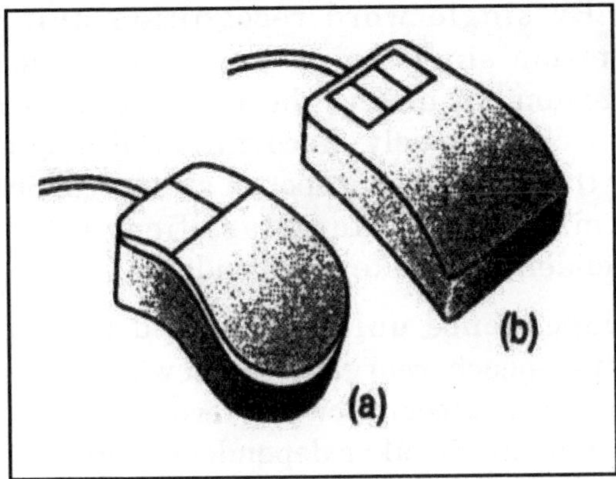

Fig. 1.28: Mouse

Fig. 1.29: Personal Computer

8. **Speech Touch Screen:** Through Speech Touch Screen the spoken human languages converting machine languages. A micro phone is used to convert human speech into electric signals. Speech input is particularly useful in the situations where commands given to a remote computers using a telephone.

Speech input units may be classified as: *(i)* Single word reorganisation unit; *(ii)* Continuous speech recognition unit. By single word recognition unit we mean recognition single word but by continuous speech recognition we means the recognition of sentences spoken continuously. Recognition of single words is easier than recognising spoken sentences. Speech input unit may be further classified as - speakers independence, speakers dependence.

The dependence unit is designed for a particular person's speech reorganisation where as a speaker independence recognition can recognising spoken input of any person. Speaker dependence unit is much more easier to design. But, speaker independence is much more difficult to design.

9. **Graphic Tablet**: The devices to input graphic information are called as graphic tablets. A typical tablet contains hundreds of copper lines from a grid. The grid is connected to the computer. Each line receives electric pulses. These pulses are picked up by electrodes embedded on the tablet. The position of the electrode which picks up a particular pulse located the x-y coordinates on its surface by the tip of a stylus position by the user and feeds this coordinates to the computer.

10. **Magnetic Ink Character Reorganisation (MICR):** It is used to read characters printed in an ink containing magnetic particles iron oxide. This is used principally for bank cheques. The code number of the bank, the customers account and cheque sequence numbers are pre-printed in magnetic ink. The MICR is the first inputting character recognition device. The magnetic ink includes a current in a reading circuit. The current includes will be proportional to the area of ink been scanned. By using MICR, special characters are encoded on the cheque that identifies numbers such

as bank account, account number, etc. The most commonly used character set by MICR devices is known as E13B font that consists of the numbers 0 to 9 and four special characters.

11. **Optical Character Reader (OCR):** OCR or Scanner is an electronic device which can read hand written, typed, printed characters directly and convert them into computer machine language as 0 and 1 and stored in computer memory. The pictures may also be read by it. In case of handwritten characters special care has to be taken to ensure that the characters are of standard size, lines marking of the characters are connected and no stylish loop, etc. are used. Otherwise, if that is type written the letters should be in a specific font type called as OCR Fonts. A wide range of fonts, using ordinary inks, can now be accepted by OCR devices. The standard fonts are used in OCR-A (American standard OCR), OCR-B (European standard OCR). The OCR also accepts computer print-outs.

    OCR devices accepts the collection of minute spots ('pixels' abbreviated for the picture elements). Once the whole character has been scaled It is compared with the characters, the machine has been programmed to recognise. Whichever pattern it matches or nearly matches is considered to the character reader. If the scanned character does not match satisfactorily with any of the fonts, it is rejected.

12. **Optical Mark Reader (OMR)**: It is a machine which recognises the marked inks as character. The marked ink are designed in a specially designed printed paper which can read data from the marks. The competitive/ recruitment examinations, recruiters data, financial or bio-profile information are feed into computer through specific papers marked in ink. The machine through which the ink is reads information is called as scanner.

CENTRAL PROCESSING UNIT

If we take the example of an industry after entering the raw materials in a specified manner into the machine, it processed and getting output. In such a manner input units are the inputting or entering devices of data like machines in an industry that is known as Central Processing Unit (CPU). Thus, CPU is regarded as cardiac and Cerberus of the computer, which means brain and heart of the computer. As the brain and heart are the important parts of human body. As brain takes decisions, CPU takes decisions for the computer system. Without CPU, computer is futile. The CPU is otherwise known as computer. All data feed through input devices will be entered into computer or CPU for processing or necessary calculation or decisions and it provides finished information or output to output devices as required by user. CPU consists of three parts as described under:

1. **Control Unit (CU):** It is the nerve centre of the computer. It is the high command. It controls the operations of all the units of a computer as its name shows. It only controls and coordinates all the components of a computer system as the nervous system of a human being. When data feed into computer through input devices it enters into the primary memory unit. It manages and coordinates the entire computer system. It obtains instructions from the programmes stored in main memory, interprets the instructions and issues signals that cause other units of the system to execute them. After execution of the programme or processing it transfers to the storage device and the final result of the programme should be released to an output device.
2. **Arithmetic Logic Unit (ALU):** The ALU of a computer is performing the arithmetic and logical operations. All arithmetic calculations, decisions and comparisons are

done through ALU. From the primary storage unit data and instructions are transferred to ALU when it found that there is any arithmetic and/or comparisons having to do for execution of that programme. After the execution of the programme again it transfers back to primary memory. The transferring of instructions to ALU is also done by Control Unit (CU).The arithmetic operations are performed by ALU are addition (+), subtraction (-), multiplication (*), division (/). The logical operations are in the form of AND, OR. Comparisons made by relational operations such as greater than (>), less than (<), equal to (=), greater than equal to (>=), less than equal to (<=), not equal to (<> or #).

3. **Memory Unit or Storage Unit:** Like human being computer has also its own remembering capacity. In which unit or device computer receives or stores data is called as memory unit. When we feed data and instructions into the computer it stores these in the memory unit or storage unit. The stored data can be taken into processing or retrieval in future. The memory is made of electronic components due to which its primary memory or main memory and secondary memory or auxiliary memory or back up memory. The BITs tend to the Binary Digits. Binary memory is the combination of 0 and 1. The BIT is the smallest unit of data. Byte is the combination of 8 BITs. Half of the byte is called as Nibble, 1024 bytes is a kilobyte(KB), 1024 KB is a megabyte (MB), 1024 MB is a Giga Byte (GB). The word length can be estimated for its length is estimated by its length in the memory locations in binary digits.

Output Devices

To view or to get output of a programme or a content is possible only through the output devices. Printers are most commonly output devices. Printout of an information on a sheet of paper for human readable form is known as hard copy. The printers can be classified into two types as impact printers and the non-impact printers.

In one hand, impact printers use the familiar type writer approach of hammering a type face against paper and inked ribbon. A dot matrix or a line printer is an example of impact printer. On the other hand non-impact printers don't hit or impact a ribbon to print because they use inks or powders and giving output printed through spray method. An inkjet or a laser printer is an example of non-impact printer. Impact printers are noisy, non impact printer are sound less. Impact printer can use carbon to print multiple copy of a print but non impact printer can print once on a single paper and no usage of carbon because it has no impact.

Classification of Printers

Printers are classified into two categories as:

1. Line printer;
2. Serial printer.

1. **Line Printer**: a line printer prints one line at a time. Printing speed differ from 15 lines to 4000 lines per minute with 96 to 160 characters per line space. Usually, 64 and 96 character sets are used with english letter. There are two types of line printers i.e. (a) drum printer; (b) chain printer.

Fig. 1.30: **Ink Jet Printer**

(i) **Drum Printer**: As the name shows a drum printer consists of a solid, cylindrical transmitted from the memory of the computer to a storage unit in the printer. This storage unit is called as Printer Buffer Register. It normally can store132 characters. The printer drum is rotated at enormous speed. A set of print hammers are for each character in a line are mounted in front of the drum. A character is printed by striking a hammer against the embossed character on surface. A carbon ribbon and paper are interposed between the hammer and the drum. As the drum rotates, the hammer waits and is activated when the character to be printed at that position appears in front of the hammer. Thus the movement of the drum and the striking of the hammer must synchronise accurately. Otherwise, the printing will not be uniform, the printer drums are most expensive.

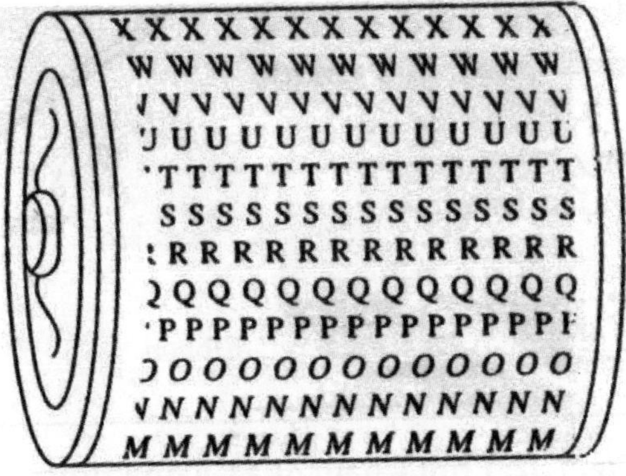

Fig. 1.31: Drum

(ii) **Chain Printer**: A Chain Printer contains numbers, alphabets and special characters pf symbols on a chain which rotates for printing. That rotating chain is called a print chain. Each link of the chain is a character font. In stead of this some models of printer use a metal or steel bank having a character set on it. For a 64haracter set printer, 4 sets of 64 characters band or chain are there, each would be embossed on the band or chain. As the print chain or band rotates, the print hammer waits and is activated when the character to be printed at that position appears in front of the hammer. In order to enhance the speed of the chain printer the hammer movement and the chain movement should be accurately synchronised. The key advantage of chain or band printer is the case with which chains may be changed, thus different fonts and different scripts may be used with the same printer.

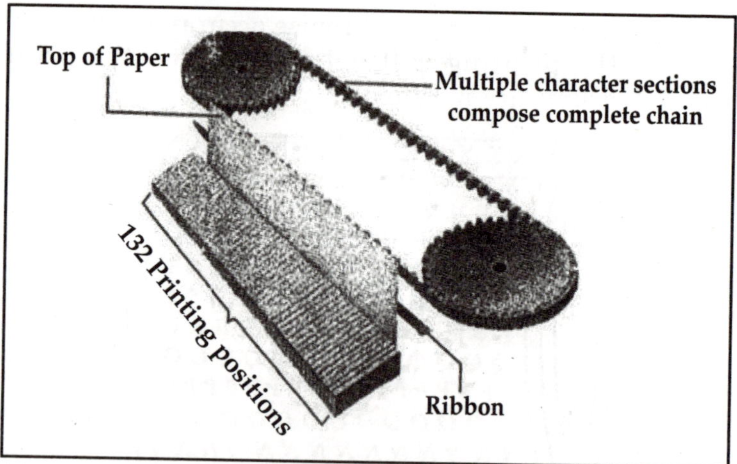

Fig. 1.32: **Print Chain of a Chain Printer**

2. **Serial Printer**: Serial printers print one character at a time, with the print head moving across a line. They are similar to the typewriter. Serial printers are normally slow. The speed is 30 to 300 characters per second. Serial printer is otherwise known as character printer. the most commonly used character printers are:

(i) Daisy Wheel Printer; and

(ii) Dot Matrix Printer (DMP)

(i) **Daisy Wheel Printer**: It uses a daisy wheel having the characters like numbers, alphabets and symbols, It provides better quality print outs than the other printer Thus it's other name is letter quality printer. For better looking output inkjet printer is used where characters are represented by sharp lines. Inkjet printer is the example of a letter quality printer or daisy wheel printer.

Each petal of the daisy wheel has a character embossed on it. A motor spins the wheel at a rapid rate, When the desired character spins to the correct position, a print hammer strikes it to produce the output. Thus, daisy wheel printers are ranged from 10 to 50 characters per second. But the modern letter quality printers print at the speed of 120 characters per second.

(ii) **Dot Matrix Printer (DMP):** DMP is a significant instance of serial printer or character printer. These printers print each character in a dotted form. The characters are the arranged set of dots. The print head comprises a matrix of tiny niddles. There are typically found seven rows with 9 niddles. Currently DMPs which have a print head with 24 pins in a vertical line are available. It strikes out characters in the form of pattern of tiny dots. Dots are arranged as characters. This printer provide high quality printed outputs and are called 'near letter quality printer'. But DMP is faster that the letter quality printers in range of 40 to 250 characters per second. DMPs are less expensive that the letter quality printers. The another advantage of DMP is there is no fixed

font of characters as compared over letter quality printer and printing is very less expensive.

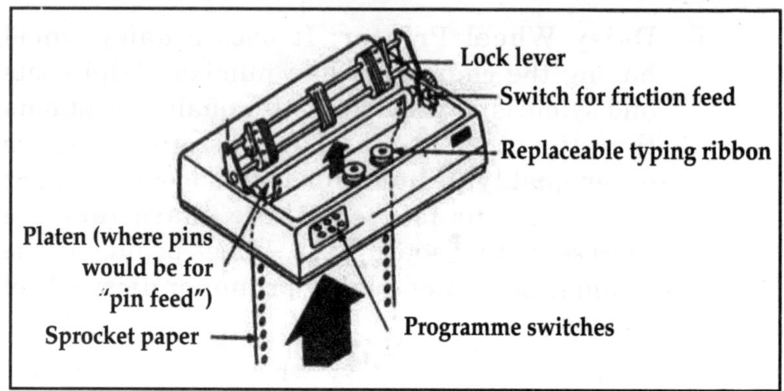

Fig. 1.33: **Dot Matrix Printer and its Head**

Page Printer: It is a non impact printer which can produce documents at speed of over 20,000 lines per minute. It is a printer in which the character pattern for a complete page is determined before printing. Page printers can produce pages of output at a rate equal to paper copier like Xerox graph, lasers, etc. Each page produced on these printers is an original one since there are no carbon copies.

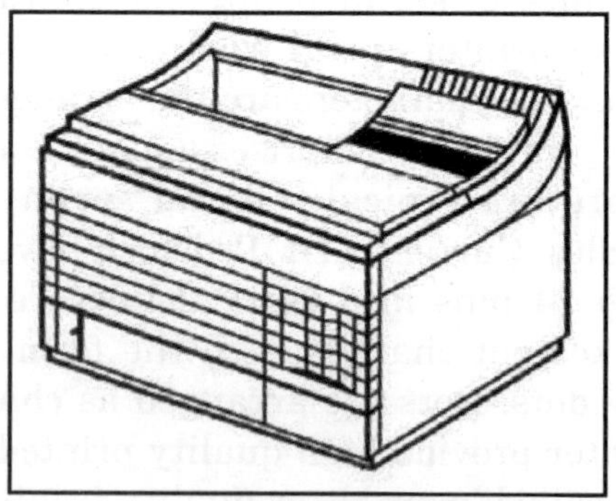

Fig. 1.34: **Laser Printer**

Plotter: Apart from printed output, in many applications, graphical output is very essential. DMPs now requiring the help of plotters to draw graphs and figures.

Some printer come with colour ribbons, the graphs and figures can be made by plotters and available in market. There are two type plotters available as Drum Plotter and Flat Bed Plotter.

Fig. 1.35: **Plotter**

(a) **Drum Plotter**: In a drum plotter, the paper on which the graph is to be drawn is mounded on a rotating drum. A pen which can move perpendicular to the direction of drum rotation, is mounted on a carriage, the drum can either clockwise or anti-clockwise. The pen can move left to right or from right to left and movement of pen from up or down. The movements of the pen and drum are controlled by the graphs and also annote them by using the pen to draw characters.

(b) **Flat Bed Plotter**: A flat bed plotter has a stationary horizontal plotting surface on which paper is fixed. The pen is mounted on a carriage which can move in either x or y direction and can move up or down. A graph plotting computer programme is used to move the pen to trace the desired graph.

Mass Storage Devices

Mass storage or secondary memory plays a significant role to store large volume of data. It is otherwise known as auxiliary memory or backup memory. It is low cost of storage unit then the main memory. It is back up storage because it stores large volume of data and retrieval is possible at any time. But, entering (input) or retrieving of data is only possible through main memory. It can not be used directly. The information has to transfer from the main memory from the secondary storage device.

Secondary storage memory devices have the particular application mainly depends upon how the stored information needs to be accessed. Basically there are two methods of accessing information i.e sequential or serial and random or direct. The sequential access method means the required location can be reached preceding other locations. But, random access means the required location can be found directly without preceding any other. Magnetic disks, magnetic drum are the example of random access device. But, the magnetic tape is an example of sequential one. As, we have to reach third file of a disk, we have to pass through the preceding two files, then we will be reach at the third one.

Typically, hardware equipments like magnetic disk, magnetic tape, magnetic drum, floppy disk, hard disk, cassette disks are the familiar secondary device. These devices are also called as mass storage device or mass storage media.

1. **Paper Tape:** It is a sequential access secondary storage device. Data is coded on paper tape in the form of punched holes. The punch is normally 1 inch wide comes in rolls and may be used in any length up to several hundred feets having 10 columns in 1 inch width. Paper tape has 8 channels. The number of characters that can be stored in a given physical space is low for paper tape storage. The input speed is very

low, it is not reusable. It is very difficult to delete, add data, edit data. Due to these draw backs paper tape is very rare today.

2. **Magnetic Tape**: It is one of the most commonly used sequential access secondary storage device for storing large volume of data similar to audio cassette. The tape is a plastic ribbon usually half inch wide that is coated on one side with an iron oxide materials which can be magnetised. The tape ribbon itself is stored in reels of to feet in a small cartridge or cassette. Like audio cassette, computer tape can be erased in it and can be reusable and durable.

   Information is recorded on the tape in the form of small invisible magnetised and non-magnetised spots on the iron oxide representing 0 and 1. The tape is divided into vertical columns or frames and horizontal rows called channels or tracks. The older tapes had 7 tracks and they used the 6 bit Binary Coded Decimal (BCD) format for data recording. The first 6 tracks are used for 6 bit BCD code. The 7th track is used for recording the parity bit. The parity bit is otherwise known as check bit. The parity bit is used to detect errors during data input or output operations.

Most of the modern tapes have 9 tracks and they are 8 bit Electronic Binary coded Decimal Interchange Coded [EBCDIC] format for data recording.

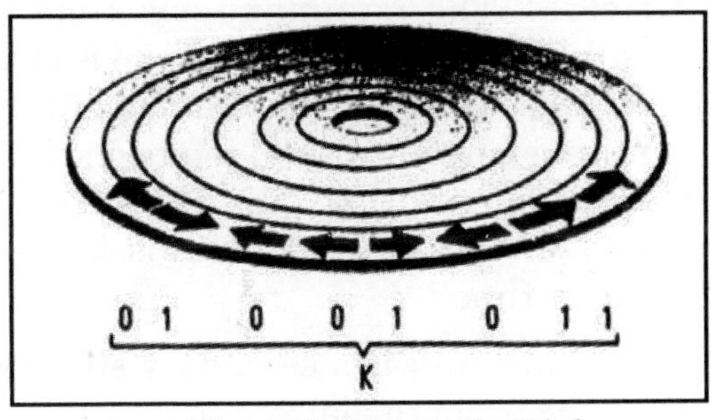

Fig. 1.36: Magnetic Disk

3. **Magnetic Disk**: Magnetic disks are the most popular medium for direct assess secondary storage .A set of magnetic plates are fixed to a spindle one below another. These smooth circular metal plates coated on both sides with a thin film of magnetic material like magnetic metallic oxide to make a disk pack. A disk pack consist of a number of these disks, three or mare mounted about half an inch apart from each other on a central shaft which rotates at the speed of 2,400 to 3,600 revolutions per minute (rpm). Thus all the disks all the disks on the disk pack move simultaneously in the same direction and at equal speed. Except the upper surface of the top disk and lower surface of bottom disk, information are stored on both side of each disk place. Each disk consists of corresponding tracks in all the surfaces are called as cylinders. Thus a disk pack having 10 disk plates will have recording surface and hence it will have 18 tracks per cylinder. Each track is divided into fixed number of sectors. Read/write operations on a disk start at sector boundaries. In general, disk store 512 bytes per sector. Hence, the total capacity of disk pack containing 64 sectors per track, 1756 tracks per surface and 10 surfaces. The total capacity of a disk is thus, 512 64 1756 10 = 53,94,43,200 or 539.4432 million bytes.

   The time taken to search the specified cylinder is known as sick time(Ts). The minimum sick time is 0 and average sick time is usually specified and is of the order of 30 mili seconds. The average rotational delay equals half the time taken by the disk to rotate once. This time is known as the latency time (Tc). The sum of average latency time (Tc) and sick time (Ts) is known as the average latency time.

4. **Hard Disk**: A hard disk is a secondary storage device. It consists of one or more platters coated with metallic oxide materials which allows data to be magnetically

recorded on the surface of the plates. The platter's range in diameter from 3.5 inch to 14 inch depending upon the drive. The disks are the series of tracks, The tracks are divided into a series of sectors when the data is formed. It is also similar to gram phone records that are stacked on a central spindle. The unique characteristics of the disk is that tnay one of the other records. As soon as a read/write command is received by the disk unit, the arm assembly in the proper direction.

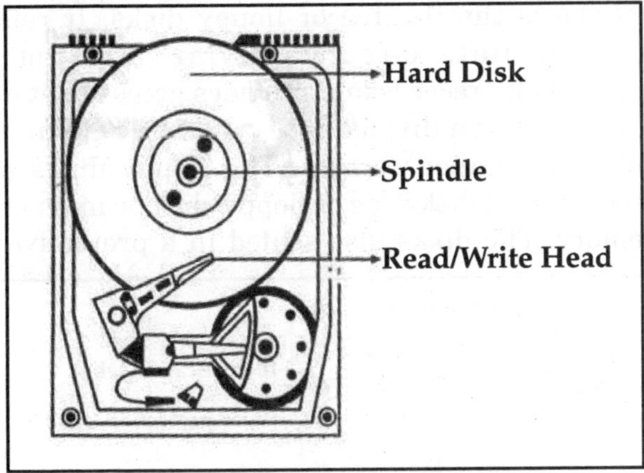

Fig. 1.37: **Hard Disk Drive**

In fact, disk pack is the device on which data is recorded the disk drive is the I/O unit writes data on the hard disk and reads data from the disk pack. A variety of hard disk drive (HDD) have been developed which are movable as well as fixed i.e. permanently mounted in the storage unit. A type of hard disk drive called as Winchester disk is often used.

5. **Winchester Disk**: A new type of disk drive developed by IBM in the early 1970s is named as Winchester Disk. The disks are coated with a special lubricants which reduces the friction when the read/write heads land on the disk surface. The sealed non-removable

right magnetic oxide coated disk, allowing very short time and high capacity storage as compared with cassette tapes or floppy disk drives. The disks are normally 5.25, 8 and 14 inch in diameter and 10, 2 and 40 MB storage space.

Fig. 1.38: **Winchester Disk**

6. **Floppy Disk**: An increasingly popular direct access secondary storage devices for micro and mini computer systems is the flexible or floppy disks. It refers to a flexible, flat, circular Mylar medium which magnetically records and provides access to stored data which has been divided into concentric circular tracks and wide shaped sectors. The floppy disks are also referred to as diskettes or floppy, disk or magnetic oxide memory. The disks also sealed in a protective square

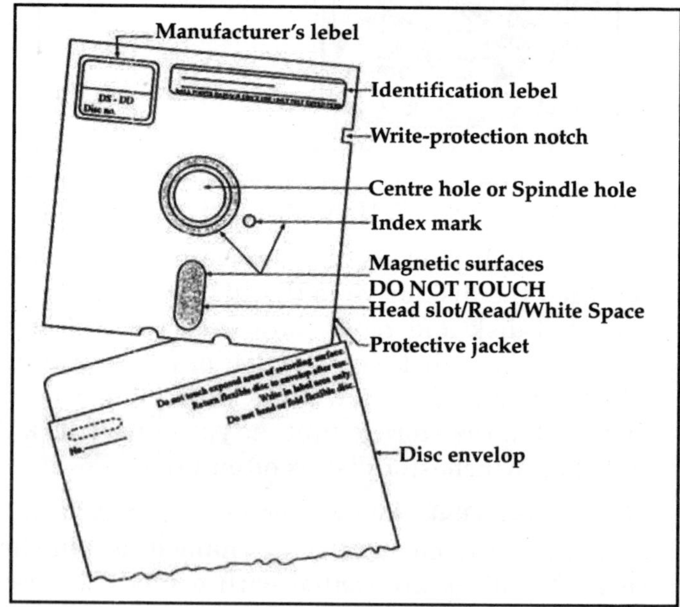

Fig. 1.39: **Floppy Disk**

cover that is lined with a soft material which cleans as it rotates. They were introduced in 1972 by IBM. They are various in size by many manufacturers like 8, 5.25 and 3.5 inch diameter. It stores 1.2 and 1.44 MB storage space. But, now these are not mostly in use. A floppy allows recording on both sides of the floppy medium and recording density of 14000 bits per inch along with each track. They are called as High Density (HD) floppies have a capacity of 1.25 MB. They are packed in a thin, hard plastic cartridge with an opening for the read/write head. These opening remain closed until and unless the cartridge is inserted into floppy disk drive (FDD). It is predicted that 3.5 inch diameter floppy stores 1.44 MB data. The disk within the protective covering is rotated at about 300 Revolutions Per Minute (RPM).

Fig. 1.40: **5.25″ Floppy Disk**

7. **Tape Cartridge:** Tape cartridge is used to store binary digits. It refers to a magnetic tape in a cartridge used with a tape drive, normally for the purpose of medium back up face disk. Moreover, tape cartridge also provide

protections against dirt and contamination, since the tape is sealed in a cartridge. A tape cartridge have relatively low data transfer rate which is typically less than 10,000 bytes per second (BPS).

Fig. 1.41: 3.5″ & 5.25″ Floppy Disk

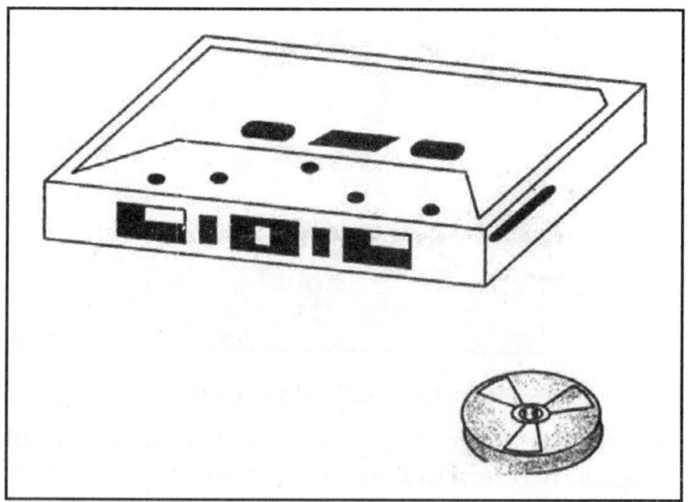

Fig. 1.42: Tape Cartridge

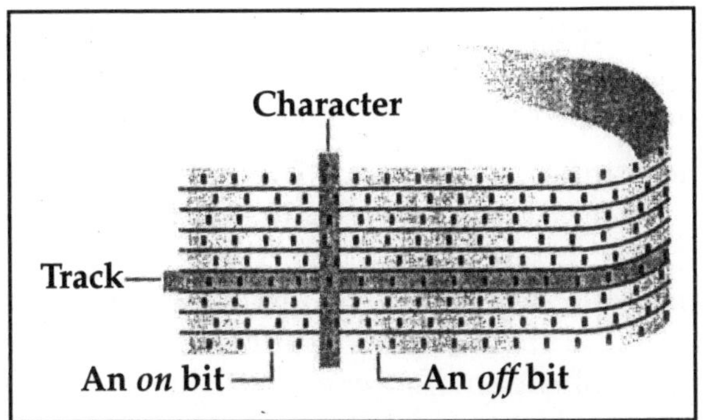

Fig. 1.43: **Internal Structure of a Tape Cartridge**

I/O Devices

The key functions of a computer is processing by input to get output. The devices through which data or something entered into the computer is called as input devices. The equipment or devices through which the result or output of the input got after processing is known as output devices. But there are some devices which have the both functions i.e. input and output which is abbreviated as I/O device. The best example of I/O devices are VDU, Magnetic Disk, Magnetic Tape, Punched Card, etc.

Blue Tooth - An Introduction of Wireless Data Communication Technology

Bluetooth is a wireless technology that allows computers, cell phones and other devices to connect to each other over a short distance (typically about 3 meters surrounding). Bluetooth uses radio waves (in 2.4 GHz) range and is designed to be a secure and inexpensive way of connecting exchanging information between the devices without data transmission cable. In other ward it is a Wireless Personal Area network (WPAN). It can be an I/O device.

Where did the Bluetooth originated - Bluetooth was originally developed by mobile phone company named

Ericsson in 1994. Looking for a unique name for the technology, this settled on "Bluetooth" after tenth century Viking king called herald Bluetooth blatant.

A more information about Bluetooth is founded from a special interest group (www.bluetooth.com) in 1998 by Ericsson, IBM, Intel, Toshiba and Nokia. According to them Bluetooth is an standard for short range transmission of digital voice & data that supports point-to-point and multipoint application. You can find Bluetooth in many of newer mobile phones, handheld computers, laptops and notebook PCs. It uses a common protocol transmission of data and voice between two Bluetooth devices of different manufacture is straight forward.

Connect the mobile with a PC to transfer files and performs backup. Most PCs and laptops do not have built in support for Bluetooth but you can add Bluetooth via USB Bluetooth adapter, which let you create cable free connection between USB desktop and PC devices. It will help you to connect 7 other devices just like printer and mobile phones simultaneously. The d-link DBT.900AP. Bluetooth access point is designed to extend LAN network services to Bluetooth enabled devices such as laptops, computers & PDAS.

What is my pass code - in order to pair two Bluetooth device pass code has been exchanged between the two devices when you first connect one machine will ask you to enter a pass code enter any 4 digital numbers. The another devices will then ask for password. Enter the some 4 digit number. It does not matter what the pass code is as long as you enter the same number at both ends.

Phone to PC - If you have a Bluetooth enabled mobile, then you can use Bluetooth to beam you photos and other objects from your phone to PCs. It needs to have Bluetooth on your pc with Bluetooth switched on both the phone and PC. You can transfer, share files now with of Bluetooth.

How to keep safe from cheaters

— when not using Bluetooth, then it off.

— set your Bluetooth mode so that it cannot discoverable.

— be careful of device that may be guessable pass code like '0000'.

Be careful when setting a device to 'trusted' or authorized as that device contain access all of your devices, services features & potentially data.

COMPUTER MEMORY

Memory - As people accepts and remembers things, computer has also its own remembering capacity. In which unit or device computer receives or stores data is called as memory unit. When we feed data and instructions into the computer it stores these in the memory unit or storage unit. The stored data can be taken into processing or retrieval in future. The memory is made of electronic components due to which its primary memory or main memory and secondary memory or auxiliary memory or back up memory. The BITs tend to the Binary Digits. Binary memory is the combination of 0 and 1. The BIT is the smallest unit of data. Byte is the combination of 8 BITs. Half of the byte is called as Nibble, 1024 bytes is a Kilo Byte (KB), 1024 KB is a Mega Byte (MB), 1024 MB is a Giga Byte (GB). The word length can be estimated for its length is estimated by its length in the memory locations in binary digits.

Types of Memory

There are two types of memory:

(i) Primary memory;

(ii) Secondary memory.

Primary Memory

It is otherwise called as main memory or Intermediate Access Storage (IAS). When data is entered its memory of the computer through input devices. It is stored in main memory. It holds the programme and data currently being used. This memory unit consists of a set of storage registers or memory cells. Each cell can store a fixed amount of information. Each memory location has a unique address. By specifying this address one can retrieve information from that location. The information stored in main memory gets erased when the power is switched off. Depending on the components it is made up of two types of memories as:

(a) Core memory (magnetic ferrite)

(b) Semi conductor memory

(a) ***Core Memory:*** It is made up of a large number of cells, each cell can store one bit. The cells may be organised as a set of addressable words, each word storing a sequence of bits. One of the components commonly used as a binary storage cell in memory units is magnetic core.

(b) ***Semi-conductor Memory:*** The semi conductor memory has placed other devices like magnetic cores and is vital in digital systems. The typical semi conductor memory consists of a rectangular array of storing 1 bit of fabricated using a semi conductor in silicon.

Memories are classified either as Metal Oxide Semiconductor (MOS) and Complementary Metal Oxide Semiconductor (CMOS). These are actually differenced according to the type of transistors used to construct the individual memory cell. The total number of cells in a memory determines its capacity.

The term 'chip' is a semi conductor type of memory device with silicon base. The transistors, capacitors, registers are known as Integrated Circuits (ICs) and this is fabricated on a single chip. The ICs are classified as Small Scale Integrated (SSI) Circuits consists of 20 transistors on a single chip. Medium Scale Integration (MSI) circuits consists of 100 transistors and Very Large Scale Integrated (VLSI) circuits consists of 10,000 circuits on a single chip.

In general faster operationally obtained with bipolar memory chips which consists of MOS and CMOS. There are the discussions of physical properties of semi conductor memories. But there are the various functions of memory. Depending on the types of functions performed by the memories, they are classified into two as: (i) Random Access Memory (RAM); (ii) Read Only Memory (ROM).

(i) **Random Access Memory (RAM)**: As the name shows it randomly selects and used any location of this memory to directly store and retrieve data and instructions. In other words when any body working with computer, RAM is used for feeding data and instructions first and the only possibility of retrieving data from any memory device through RAM. The inputting and output both can only performed by RAM. It is thus referred to as read-write memory, because information can be read from it and can be written into it. The RAM is volatile in nature and all the user data and instructions stored in this part of the main memory of the computer. The volatility emphasises the loss of the power of computer or switch off which loses data.

RAM is sub-divided into:

(a) Dynamic RAM(DRAM)

(b) Static RAM(SRAM)

(a) ***Dynamic Random Access Memory*** (***DRAM***): DRAM chip contains the transistor that acts as in much the same way as a mechanics on and off light switch. It can holds electric charge depending on the action of the transistor. The transistor or capacitor either contains no change that mean 0 or does not hold a charge is 1. the storage charge must be refreshed every two mili seconds. In this conclusion we came to know that it provides voltage and the data stored are lost in the event of power failure.

(b) ***Static RAM(SRAM)***: SRAM chip is also called as voltage storage device. There is no required special generation circuits to return the stored data as long as it takes more transistors and other devices to store a bit. Thus, SRAM is used in specialised complex applications. SRAM are faster than DRAM. Access time of SRAM is 10 to 20 nano seconds which means that it read from or write into any memory locations. But, in the other hand DRAM has an access time of 60 to 80 nano seconds. Hence, SRAM is more expensive i.e. 10 times faster than DRAM. So, it is not used for large memories.

(ii) ***Read Only Memory (ROM)***: A ROM is one in which information is permanently stored. The information from the memory can only be read and it is impossible to write any information into it because it is read only in nature. The information written in ROM is made by the manufacturing company. When the power is off as the main memory, the data in the main memory can be lost. such memories are called as field stores, permanent store or deal store. The important application on DRAM is to store tables which do not change. For example trigonometric function table is stored in ROM. A variation of ROM chip is Programmable Read Only Memory (PROM). The programming through ROM is only possible if the user is possible to customise a system by converting his own programmes to micro programme and storing them in a PROM chip. Once the user programmes stored in the PROM chip, they can be usually executed as the programmes in ROM functions. And also PROM is non

volatile as ROM. In ROM and PROM all information are non-volatile when power is off. But, there is another memory chip called Erasable Programmable Read Only Memory (EPROM). As name indicates it is volatile in nature. It is programmed by PROM chip. It is frequently used in research and development (R&D) department. Research in case of experiments being made by R&D department because every time they have to change the programmes to take new experiments. There is also another type of ROM i.e. Electrically Erasable Programmable Read Only Memory (EEPROM) which can be performed by certain instructions as the programmes executions made by the computer.

Thus, the memory unit can be given the birds eye view with the schematic diagram given below:

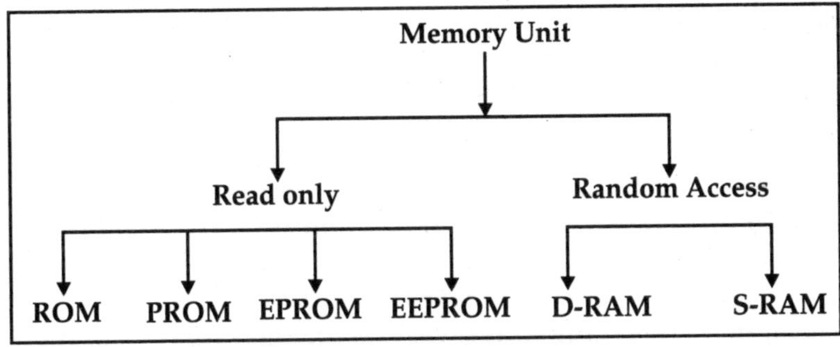

Fig. 1.44: **Memory Unit**

Cache Memory: It is another type of memory unit which is used to increase the speed of processing by making current programmes and data available to the CPU at the rapid rate. It is only unit to speed the processing of the programme into computer. The processing speed of computer depends upon the speed of the cache memory. Cache memory makes main memory appear to the faster and larger than quite really it is very expensive than the main memory. The most significant affect of cache memory is in improving the memory transfer rates and thus raising the processor speed. It is otherwise known as buffer.

Secondary Memory

Secondary memory plays a significant role to store large volume of data. It is otherwise known as auxiliary memory or backup memory. It is low cost of storage unit then the main memory. It is back up storage because it stores large volume of data and retrieval is possible at any time. But, entering (input) or retrieving of data is only possible through main memory. It can not be used directly. The information has to transfer from the main memory from the secondary storage device.

Typically, hardware equipments like magnetic disk, magnetic tape, magnetic drum, floppy disk, hard disk, cassette disks are the familiar secondary device. These devices are also called as mass storage device or mass storage media.

DATA PROCESSING

Introduction

The key function of a computer is data processing. A computer data is a key fact or raw material for a computer. The meaning of data processing is mainly tends to the Electronic Data Processing (EDP). After processing of data through a processing unit gives the meaningful information. Thus, data is used during processing to get information. This process is called data processing. Before we analyse in depth of information requirement data processing, first we shall have an overview of data and information.

Data

Data us a collection of facts, figures, observations, assumptions, conditions, situations, objects. For instance the inventory figures, financial records, customer name, address, the result and marks of students, the weather report. Even photographs, drawings, maps are the part of data. Thus, data may be alpha-numeric or in the form of drawings. The data are basically the raw facts in isolation, which when placed in a meaningful contest by a data processing operation, allow inferences to be drawn.

The basic purpose to process the data us to process the data is to produce information. The very need to capture data and process the data is governed by the information, objectives. The data processing whether done manually or with the help of a computer, shall guarantee that data will be processed in accordance with the need of the user. Data are the plural form of the word 'datum' which is the collection of facts, figures, observations, etc.

Information

As defined earlier data is prerequisite for processing, data is a raw facts. This raw data are processed to generate information. After processing of data the information will be obtained. So, information is the output or finished product of the raw fact or data. The processing takes all arithmetic calculations, decisions, merges, sorting, classification of data. We can compare a flour mill as processing unit of the raw material 'wheat' to get the output as processed product 'flour'. Information can thus be defined as anything which increases the recipient's and an information system can be defined as the means by which the information is generated and communicated to the people involved.

Information is the key ingredient in the decision making process for most individuals, although it alone will not guarantee proper decision making. The action may generate further data which may have to be processed. The information of one processing may be data for others. If it is data for others, it may be processed further. And in some cases the information can also used repeatedly for any other processing, so the information used as data and process further.

Stages of Data Processing

As mentioned above data processing, information, data processing consists of the following basic stages as input, process and output:

1. **Input:** This is the initial stage of data processing. Input refers to the concept of entering data in the computer. The data can be inputted by the help of some devices are known as input devices.

2. **Process**: In this stage the inputted data are refining from other information with data to give required form of data which is called as processing. In other words, the necessary arrangement to get data into required form is called as processing. The became more meaningful after processing.

3. **Information**: After processing of data the output is called as information. So, the outcome after processing of data is called as information. Processing is the media to convert data into information.

   In spite of these three main stages of data processing there are other stages of data processing as.

4. **Origination:** This process tends to process of collecting original data. An original data record is called source document.

5. **Preparation**: The collected should be transferred into some convenient form for input. It has to prepare in such a form that data will be prepared first then inputting data into the computer would be easy and useful.

6. **Storage**: Data storage is essential for future retrieval or further input for processing. In computer there are so many storage media are used for storing data for future use.

7. **Reporting**: Report is the step by which results of data processing are made available to others. The processing

of data may be reported in a number of ways. In some cases results are printed in a report which may be used further as data.

8. **Reproducing**: A multiple copies of a certain data is required, Data may be reproduced in readable form by hard copies which implies the duplicating or photo coping or printout by printer.

9. **Data Structure**: The data is recorded in the structure as character, data item, record and file.

Character

It is the smallest unit of data used for the purpose of recording. The characters are as follows:

(i) **Alphabets** - Alphabets in lower case (small letters) and upper case (capital letters) as a, b, c, d, . . ., x, y, z, A, B, C, D, . . ., X, Y, Z

(ii) **Numeric** - The numbers consisting of digits 0, 1, 2, 3, 4, 5, 6, 7, 8, 8, 9

(iii) **Special characters or symbols** - = +_ \ I) (* & ^ % $ #v @ ! ~ ` " ' ;: > < ? / . ,

Data Item

Data items are called as data fields or facts or data elements. A field is a meaningful collection of related characters. It is the smallest logical data entry that is treated as a single unit in data processing. For example, employee name, employee code, identification number, basic salary, DA, HRA, GPF, LIC, Net Pay, etc. Data items are classified as under.

(iv) **Alphabetic:** A data item consisting of alphabets both in lower case and upper case student name, employee name, etc.

(v) **Numeric:** A data item consisting of digits only as basic pay, DA, HRA, Net Pay, phone number, etc.

(vi) **Alphanumeric:** A data item consisting of data consisting of both alphabets, digits and/or symbols as PAN number as ALKPP5439P, Roll Number like 21G40/5, etc.

Elementary Data Item

The data item which are not further subdivided and are always used as single unit.

Grouped Data Items

The data item which may further be subdivided into elementary data items. There exists a provision to refer to the complete group data item as well as its sub parts. The group of data is illustrated as DATA consisting of Day, Month and Year. If we will take employee data divided as Male and Female, again subdivided as Married and Unmarried, again can be subdivided as castes of both male and female, like this.

Record

A record is a group of all the data items for one object of data processing. Data can be processed only often the values for all the data items within a record have been made available. The data is recorded in terms of these records.

File

Records are grouped to form of a file. A file is a numbers of related records that are treated as one unit i.e. file. We may take an example of collection of data of all employees consisting of several records of a company which will be stored in an unique name as file called as file name.

File Organisation

System designers or the users choose to organise, access and process records and files in different ways depending on the types of applications required. Then data is stored in a secondary storage device i.e. disks. It must be logically

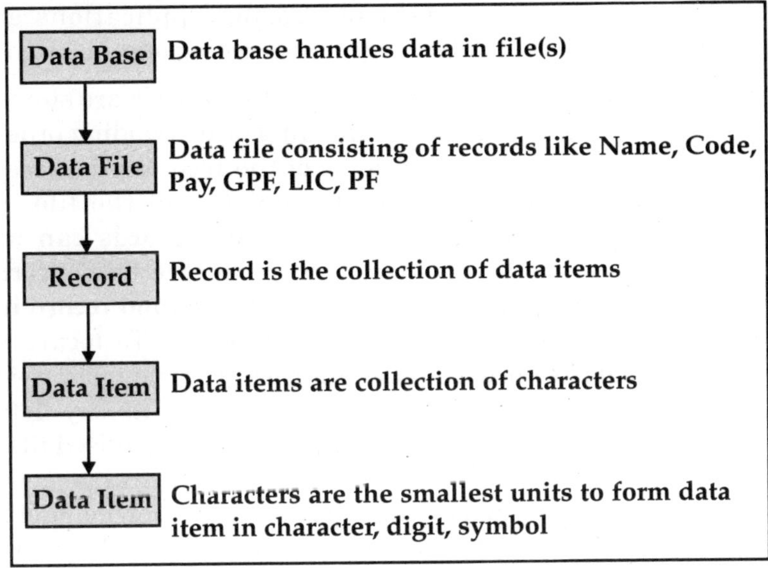

Fig. 1.45: **Data Structure**

organised into files, the files named as the related names of data consistence to identify easily. The file name divided into two parts as primary name and extension name. Primary name is the name of the file to identify the nature of data consisting and the extension name indicates the nature of file. The primary name and extension name is separated by a dot (.) as STUDENT, DAT, EMPLOYEE. DBF, PAY. PRG, etc. The primary name should be in 8 characters and extension name should not exceed 3 characters, In the primary name should not contain any symbol except a symbol - i.e. underscore. In WINDOWS system more than eight characters can be used in primary name, when we will see the file name in DOS environment, we will find the primary name converted into eight characters. In DOS environment we can not give more than 8 characters in primary name. If we will give more than 8 characters, the first 8 characters will be taken automatically by the system as primary name. There are three major file organisations used in data processing applications as sequential, direct or relative and indexed or organisation.

1. **Sequential File:** In a sequential file records are stored one after another in an ascending or descending order determined by the key fields of the records. To access these records, the computer must read the file in sequence from the beginning. The records can be retrieved one by one. In other words, the first record is read and processed first. Then the second record in the file sequence will read and so on. To locate a particular record, the computer programme must read in each record in sequence and compare its key field to the one that is required. Sequentially organised files generally stored on the storage media such as magnetic tape, punched paper tape, punched card or magnetic disk. The file organisation is time consuming. It is very inefficient and uneconomical. Transactions must be stored in a sequential order, prior to it the user have to prepare the record and input it.

2. **Direct File:** A relative or direct file consists of records organised in such a way that it is possible for the computer to directly locate the key of the desired record without searching through a sequence of other records. It implies that for retrieving of a file will take less time than the sequential file. Once a record is stored in its relative location within a relative file it can be retrieved either sequentially or randomly. The more common access media for relative or direct files, however it randomly access. The direct access storage device (DASS) such as magnetic drum. Magnetic disk, diskette, hand disk, pen driver, etc. used for direct files.

3. **Indexed File:** Records stored in indexed file is in an ascending or descending order of sequence based upon the key fields. An index table is used to speed up access to the records without requiring a search of entire file.

Here, the word 'index' means a table of contents. It also refers to an alphabetical register of subject with page or folio references. It implies anything that gives an indication. An indexed file can access records sequentially or randomly. Sequentially accessed records in an indexed file can begin with the first record in the file in continue through the file. In an indexed file random access of a records searched until the key fields of the record to be retrieved. Random retrieval is faster than in case of index files because an index does not have to be searched when using relative files. Indexed files offers a compromise between sequential or relative files.

The computer files are categorised according to its types as:

1. **Master File:** It refers to a computer file which contains relatively permanent information, generally updated periodically. The master files need frequently updating with respect to transaction files currently prepared. More than one files are used in a single master file. It is used as an authoritative source of data in carrying out a particular job on the computer.
2. **Transaction File:** Transaction files are called movement files and are purely temporary files which are used for updating master files.

File Manipulation and Maintenance

Data processing is a process of collection, storage, processing and distribution of processed data. It is the process of restructuring, manipulating of data by people or machine like computer to increase their usefulness and value for some particular purpose. It is otherwise known as file utilities. File utilities consists of routine which perform a variety of generalised operations on data files. To bring order to the data and procedure meaningful results, some basic data operations must be performed. These are described below:

1. **Capturing and Recording of Data:** Data need to be captured first from the source of its organisation. It should be recorded in hand written or typed or in computer in a human readable form. There is first record, called as source document. The data may be stored in a card or magnetic tape or floppy disk. This data should be transferred to the computer. The data transferring and recording from one medium to another is known as transcription. If any error in the data recording or collection is done, it will occur error in other steps. Thus, all necessary precautions and utmost care should be taken in this stage. So data processing should give accurate result.
2. **Variety Data:** The capturing of data recorded should need to be verified for its accurate before starting the process of manipulating it. There are chances of error in the capturing of data or its results.
3. **Verification and Coding of Data:** Classification involves grouping of likely items of transactions. It places data elements into specific categories which provide meaning for the user. It is a process of identification and separation of data for all kind or another. Classification also requires coding. It requires unique code numbers. The code identify and separate different items or groups of data from one another. A coding system may consist of alphabetic, numeric or alphanumeric code.
4. **Sorting of Data:** The process of arranging the various records within a file in a given order or sequence is known as sorting. Sorting is a very common requirement during data processing for the convenience of reference by the user. For example, the result of the students may be referred according to ascending order of Roll Numbers, merit list is sorted in descending order with concerned roll number,. The name is sorted in ascending order to allot roll number.

5. **Searching of Data:** Searching is the process of scanning a file to find a particular record. After sorting data searching become easy and convenient. The required data should be sought for the file. For example to search a particular record in a sequential file, the file is scanned sequentially beginning with the first record and the desired key field is compared one-by-one with the key field to each record. The search process terminates when the machine key is found. But, direct file organisation enables the programme to have immediate access to the desired record.

6. **Merging of Data**: Merging is combined two or more sets of sorted similar data in a file. It may be the combination of records from two or more ordered files into a single ordered file. For example, the merit lists of students in two different classes may be combined according to grades to get single merit list.

7. **Storing, Updating and Retrieving of Data:** Storing is the process of saving data in some accessible form for further reference. Retrieving of data is the process of searching and locating the necessary data from stored data file. The process of storing helps updating the data further. It may be updated, retrieved, copied as and when required. At the time of updating the data, data to be retrieved form file. For example, a bank keeps data of account holders with the data of name, address, transactions of deposits, withdrawls, loan, recoveries, interest, etc. They updates these as and when transactions made, prints report as the account holder requires, erases when the account closes, etc. Retrieving is the o.

8. **Reporting of Data:** To get an information, data file to be retrieved to get particular data or information to make it in specific order or form. That may be printed through printer or may be reported on line or in softcopy. The printed data on paper is called as

hardcopy. For example, any account holder can get a statement of transactions from bank for their respective account. That data is to be retrieved and printed on a paper as statement of account containing name, account number, opening data, and address of the account holder with all the transactions with data of transaction, description of transactions, debit/credit amount, balance.

9. **Communicating:** Communication means sending of data from one place to other. For example, the information about customer's order must often be sent within a business organisation from the sales department to the inventory department for checking of stocks and from there to the delivery and shipment department and finally to the billing section. Observe the different steps of data communication. Each communication for reporting need data processing.

Techniques of Data Processing

Depending upon the technology and man-machine interface, data processing are classified as manual and mechanised.

Manual Data Processing: Manual data processing implies that the data being processed by human being to get information. The data are being processed by exercise, both physical and mental. But, human being have another limitation for continuous working. It is low processing. It is some times less accurate.

However, the manual data processing system have one advantage. The previous knowledge and experience of the executive helps him to take a more realistic decision in a given environment.

Mechanical Data Processing: The data processing through machine is known as mechanical data processing. The machines are used to supplement the manual system to make it more effective and efficient system of data processing as a whole. The repetitive work can be done through mechanical data processing system. It has the advantage that it increases speed and keeps accuracy and consistency of working without any kind of subjectivity and bias.

Electrical and Electronic Data Processing: Electrical/ Electronic data processing system is much faster than others which can be an automated system. Calculator is the introduction of electronic calculating machine. Computer has revolutionised electronic data processing system. It receives data through input devices, processes in central processing unit (CPU) and gives output through output devices. The printing out of information is possible through printer on paper. The programme developed and stored in the computer which can handle data through input, processing, retrieval, reporting, sending, receiving of data from one place to another, from one computer to other, from one person to other(s). It offers a vast data handling capacity beyond the human imagination and million times faster than man.

Modes of Data Processing System: As complexities of business increases in an organisation, consistently the complexity of data . Data processing may also increase. The necessary data processing may be carried manually, mechanically or electronically. The data processing must be responsible to supply information when it is required, so as to make the performance of the organisation optimum. The manual methods fail due to its processing is time consuming, inconsistency and unreality. From the above discussion, it is opined that the methods of data processing depend on processing requirements. The processing requirements determined by volume of data complexity of data processing, processing time constraints, computational requirement.

Let it examine the methods of types of data processing system as:

1. **Batch Processing**: It is the oldest and least costly system to run programmes when the entire computer system is dedicated to a single job, the system is said to be operating in batch processing mode. In this processing, the transactions are manually assembled over a given period of time before feeding the whole as a single batch to the computer for validation and processing such application need only for periodic processing e.g. a payroll system has to run only once in a month for calculating the salaries of the employees. The various transaction relating to the employee like their attendance record, reductions, DA, HRA, increment, etc. are manually collected for the month and then send as single batch to the computer in last week of the month for processing.
2. **On-Line Processing:** On line processing is refers to the processing of the individual transactions as they occur from the point of origin. In an on-line processing system the user has direct connection to the computer by the terminals' i.e. VDU and keyboard installed in the work station. It may be considered as midway between the batch processing and real time processing. Inventory control system is the example of real-time processing where the user can check the availability of stock for the desired items or print out the list of all the items balance with its quantity, so this can be checked for sufficient to supply or procurement can be made.
3. **Real-Time Processing**: The real time processing refers to the technique of updating files with transaction of data immediately after the event to which it relates. In such system the time is key-essence, data is collected by the computer through on-line terminals. In real-time processing the terminals are enquiry driven. The data must be processed immediately. The CPU i.e. on-line to several terminals will accepts and operate any

one input at a time. In real time processing programme is allotted a certain fixed CPU time is called response time. This method of processing programme is generally using in railway reservations, ticket booking system in ports, bus stops, banking transactions, etc. In reservation/ticket booking counter, the request must be processed by the system immediately after it is made. So, that the complete up-to-date picture of availability of seats are maintained by the computer in every workstation.

4. **Time Sharing Processing:** A real time processing makes time sharing processing. Time sharing processing allows a large number of users at various remote terminals simultaneously, use a centrally located computer (CPU) for problem solving. Each user operate independently and receives such a response that s/he has the impression as if s/he is the only user. In time sharing, each programme is allotted a certain fixed CPU time called time slice. A very common time slice is mili seconds. The basic ideas of time sharing method is to allot a small share of time to each programme and thus execute simultaneously all the programmes in the main memory due to extension time of the CPU is higher.

5. **Distributed Data Processing:** Some business organisation like financial institutions, airlines, etc. are distributed over a wide area and each one requires access to common business information. There will be a centrally located CPU and each of the officers are directly connected to the central computer. Where a request made by a terminals at branch office or counters the central computer process it and immediately provides information at the same branch office or counter. One computer may be performed tasks for hundreds of users on-line at individual terminals. If the computer/CPU fails, all the terminals will halt.

But, the failure of a computer/terminal at head office does not affect the terminals located in different branches or counters. In short this system does not affect the entire system as in real-time processing.

SELF EXERCISE

- Computer is an electronic machine which is used for arithmetic calculations at an enormous speed.
- 'Data' is a plural word derived from the singular form 'datum'.
- Data are a raw material to computer for information.
- Computer has enormous calculation speed, free from error, diligence, versatility, higher storage capacity, no feeling, no Intelligency question.
- Computer is versatile in nature because it has no diligence and in a fraction of time, several types of jobs can be done.
- The other name of 'Abacus' is soroban. It was developed in 350 BC in China. It was the 1st digital computer.
- Napier's logs and bones was developed by John Napier, a Scottish mathematicians developed in 17th century. He developed logarithmic table with base e end 10.
- Pascal's adding machine was developed in 1642 by Blaise Pascal, a French mathematician.
- It is the evolution of mechanical calculator. G Leibitz's Stepped Reckoner was developed in 1673 by Gottfried Wilhelm Von Leibnitz.
- Introduction of Binary digits Os and 1s.
- The British Prof. Charls Babbage had invented Analytical engine, a mechanical calculator in 1822. He is regarded as father of computers due to the development of analytical engine.

- The key driven adding box called mercury box developed by D.E. Felt in 1887. O J.R. Mercury developed key board calculator in 1911.
- The 1st card punching machine was developed by Herman Hollerith in 1890 for U.S. Census Bureau.
- The old name of IBM was Tabulating Machine Company (TMC).
- The 1st automatic computer Havard Mark-l was developed by Hatheway Aiken and John H. Nipe in 1837. It was an electromechanical device.
- Atanasoff Berry Computer (-ABC) was developed by Vincent Atanosoff and his assistant Cliford Berry. It was activated by Vaccum tubes.
- ENAIC was the 1st electronic computer developed in 1946 by Prof. J. Presper and J. Maucheley at Moore School of Electrical Engineering, USA.
- ENAIC, EDVAC, EDSAC are the 1st generation computers.
- Semiconductor memory was introduced in 2nd generation of computers. Transistors are used in 2nd generation computers, magnetic core memory was invented in this generation.
- FORTRAN, COBOL, ALGOL, SNOBOL and Assembly languages were developed in 2nd generation of computers.
- Integrated Circuit (IC) was developed in 3rd generation of computers. The IC was invented by Jack Kilby at Texax Instrument in 1988.
- Microprocessors are developed in 4th generation of computer in which the entire computer circuit remain in a single IC or Chip.
- VLSI techniques are developed in 4th generation.

- The Knowledge Information Processing System (KIPS) based functions meet intelligency using knowledge based techniques. That is called as Artificial Intelligency which was developed in 5th generation of computers.
- Computer has a vital role in the field of data processing
- Computer system consists of two elements the physical structure called hardware and the internal or logical structure which helps in the activities of hardware called software.
- SW refers to the set of computer programmes which enhance the capabilities of the hardware.
- Software is a sequenced set of instructions to be given by the programmer or user to the computer for solving a required problem.
- The programming languages are classified as - Low Level Language-i. Machine Level Language, ii. Assembly Language, b. High Level Language (HLL)- i. Problem Oriented Language, ii. Special Purpose Language or package.
- Liveware means all the personnel dealing with the computer system and their perform different duties
- Firmware refers to a sequence of programme or software that is substituted for hardware and stored in computer memory supplied by manufacturing company.
- The physical components of computer refers to hardware.
- The availability of software are required in the computer to utilise hardware for the solving the required solution.
- In stead of software, hardware is meaningless. Hardware and software altogether form computer system.

- The computer is typically equipped with four significant ingredients viz. input, output units or devices, central processing unit (CPU) and memory unit.
- CPU consists of Arithmetic Logic Unit (ALU), Control Unit (CU), primary memory and registers. The memory unit envelops primary memory, secondary memory.
- There is an unit named as I/O device abbreviated for Input and Output which are called as peripherals.
- In which unit or device computer receives or stores data is called as memory unit. When we feed data and instructions into the computer it stores these in the memory unit or storage unit.
- The memory is made of electronic components due to which its primary memory or main memory and secondary memory or auxiliary memory or back up memory. The memory is made of electronic components due to which its primary memory or main memory and secondary memory or auxiliary memory or back up memory.
- The BITs tend to the Binary Digits. Binary memory is the combination of 0 and 1. The BIT is the smallest unit of data.
- A Byte is the combination of 8 BITs. Half of the byte is called as Nibble, 1024 bytes is a Kilo Byte(KB), 1024 KB is a megabyte (MB), 1024 MB is a Giga Byte (GB).
- The word length can be estimated for its length is estimated by its length in the memory locations in binary digits.
- There are two types of memory - primary memory, secondary memory.
- Primary memory is otherwise called as main memory or Intermediate Access Storage (IAS). When data is entered into computer through input devices which receives and stores in main memory.

- Depending on the components primary memory is made up of two types of memories as (a) core memory(magnetic ferrite), (b) Semi conductor memory
- Semi Conductor Memories are classified either as Metal Oxide Semiconductor (MOS) and Complementary Metal Oxide Semiconductor (CMOS). They are differenced according to the type of transistors used to construct the memory cell.
- The 'chip' is a semi conductor type of memory device with silicon base. The transistors, capacitors, registers are known as Integrated Circuits (ICs) and this is fabricated on a single chip.
- The processing speed of computer depends upon the speed of the cache memory. Cache memory makes main memory appear to the faster and larger than quite really it is very expensive than the main memory.
- Hardware equipments like magnetic disk, magnetic tape, magnetic drum, floppy disk, hard disk, cassette disks are the familiar secondary device. These devices are also called as mass storage device or mass storage media.
- Physical components of a computer system is called as hardware.
- The programming techniques which is required to handle the hardware is known as software(SW).
- A computer is divided into three parts as input device, output device, CPU.
- CPU consists Control Unit which controls the entire computer system.
- Arithmetic Logic Unit (ALU) tests the logical and arithmetic operations and memory unit.
- Memory unit consists of two parts as primary and secondary memory. Primary memory consists of ROM, RAM mainly.

- RAM is volatile in nature i.e. when power is OFF, the memory in RAM will be deleted. So, RAM is temporary in nature. ROM is made by the computer manufacturing company which can not be changed or deleted.
- Secondary memory is otherwise known as auxiliary or backup memory. For storing of data for future storage and retrieval secondary memory devices like floppy disk, hard disk, compact disk, magnetic tape, etc. are used.
- Few input devices are keyboard, mouse, light pen, punched card, magnetic disk, floppy disk, etc.
- The machine reads data from a punched card is known as card reader.
- Bar codes are certain vertical bars representing alphabets and numbers used in consumer products.
- MICR is used to read the magnetic ink characters of cheques.
- OCR is used to read handwritten, typed, printed matter to input into computer.
- CPU is the heart and brain of a computer system. CPU is otherwise called as computer.
- Control unit (CU) is the traffic controller of a computer.
- BIT represents binary digit which is the measuring rod of memory. BIT is either 0 or 1.
- 8 BIT=1 Byte, 4 BIT =1 Nibble, 1024 BIT=1 Kilo Byte (KB), 1024 KB=1 Mega Byte (MB), 1024MB=1 Giga Byte (GB).
- Primary memory is otherwise called as Intermediate Access Storage (IAS).
- Memories are divided into tow types according to its materials i.e Core memory and Semiconductor memory. Semiconductor memories are classified into two Metallic

Oxide Semiconductor (MOS) and Complementary Metallic Oxide Semiconductor (CMOS). CMOS is an important memory in PC in which the structure of the PC is stored with its peripherals.

- Chip is an example of semiconductor memory. Its base is silicon.
- RAM is relative in nature, divided into two types i.e Dynamic Ramand (DRAM) and Static RAM (SRAM). SRAM is faster than DRAM.
- Printer is a most commonly used output device. It is divided into two types as impact and non-impact printer. Dot matrix printer is the example of impact printer. Ink jet, laser printers are examples of non-impact printer.
- The printouts on the paper is called as hard copy. The output on the screen or VDU is known as softcopy.
- The physical elements of a computer is known as hardware.
- A set of instructions written to solve a specific problem on a computer is called or software (SW). Software handles hardware.
- SW consists of three types as system software, application software, programming languages.
- Programming language consists of low level language, High Level Language (HLL).
- Low level language consists of machine level language and assembly language
- HLL consists of problem oriented language and special purpose language.
- A programme consists of a set of instructions written sequentially in a file to perform a specific task.
- Machine level language is written in machine understandable language i.e. binary language

consisting of 0s and 1s. Every input of data transforms user language to machine level language.

- Assembly language used mnemonics (symbols) in opcodes (operation codes) and macros to communicate instructions into computer.
- System software is otherwise called as system package. It is a programme of a set of programme consisting of set of instructions in the programme which performs a specific task by controlling the architecture of a computer system.
- Data is a collection of facts around us..
- 'Datum' is the singular form of 'data'. So, 'data' is the plural word.
- Data is essential for processing to get information.
- After processing of data the out come will be information. Information is the finished form of data.
- Input-Processing-Output is the major steps of data processing.
- Data items are called as data fields or facts or data elements.
- Record means a group of relevant data items.
- File stands for a group of relevant records which is called a data file.
- A database consisting of group of data files.
- A file name must not exceed 8 characters and its extension name is of three characters separated by a dot (.).
- In a sequential file data are stored and retrieved in sequential process.
- Master file stores permanent information.

- Transaction files are called as movement files and purely temporary.
- Data processing divided into manual and mechanical.
- In real time processing, programme allocates a certain fixed time to CPU for data processing which is called as response time.
- In time sharing processing, the time taken by CPU for data processing is called as time scale.

2

Applications of Computer (IT) in Different Fields

The application of computer became a recent trend towards general purpose usage. Every business to scientific application are computer usage with information database which is called as information highways. This information highway enabled database system is updated by database management system (DBMS) which is called as information technology. Any information can be accessed from the database through computer is called as information technology (IT). Hence, today's age is IT age. So, IT is applicable in every walks of life which is described under.

IT in Business Applications

Every business requires data handling and processing in a large volume. It requires more report generation and calculations. It emphasises high speed input and output. It facilitates transformation of data into information or report as per requirements.

Computer stores the stock of products and its descriptions, updates the input, setting and balance which is called as inventory control. In this process there is a billing system included while selling the product, every product has been defined this process there is description, rate, etc. to computer and generates bill total product cost printing on a billing paper. It also updates the number of products out from stock to outlet or sales point or sold. Now-a-days, every shop including hotels arranging computer with their product database to deliver their product to customer through computerised billing. People become computer savvy and aims to identify the standard business firm who has computerised billing system. The electric department, telecom and cellular services, whole sales, companies, firms, etc. are working with computerised billing system. In the recent trend, online trading become so popular which become possible through IT and internet. Both the buyer and seller are beneficiaries through this system which become success by IT developments.

IT in Reservation System

The airlines, railways, roadways, transporting companies makes databases of their seats, fairs, mode of travelling or transportation, etc. and makes reservation in advance with their terminals over the area they covered. IT is only medium which made easier to the public in information highways. In mobile technology, people also accesses the vacancies, timing, etc. before reservation and also confirmation of reservation if reservation booked in waiting.

IT in Banking

Bank is an important institution which gives public and government more easier ways grow and transact their money in easiest way. Most of the banking institutions are computerised updating transactions, printing of passbooks of account holders, statements for a specific period. core banking service (CBS) to transact the concerned account in any of the branch of the specific bank, ATM service for 24 hours transactions any where in the bank network, internet banking for online transactions, etc. which are only possible through IT banking organisations issues debit cards, credit cards which gives safety to the account holders from frauds, thefts, robbery, pick pocketing and headache for it. It is an easy way to travel, sleep in home peacefully, shopping in an easier way. The shopping of consumer products also carried by banking organisations and the shopping centres receives debit cards and credit cards with a specific machine which transfers the billing amount transfer from bank account of the customer/card hold to shop account. Hence, IT made the society "cash less", grows market sharply with more firms and customer. Except CBS transactions, where the branch of the bank is not in service money transfer can be possible electronically. It is possible through IT where the money is transferred to the particular bank account. It is applicable money transfer from one country to another. There is no need to make money order, bank draft, etc for sending money from one place to other. The EFT (Electronic Fund Transfer) can transfer fund from one account to another on line any where in the network.

IT in Scientific Applications

In general concept computer is only for scientific applications. In scientific calculations computers are used as suitable device for accuracy and timeliness. Except this computer is used for weather forecasting, measurement of pressure, temperature, humidity, etc. It is used in scientific research such as space research. It is used in military applications.

IT in Data Processing

The IT has its significant role in data processing. The IT controls data from input to providing necessary forms of output to user. In every business organisation, IT played vital role in inventory control, maintenance of stock, financial calculations and billing system.

IT in Financial and Cost Accounting

In business firms and big organisations or industries financial transactions are required as management information system of the organisation. It gives financial pictures of the organisation for investors, creditors, income, expenditure, cash and bank position, liabilities and assets, losses and profits, balance sheet, trial balance in systematic accounting method. It maintains costs of production, tax records, share holders and partners data, operation, control, product details, etc. which needs the immediate and periodical requirement of reports to the organisation, share holders, government, tax departments, auditors, financial statement. The IT enabled financial accounting deals with wages and salary like pay-bill, benefits, over time, allowances, deductions. It also deals with billing, receipts, payment, inventory, cost of production, loss and profit, etc. It gives sales report, receipt and payment, purchase report, etc.

IT for Payroll Applications

Every organisation is paying wages and salary in computer generated paybills. This system consists of data on name of employee, worker details, attendance, overtime, wage structure, deductions in every period of payment, and a final slip printed on, to pay him/her which enable the worker to know how much his earnings with the details of deductions and net salary or wage receivable and the slip can be recorded by him/her. It also helps to get the total data of employees and payment and deduction details in any period of time and for calculations in financial year. It consists of data of employee name, address, employee code/ id number, PF Number, Bank Account Number, nature of job-regular, *ad hoc*, temporary, NMR; designation, Department, wage-daily/weekly/fortnightly/monthly; over time, incentives, house rent, dearness allowance, city allowance, uniform allowance, bonus in earning side and deductions like PF, LIC and other premiums, contributions, donations, fines and penalties (if any), etc. in deduction side and the net salary/wage payable/paid to the concerned employee to be printed on the end of a salary/wage period. Its data can be retrieved as and when required.

IT in Health Care and Diagnosis

Doctors and medical practitioners using computer for health care and diagnosis. Many of the health care tools developed which predicts specific health conditions and the tool is connected to a PC which specified the disease and its suggestions for remedy and care. For this specific programs developments made by super IT programmers with medical theorists. There are many software which are used by doctors in general for suggestive medicines and precautions for a specific disease. In internet there are many sites on medicinal improvements, new inventions of remedy for many diseases, new diseases found and precautions, etc used by the hospitals and diagnostic houses.

For paralysed person the messaging technology can be used for remedy through computer. The laser technology helped the physically challenged persons those who are using artificial limbs which can be connected with computer. That limbs can be functioned somehow by computer. By laser scanners, the printed matters can be converted into speech which can be read out by blind people on hearing from computer. It enabled several testing equipment of health to PC which can be detected the disease and diagnosis by Doctor. The patient monitoring system can also be performed by IT.

IT in Education

From school education IT is included in the study. Every subject become IT enabled study. Education packages are readily available in the market. For each subject, disks are available, The publishers are also accompanying subject disks with theoretical and power point, graphic presentation to make the subject lucid and attractive which is accompanied with the book. Teachers also developing such packages for class room teaching. They are using PC with projector to teach. Now-a-days, education become internet savvy. For any reference it becomes easy to get information and details from internet. Most of the publishers made their sites to get information of their books and contents. Many courses are open through internet. The student or professional can admit, study and give examination on line and can be awarded easily by studying before PC. Computer can be used for education in two ways Computer Aided Learning (CAL), Computer Aided Instruction (CAI). There are another made of training called as Computer Based Training (CBT).

IT in Entertainment

Computer is used for entertainment purposes by major part of the users. The users are playing, listening songs and music, viewing movies, etc. Now-a-days the day to day its developments are going on. The development of internet, mobile technology, blue tooth technology, people become more savvy on computer for entertainment. For entertainment through IT even uneducated people can handle it. So, computer is mostly possible for entertainment.

IT for Multi-lingual Applications

The best language for data transmission in It is Sanskrit. Because, development of computing and computer are from India. But, its major developments up to recent age is at America, Japan, Korea, Taiwan, etc. So, English became a global common language used in computer. But, computer is used for several language. In word processing software there are several types of languages developed for western countries. In our country, 14 regional languages are developed as IT enabled for word processing and documentation. The state governments enabled IT for their day to day operations and transactions through their local languages. It become possible more and more publications, print media and printing works become easy through IT enabled regional language enabled IT. The IT become a blessing for development of publication and research in local languages.

IT in Reservation System

The reservation system first of all adopted by Railway Department in India with networking technology. The workstation, reservation, billing, etc. first seen by public in Railway Reservation counters. The networking for reservation made by them are through telephone lines which is called a TeleNet. Now-a-days, every transaction system become IT enabled. Any information can be got thorough mobile network and internet. The airports, ports, roadways, transports, railways, public carriers, cargo, parcel services are updating and billing through computerised offices. They also developed web sites as service providers for giving information online and enabling online reservation, reservation connected to internet banking system for bill payments. The ATM counters are also enabling internet banking for reservation bill payments. The bills can be paid through debit and credit cards also. It facilitated to the customers and general public for easy reservation not standing on queue or not searching or moving to reservation counters.

IT in Software Development

In the company list of the world's mostly growing companies IT, Software development, Pharmaceutical, FMCG companies are in the forefront. IT and software developers and service providers are marching ahead sharply, because the recent age is IT enabled age in any field of work. So, more and more software are required bb the organisations, firms, industries, companies, banks and other financial companies, are developing and orderly supplying software and earning more profits. So, more and more software development firms and software parks are opening day by day. Every organisation adopting IT as a tool of their functionaries and people measuring IT enabled firm a trusted one. So, programs and packages, games, fun and laughing programs, educational packages, etc. are demanding more and more in the market. The multinational IT companies and software developers developing the commonly used software packages in regional language to reach among common people and to check piracy, to sell more and more locally to get good revenue and profit worthy.

IT in E-Commerce

Electronic Commerce, commonly known as (electronic marketing) e-commerce or eCommerce, consists of the buying and selling of products or services over electronic systems such as the Internet and other computer networks. The amount of trade conducted electronically has grown extraordinarily with widespread Internet usage. The use of commerce is conducted in this way, spurring and drawing on innovations in electronic funds transfer, supply chain management, Internet marketing, online transaction processing, electronic data interchange (EDI), inventory management systems, and automated data collection systems. Modern electronic commerce typically uses the World Wide Web at least at some point in the transaction's lifecycle, although it can encompass a wider range of technologies such as e-mail as well. A large percentage of electronic commerce is conducted entirely electronically for virtual items such as access to premium content on a website, but most electronic commerce involves the transportation of physical items in some way. Online retailers are sometimes known as e-tailers and online retail is sometimes known as e-tail. Almost all big retailers have electronic commerce presence on the World Wide Web. Electronic commerce that is conducted between businesses is referred to as business-to-business or B2B. B2B can be open to all interested parties (e.g. commodity exchange) or limited to specific, pre-qualified participants (private electronic market). Electronic commerce that is conducted between businesses and consumers, on the other hand, is referred to as business-to-consumer or B2C. This is the type of electronic commerce conducted by companies such as

Amazon.com. Electronic commerce is generally considered to be the sales aspect of e-business. It also consists of the exchange of data to facilitate the financing and payment aspects of the business transactions.

IT in E-Governance

For SMART governance, e-governance is the tool of its application which can accelerate the pace of community development. e-Governance in general have the dimensions of interface as G2C (Government to Citizen), G2B (Government to Business). It can enable 4 dimensions of interface in panchayats of rural India i.e. P2P (Panchayat to Panchayat), P2B (Panchayat 2 Business), P2G (Panchayat to Gram Sabha), P2E (Panchayat 2 Employee). The panchayats governed with e-Gov. us called as e-Panchayat. E-Panchayat or e-Gov. centres will be equipped with all electronic devices as computer, telephone, internet (VSAT with application), telephone, scanner, printer, projector, video camera connected to computer and individual. E-Governance has proven its usefulness in implementation of various welfare schemes for citizens as weather forecasting (farmer, fishermen, tourist), e-learning project, tele-medicine, e-voting, etc. It is helpful to get policy and project knowledge of Government and other agencies, e-library and many more.

The Concept of e-Governance has originated in India in Seventies focussing in house government operations in the area of defence, economic monitoring and planning, managing data of election, census, tax, administration, etc. In Eighties with the initiation of National Information Centre (NIC) to connect all the state and district headquarters. In the beginning of Nineties, IT supplemented with ICT technology, it has enabled wide sectoral applications with policy emphasis on reaching out to rural and taking the help of NGOs and private parties to spread the services to citizens of remotest areas. The services of e-Governance has been extended up to public grievance system, tax payment, information gathering, payment of bills, poverty alleviation initiatives, land record information, driving licence-residential certificate collection, health assistance, judicial assistance, passport services, banking and railway services, etc. At the time of general election Government has initiated to join the citizens in the governance has launched a web portal www.nationalelectionwatch.org to know about the candidates contesting in the election and other information. It is also meant for an idea to look at large picture of accountability and governance. The website empowering India set up for comprehensive information on election, the past results, the candidates and voting patterns in www.empoweringindia.org. The services of e-Governance has been varied from state to state. Most of the state governments has initiated to form citizen centric services through Community Service Centres (CSCs) with the technical assistance of NIC. There are several projects in different states under National e-Governance Project with their initiatives on service rendering for their citizen are as under. E-Governance as an initiative through Information Technology (IT) and networking through internet for Information Communication Technology (ICT) for connectivity, communication, information gathering with other friends, relatives, offices. It gives a chance for bridging the distance between rural and urban, government and citizen. E-governance is n information highway for citizens in rural areas without moving to urban areas, government offices, agencies. In such a system, corruption, delay in delivery of service has been avoided maintaining transparency.

IT in Data Warehouse

A data warehouse is a repository (collection of resources that can be accessed to retrieve information) of an organization's electronically stored data, designed to facilitate reporting and analysis. This definition of the data warehouse focuses on data storage. The main source of the data is cleaned, transformed and cataloged and is made available to be used by managers and other business professional for data mining, online analytical processing, market research and decision support. However, the means to retrieve and analyze data, to extract, transform and load data, and to manage the data dictionary are also considered essential components of a data warehousing system. Many references to data warehousing use this broader context. Thus, an expanded definition for data warehousing includes business intelligence tools, tools to extract, transform and load data into the repository, and tools to manage and retrieve metadata. Data warehousing arises in an organization's need for reliable, consolidated, unique and integrated analysis and reporting of its data, at different levels of aggregation. The practical reality of most organizations is that their data infrastructure is made up by a collection of heterogeneous systems. For example, an organization might have one system that handles customer-relationship, a system that handles employees, systems that handle sales data or production data, yet another system for finance and budgeting data, etc. In practice, these systems are often poorly or not at all integrated and simple questions like: "How much time did sales person A spend on customer C, how much did we sell to Customer C, was customer C happy with the provided service, Did Customer C pay his bills" can be very hard to answer, even though the information is available "somewhere" in the different data systems. Another problem is that enterprise resource planning (ERP) systems are designed to support relevant operations. For example, a finance system might keep track of every single stamp bought; When it was ordered, when it was delivered, when it was paid and the system might offer accounting principles (like double bookkeeping) that further complicates the data model. Such information is great for the person in charge of buying "stamps" or the accountant trying to sort out an irregularity, but the CEO is definitely not interested in such detailed information, the CEO wants to know stuff like "What's the cost?", "What's the revenue?", "did our latest initiative reduce costs?" and wants to have this information at an aggregated level.

Yet another problem might be that the organization is, internally, in disagreement about which data are correct. For example, the sales department might have one view of its costs, while the finance department has another view of that cost. In such cases the organization can spend unlimited time discussing who's got the correct view of the data. It is partly the purpose of data warehousing to bridge such problems. It is important to note that in data warehousing the source data systems are considered as given: Even though the data source system might have been made in such a manner that it's difficult to extract integrated information, the "data warehousing answer" is not to redesign the data source systems but rather to make the data appear consistent, integrated and consolidated despite the problems in the underlying source systems. Data warehousing achieves this by employing different data warehousing techniques, creating one or more new data repositories (i.e. the data warehouse) whose data model(s) support the needed reporting and analysis.

IT in Data Mining

Data Mining is the process of extracting patterns from data. Data mining is seen as an increasingly important tool by modern business to transform data into an informational advantage. It is currently used in a wide range of profiling practices, such as marketing, surveillance, fraud detection, and scientific discovery. The related terms *data dredging, data fishing* and *data snooping* refer to the use of data mining techniques to sample portions of the larger population data set that are (or may be) too small for reliable statistical inferences to be made about the validity of any patterns discovered. These techniques can however, be used in the creation of new hypothesises to test against the larger data populations.

The manual extraction of patterns from data has occurred for centuries. Early methods of identifying patterns in data include Bayes' theorem (1700s) and regression analysis (1800s). The proliferation, ubiquity and increasing power of computer technology has increased data collection and storage. As data sets have grown in size and complexity, direct hands-on data analysis has increasingly been augmented with indirect, automatic data processing. This has been aided by other discoveries in computer science, such as neural networks, clustering, genetic algorithms (1950s), decision trees (1960s) and support vector machines (1980s). Data mining is the process of applying these methods to data with the intention of uncovering hidden patterns. It has been used for many years by businesses, scientists and governments to sift through volumes of data such as airline passenger trip records, census data and supermarket scanner data to produce market research reports.

Before data mining algorithms can be used, a target data set must be assembled. As data mining can only uncover patterns already present in the data, the target dataset must be large enough to contain these patterns while remaining concise enough to be mined in an acceptable timeframe. A common source for data is a datamart or data warehouse. Pre-process is essential to analyse the multivariate datasets before clustering or data mining. The target set is then cleaned. Cleaning removes the observations with noise and missing data.The clean data are reduced into feature vectors, one vector per observation. A feature vector is a summarised version of the raw data observation. For example, a black and white image of a face which is 100px by 100px would contain 10,000 bits of raw data. This might be turned into a feature vector by locating the eyes and mouth in the image. Doing so would reduce the data for each vector from 10,000 bits to three codes for the locations, dramatically reducing the size of the dataset to be mined, and hence reducing the processing effort. The feature(s) selected will depend on what the objective(s) is/are; obviously, selecting the "right" feature(s) is fundamental to successful data mining.

Data mining commonly involves four classes of tasks:

- **Clustering** - is the task of discovering groups and structures in the data that are in some way or another "similar", without using known structures in the data.
- **Classification** - is the task of generalizing known structure to apply to new data. For example, an email program might attempt to classify an email as legitimate or spam. Common algorithms include decision tree learning, nearest neighbor, naive Bayesian classification, neural networks and support vector machines.
- **Regression** - Attempts to find a function which models the data with the least error.
- **Association rule learning** - Searches for relationships between variables. For example a supermarket might gather data on customer purchasing habits. Using association rule learning, the supermarket can determine which products are frequently bought together and use this information for marketing purposes. This is sometimes referred to as market basket analysis.

Conclusion

Applications of computer commonly called as IT (information technology) which is ubiquitous in such a manner that men became mechanical. In every sphere of life like there are applications of IT as IT in Railway Station Ticket counter, Bus stand Ticket Counter, Air Port, Traffic control, diagnosis, in Law and Justice, Weather Forecasting, Horoscope, Translating books one language to another, Science and Research, Satellite, searching words from a book, etc. computer will be mostly helpful. In stead of these in Schools, Colleges, Hospitals computers are mushroom. Today in home also the personal computers are used for funny and playing games. By the use of computer we become free and avail the facilities of time saving, complete accuracy, easy going, easy memory capacity. It is also helpful in Office automation, used in banking system, used for inventory control, payroll calculations, etc. The IT is a more effective tool for modern men. The developments are going on which make the men more easier.

3

Problem-solving Techniques

Introduction

Computer system consists of two main components, e.g. hardware and software. Hardware is the physical components of a computer system. Software is the knowledge built into the hardware to put it into the hardware in the form of computer programmes. In other words, software is the technique or the required knowledge to process data to get specific output. The programme is a set of instructions given sequentially which achieves specific task or results. Software handles the hardware properly.

Before using hardware with the software for solving a specific problem, the programme planning or programme technique to be developed in a step by step manner. Such a planning is sequentially represented symbolically with the help of flow chart, a computer logic. Logic is the essence of flow chart. It is an important tool of system analysts and programmers for tracing the information flow and the logical sequence in data processing.

Flow Chart

Flow chart, as its name indicated, it is a pictorial (figurative) representation of instructions need to be carried out in a given sequence (flow) for a programme. In other words, a flow chart is a given problem indicating the flow of the entire processing i.e. the sequence of data input, operations, computations, decisions, output and other processing.

Flow charts can be drawn for simple as well as complex operations and are possible even in a non-computational environments. Trial and error of a specific task can be avoided in front of the computer, because time is most precious. Computerisation of data without flow chart is just a construction of building without foundation and design. Once flow chart is ready accurately, it is quite simple to convert this in the form of programme in any programming language through computer.

Kinds of Flow Chart

Flow charts can be classified into two broad categories e.g. system flow chart and programme flow chart:

1. **System Flow chart** - A flow chart that gives only the main logic without the details of each step is called a system flow chart.
2. **Programme Flow chart** - A flow chart that step-by-step description of each details involved in the solution of a programme is called a programme flow chart. In a programme flow chart absence of detail may lead to errors and omissions.

These are used generally by the programmers to describe the sequence of operations and decisions for a particular problem. The programmers are recommended to prepare a detail programme flow chart for building the logic of a given problem which should include the basic step like expanding to a level from which instructions can be directly coded. In all the High Level Language (HLLs) and packages before preparing programme, flow chart should be prepared.

A flow chart is frequently used in planning, development and structuring of an algorithm for solving a complex as well as simple problem. The main purpose of a flow chart is to depict the sequence of operations, data flow and control flow. It is usually regarded as an essential part of the documentation of any computer programme translation of the original algorithm.

Algorithm

The world 'algorithm' simply means a procedure of rules for achieving a goal or object. It is a series of step by step procedure to solve a specific task. It helps to write a complete programme with the help of subsequent steps. To get clear idea about algorithm, let us take a few examples as:

Question 1: Reema have to make a cup of tea. How she will prepare it?

Ans:

Step - 1 Reema will go to kitchen.

Step - 2 Take an utensil, keep on the stove, pour a cup of water on it.

Step - 3 Fire the stove which boil the water.

Step - 4 Add milk to it.

Step - 5 Add sugar and leaf tea on the boiled liquid.

Step - 6 Purify the boiled liquid with purifier.

Step - 7 Serve the tea on a cup.

Question 2: Rakesh have to wash his cloth. How he will perform it?

Ans:

Step - 1 Rakesh will take a bucket with required water and detergent.

Step - 2 Rinse the dirty cloth in it.

Step - 3 Wash the cloth

Step - 4 Hang the washed cloth in the hanger.

Question 3: A person earns 50 rupees per day, the contractor wants to know how much he is earning in a specific period of time.

Ans:

Step - 1 Accept the number of working days in the specified period.

Step - 2 Multiply 50 with the number of days given as working day.

Step - 3 Display the product as the total earning of the worker in the given period

Step - 4 End.

Question 4: Calculate the total emolument of an contractual employee for a given period of time.

Ans:

Step - 1 Accept the number of working days in the specified period.

Step - 2 Accept per day remuneration of the employee on contract.

Step - 3 Multiply both the working days with the per day remuneration

Step - 4 Display the product as the total emoluments of the worker in that period

Step - 5 End.

Developments of Flow Chart

The first flow chart was developed by John Von Neumann in 1945 on his lecture on Electronic Digital Computers explaining the idea of storage programme concept. But, conventionally it is said that further symbols of flow charts were developed by International Standard Organization (ISO). A flow chart consists of different types of boxes called as symbols and arrow lines connected the boxes called as flow lines. A box tells us what to do and arrow lines indicates us the flow of sequence of instructions to be performed in further steps. A flow chart, as the name shows gives a pictorial representations (through several boxes) represents given sequence (flow) of operations indicating flow lines (arrows). It will depict the clear picture of functioning of the instructions for specific task.

Types of Instructions Used in Flow Charts

There are several types of instructions which can be carried out in flow chart.

Need of Flow Chart

Flow chart will help the programmer to develop the program logic and to serve as documentation for a completed program which are discussed below:

1. It gives convenient methods of communication
2. It clears the logical complexities of program.
3. It is key to debugging the program.
4. It helps in planning and designing of programs.
5. It indicates clearly the sequence of instructions to be followed.
6. It provides an over view of the system and also demonstrates the relationship between various steps.
7. It promotes logical accuracy.
8. It takes confident to get accurate result.

Symbols Used in Flow Chart

Being a symbolic representation of sequence of instruction of a program, flow chart have several symbols for different types of instructions.

1. **Terminal box or oval:** It is used fore START/STOP. START is the first symbol of the flow chart. STOP is the last symbol of instructions. START indicates beginning and STOP indicates completion of instructions.

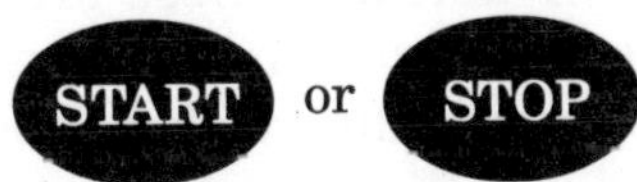

2. **Processing box or rectangle:** It processes data. For arithmetic instructions this box is used.

3. **I/O box or parallelogram:** It is used for READ and WRITE instructions. It implies that the symbol is used for instructions input data and get output of a program. READ is used to input data and WRITE is used to get result.

4. **Decision box or diamond or Rhombus:** It takes decisions for logical instructions. This symbol is used to take decisions in the flow chart.

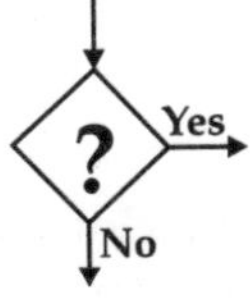

5. **Connector or circle:** It is used to connect the flow of the divided part of a flow chart. When the program is very large, takes one after one page, it is used at the last of the first page and at the beginning of the next page and so on to indicate the connection of flow of instructions. A number or alphabet can be written in the circle or connector to be more convenient to know the connection.

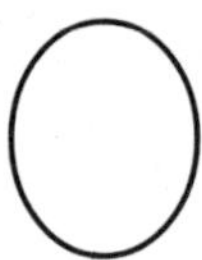

6. **Flow lines or arrows:** These are indicating the flow of the sequence of instructions towards the face of the arrow. It connects the symbols one-by-one.

7. **Comments or annotations:** It is used to write the comments or annotations inside the bracket to get the logic of instructions easier.

.... [or .... [

8. **Document or printout:** It is used to indicate the printout requirement through printer.

9. **Visual display:** It is used when the display of result is required visually through VDU or monitor. This is normally used in query programs.

10. **Pre-defined process:** Before writing an instruction something can be written to pre-define the process of instructions, this symbolic is used.

11. **Manual operation:** It there is any requirement of manual operation i.e. by the programmer, a task to be done for computerisation, this symbol is used in flow chart.

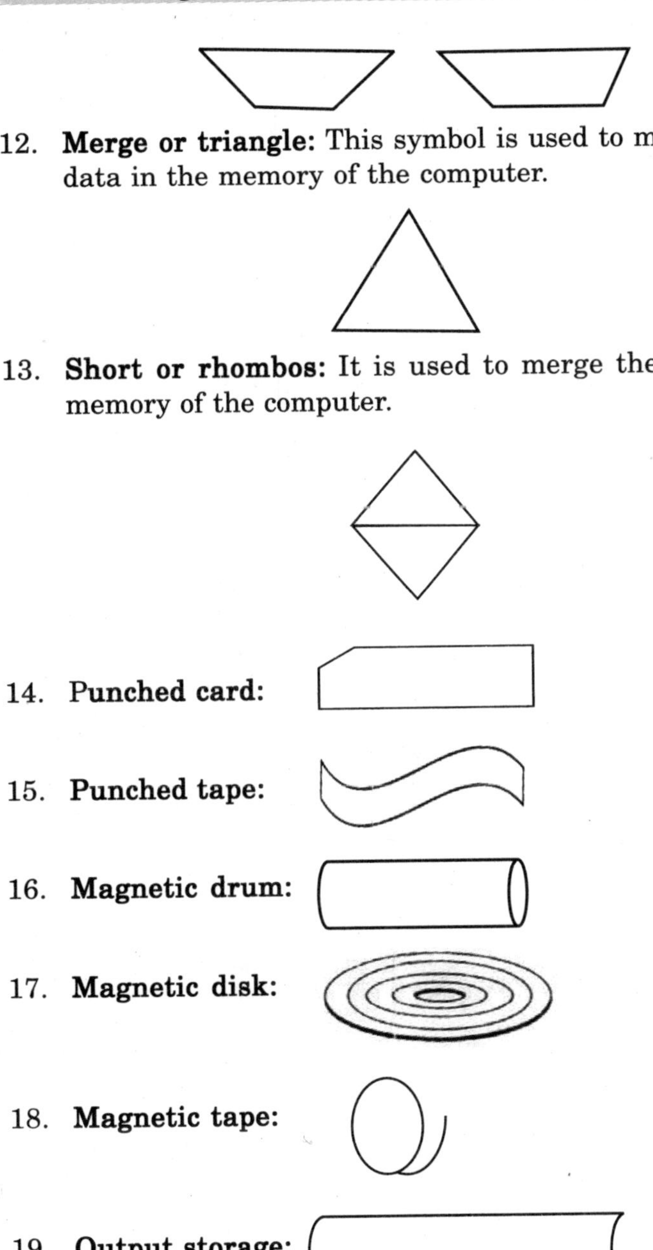

12. **Merge or triangle:** This symbol is used to merge the data in the memory of the computer.

13. **Short or rhombos:** It is used to merge the data in memory of the computer.

14. **Punched card:**

15. **Punched tape:**

16. **Magnetic drum:**

17. **Magnetic disk:**

18. **Magnetic tape:**

19. **Output storage:**

20. **File or cards:**

21. **Auxiliary operator:**

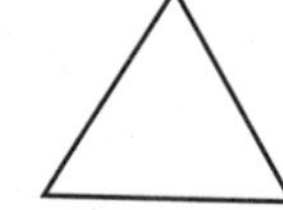

22. **Extract:**

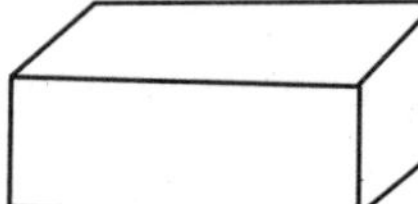

23. **Deck of cards:**

24. **Core:**

Techniques of Drawing Flow Charts

Flow chart is a step-by-step procedure of algorithm. Thus for understanding the drawing techniques of flow chart, a few examples are illustrated below. The following exhibits the simple algorithm of a flow charts.

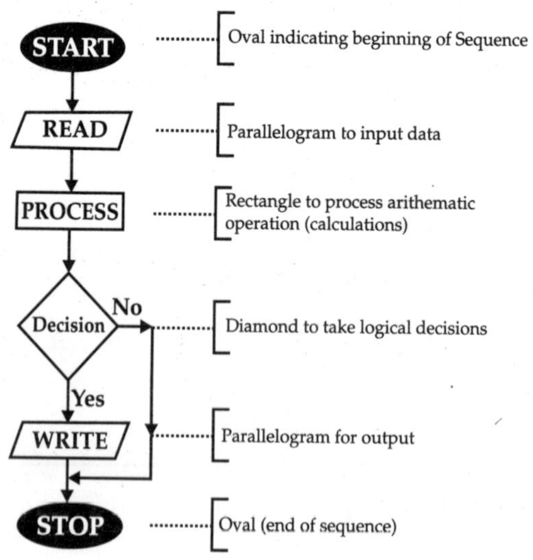

Example 3.1

Draw a flow chart to calculate and print the value of the expression C = (A+B).

Algorithm

Step - 1 Start

Step - 2 Let A be the variable with the value of 10

Step - 3 Let B be the variable with the value of 5

Step - 4 Add A and B and store the result in the variable C

Step - 5: Write the value of C

Step - 6: Stop

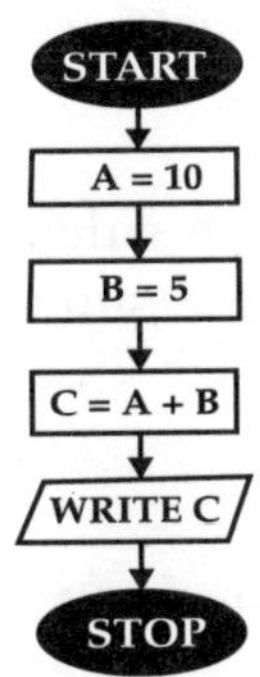

Flow chat 3.1

Example 3.2

Draw flow chart to calculate the value of C as, C = A + B for any value of A and B.

Algorithm

Step - 1 Start

Step - 2 Read the value of A

Step - 3 Read the value of B

Step - 4 Add A and B, and store it in C (as C = A + B)

Step - 5 Write C

Step - 6 Stop

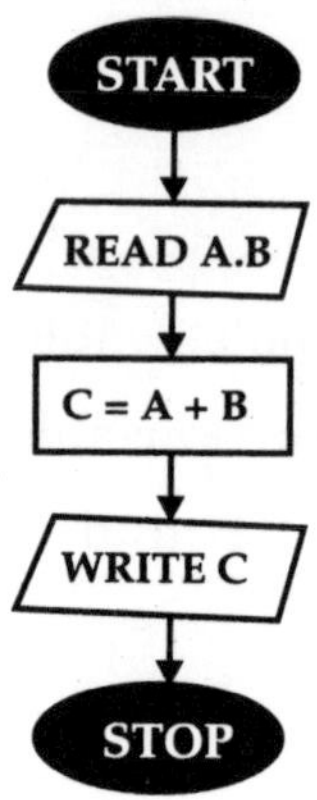

Flow Chart 3.2

Example 3.3

Draw a flow chart to calculate and print the total marks of a student of three subjects are given.

Algorithm

Step - 1 Start

Step - 2 Let the value of A is 50

Step - 3 Let the value of B is 60

Step - 4 Let the value of C is 75

Step - 5 Add, A, B and C, store the result in T

Step - 6 Write T

Step - 7 Stop

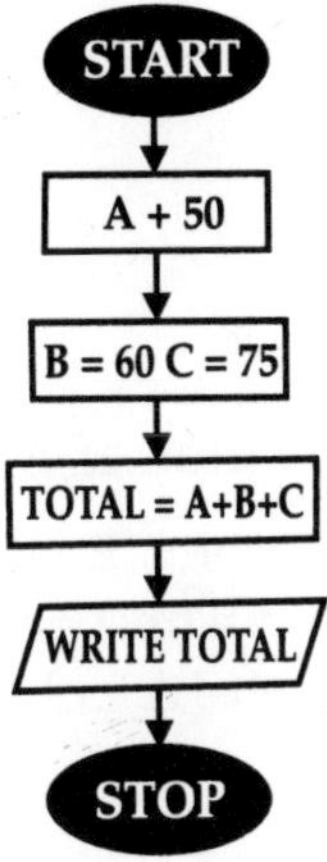

Flow Chart 3.3

Example 3.4

Draw a flow chart to find largest among two numbers.

Algorithm

Step - 1 Start

Step - 2 Read the value of A, B

Step - 3 Check if A is greater than B, Write A is big else B is big

Step - 4 Stop

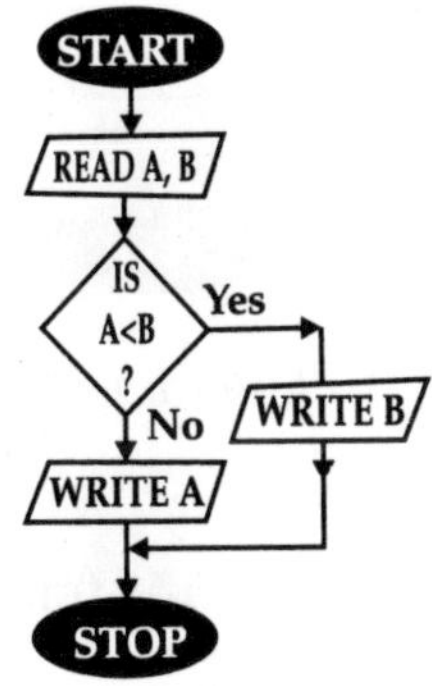

Flow Chart 3.4

Example 3.5

Draw a flow chart to calculate and print the biggest between three numbers.

Algorithm

Step - 1 Start

Step - 2 Read the value of A, B, C

Step - 3 Check whether the value of A is greater than B then find whether the value of A is greater than C, write A is Biggest.

Step - 4 Check if A is not greater than B then check if B is greater than C, write B is biggest else write C is biggest.

Step - 5 Stop

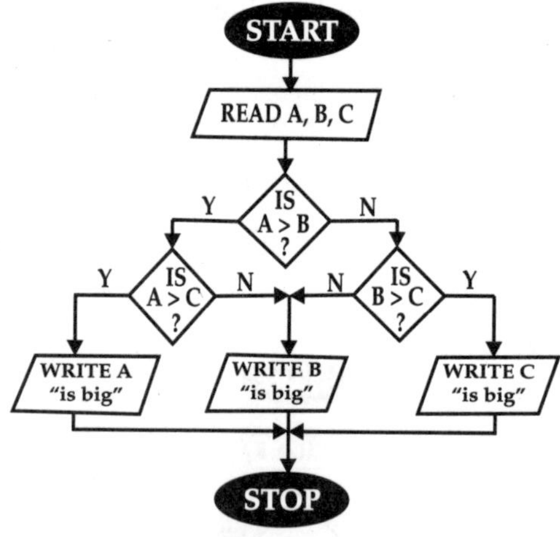

Flow Chart 3.5

Example 3.6

Draw a flow chart to print temperature in Fahrenheit by the value input in Celsius.

Algorithm

Step - 1 Start

Step - 2 Read C

Step - 3 Calculate the formula F = (C*9/5) + 32

Step - 4 Write F

Step - 5 Stop

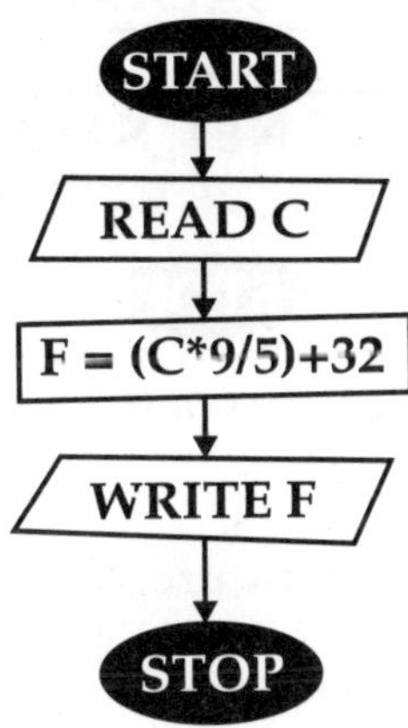

Flow Chart 3.6

Example 3.7

Draw a flow chart to calculate the net salary by the employee by designing, 3/4th of the salary in expenditure.

Algorithm

Step - 1 Start

Step - 2 Read salary

Step - 3 Expenditure = Salary* 3/4

Step - 4 Net _ salary = Salary-Expenditure

Step - 5 Write Net _ Salary

Step - 6 Stop

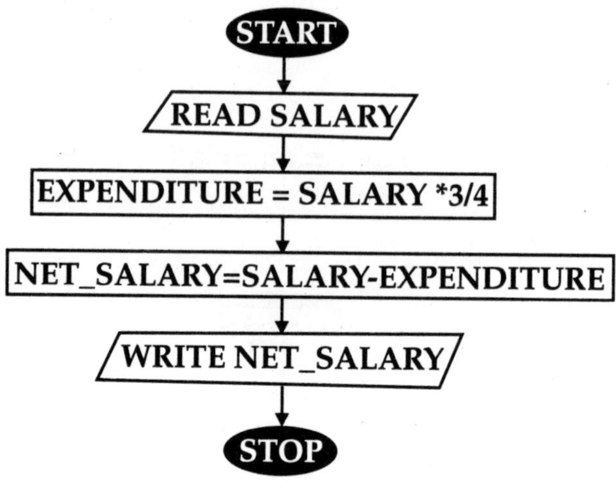

Flow Chart 3.7

Example 3.8

Draw a flow chart to prepare the mark sheet of a student having three subjects English, mathematics and G.K. with his/her name, roll No.

Algorithm

Step - 1 Start

Step - 2 Read Name $, Roll _ No.., Eng., Math, G.K

Step - 3 Add Eng., Math and G.K., store the result in Sum

Step - 4 Write Name $, Roll _ No., Eng., Math, G.K., Sum

Step - 5 Stop

Hints: The string variable like name should follow $ symbol when it was used for BASIC programming else garbage.

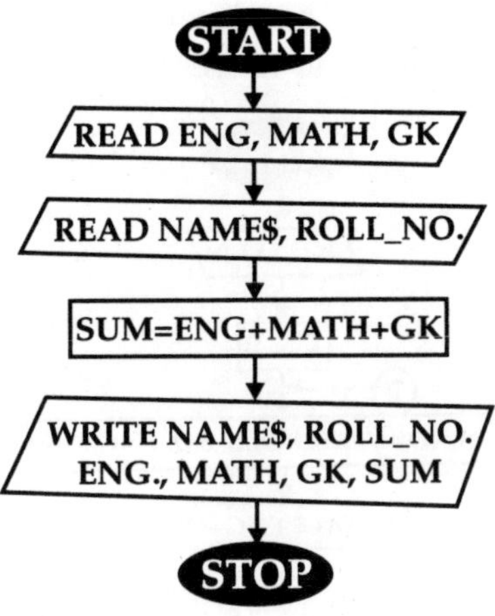

Flow Chart 3.8

Example 3.9

Draw a flow chart to calculate a number of students of example 3.8.

Algorithm

Step - 1 Start

Step - 2 C = 0

Step - 3 Read "No. of Students", N

Step - 4 Read NAME$ ROLL _ NO, ENG., MATH, GK

Step - 5 Add ENG., MATH and G.K, store the result in SUM

Step - 6 Write N, NAME$, ROLL_NO., ENG., MATH, GK, SUM

Step - 7 Check if C<N then goto Step-3

Step - 8 Stop

Hints: Step – 3 will display the message while receiving the data for the value of N which is within quotes (" "). It make the input easier and more convenient to the user.

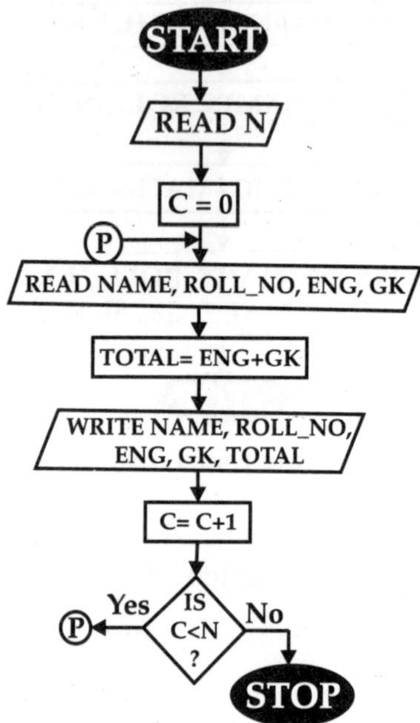

Flow Chart 3.9

Example 3.10

Draw a flow chart to calculate the person whether eligible to vote and print his/her name, age, eligible or not.

Algorithm

Step - 1 Start

Step - 2 Read NAME$, AGE

Step - 3 Check if AGE is greater than 18 write "Eligible to vote" else go to

Step - 4 Write NAME, AGE

Step - 5 Stop

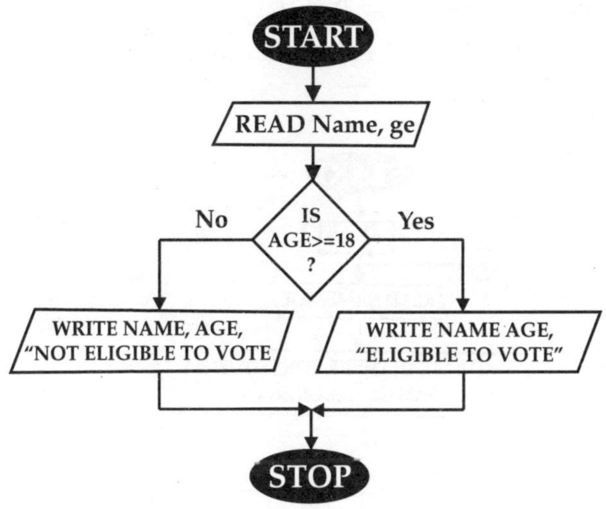

Flow Chart 3.10

Example 3.11

Draw a flow chart to print the name and age, who can vote in a city named as Brahampur, at Ganjam district, of Orissa state of 11,10,550 people. The eligible age for vote is 18 or more.

Algorithm

Step - 1 Start

Step - 2 Take 1 as the value of N

Step - 3 Rad N$, AGE

Step - 4 Write "Brahamapur Constituency, Brahamapur, Ganjam, Orissa."

Step - 5 Write "______"

Step - 6 Check whether age is greater than or equal to 18, go to step 7

Step - 7 Write N, N$, AGE

Step - 8 Take N as N + 1

Step - 9 Check if N > = 1110550, goto Step 3

Step - 10 Stop

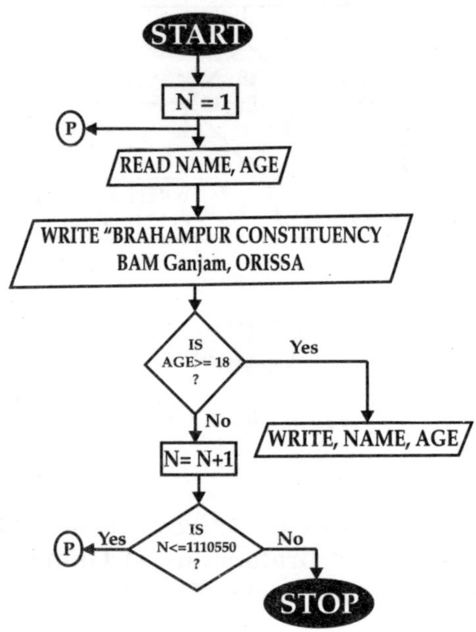

Flow Chart 3.11

Example 3.12

Draw a flow chart to find the sum of N numbers.

Algorithm

Step - 1 Start

Step - 2 Read N

Step - 3 Take 0 as the value of S

Step - 4 Take 0 as the value of C

Step - 5 Read the value of A

Step - 6 Take the value of S is S + A

Step - 7 Take the value of C is C + 1

Step - 8 Check if C is less than N go to Step 5 else write S

Step - 9 Stop

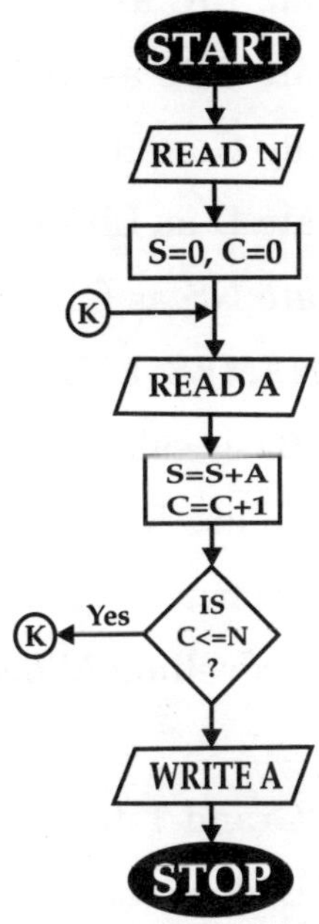

Flow Chart 3.12

Example 3.13

Draw flow chart to calculate net salary of an employee with the conditions as HRA, DA, TA, deductions like LIC, GPF are 10%, 138%, 28%, 18%, 08% of the basic salary respectively. Prepare the pay bill as employee name, employee code number, net payable salary with the details of payments.

Algorithm

Step - 1 Start

Step - 2 Read NAME$, EMP_CO, BP

Step - 3 Calculate HRA as BP*10/100

Step - 4 Calculate DA as BP*138/100

Step - 5 Calculate TA as BP*28/100

Step - 6 Calculate LIC as BP*18/100

Step - 7 Calculate GPF as BP*8/100

Step - 8 Calculate G as BP + HRA + DA + TA

Step - 9 Calculate D as LIC + GPF

Step - 10 Calculate NS as GD

Step - 11 Write NAME$, EMP_CO

Step - 12 Write "Basic salary", BP

Step - 13 Write "House Rent Allowance", HRA

Step - 14 Write "Dearness Allowance", DA

Step - 15 Write "Travelling Allowance", TA

Step - 16 Write "______"

Step - 17 Write "Grand Total = G

Step - 18 Write "Deductions"

Step - 19 Write "Life Insurance Corp.", LIC

Step - 20 Write "Gen. Provident Fund", GPF

Step - 21 Write "______"

Step - 22 Write "Net Deduction =", D

Step - 23 Write "______"

Step - 24 Write "Net Salary Payable", NS

Step - 25 Write "______"

Step - 26 Stop

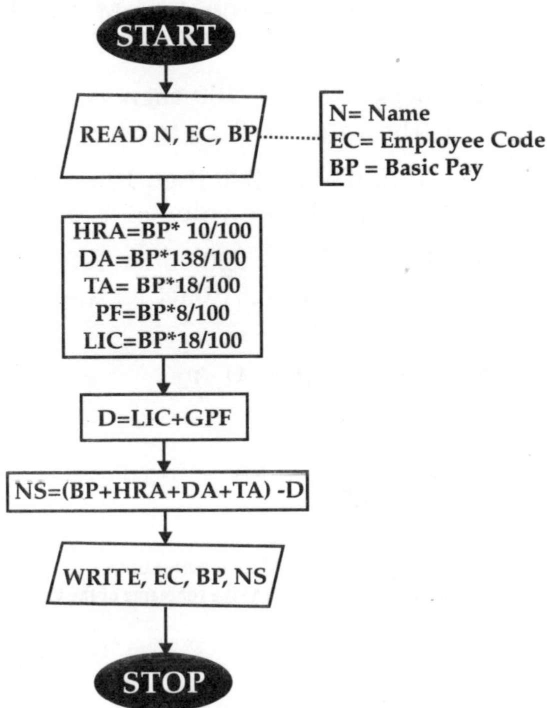

Flow Chart 3.13

Example 3.14

Draw a flow chart to calculate the monthly telephone bills as the condition follow

Minimum Re. 1 for first 100 message units

for next 60 units Re. 0.06 per unit

for next 60 units Re. 0.05 per unit

for more than that Re. 0.04 per unit should be charge

Algorithm

Step - 1 Start

Step - 2 Read message units as the value of M, name as NAME$

Step - 3 Check if M < = 100 them M*1 is the value of T, go to Step 7

Step - 4 Check if M < = 160 then 100+(M-100)*0.06 is the value of T, go to Step 7

Step - 5 Check if M <= 220 then 100+(60*0.06) + (M-160)*0.05 is the value of T, go to Step 7

Step - 6 Check if M >= 220 them 100 + (60*0.06) + (60*0.05+(M-220)*0.04 as the value of T, go to Step 7

Step - 7 Write NAME$, M, T.

Step - 8 Stop

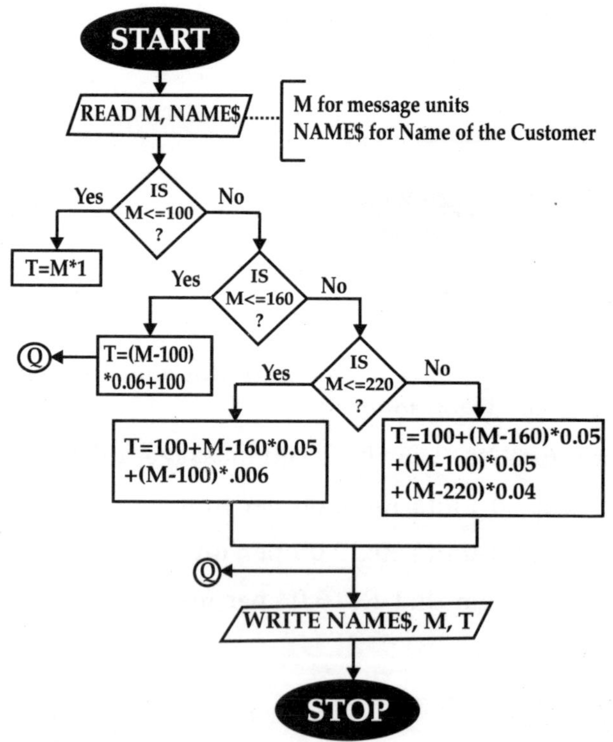

Flow Chart 3.14

Example 3.15

Develop a flow chart listing all the steps required to make telephone calls of a person assuming the following procedural steps are the performed in the given order:

(i) To begin to lift the receiver.

(ii) Dial the number.

(iii) If the line is engaged the receiver is to be put down, wait or some time and dial again.

(iv) Otherwise call for the person.

(v) If the person is attending, talk to him or her.

(vi) Otherwise, leave the message.

(vii) Replace receiver to end.

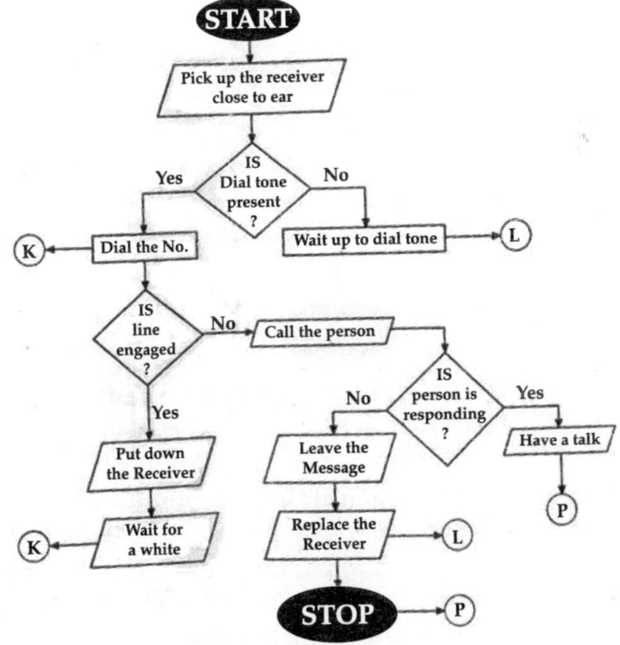

Flow Chart 3.15

Example 3.16

After reading the three angles, a triangle to be identified as equilateral, scalene, isosceles, right angle or only isosceles triangle. Develop a flow chart.

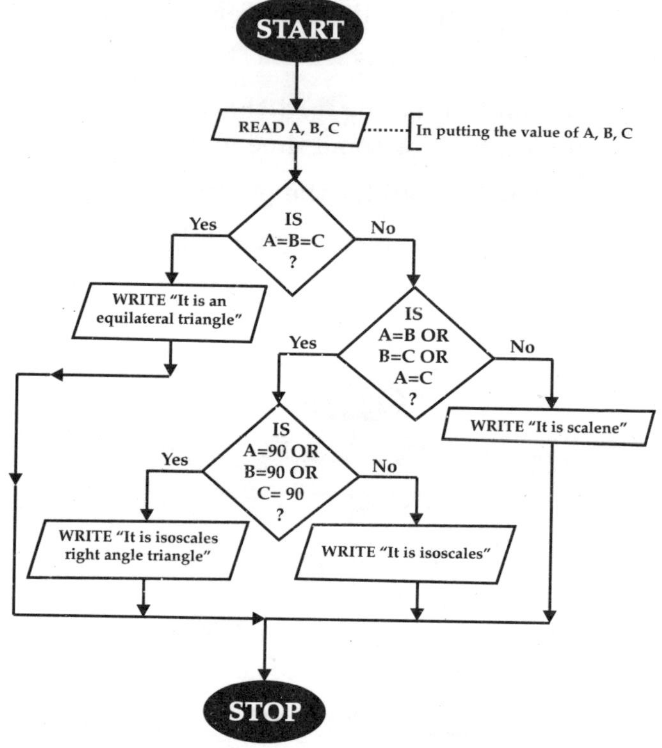

Flow Chart 3.16

Example 3.17

A carpenter has a number of planks of wood from which he has to cut length of 2 meter each. He takes the planks one after another, measures the length, rejects those planks are smaller than 2 meter and selects the planks are just 2 meters. From those which are longers, he cuts as many pieces of 2 meter as possible. He continues his job till the last plank. Develop a flow chart to complete the job.

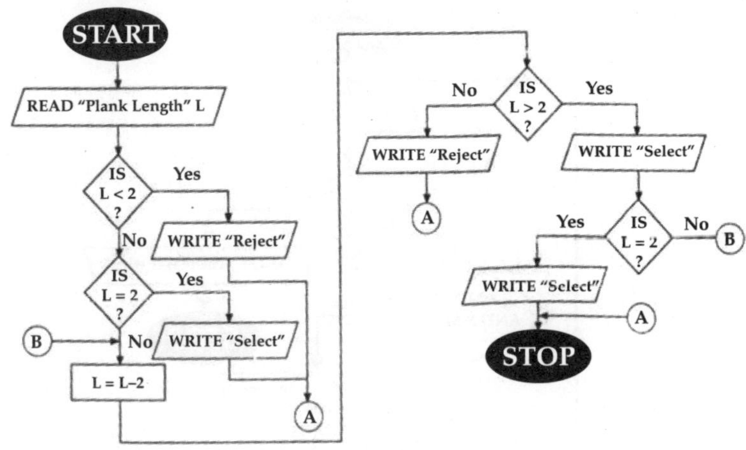

Flow Chart 3.17

Example 3.18

John and Nisa play a game using 2 dice. The game is described by the following rules

1. Decide who plays first.
2. Player throw 2 dice.
3. If numbers are same the player who has just thrown the dice wins and game stops.
4. Otherwise, if numbers are even the same player gets another chance.
5. Otherwise, the other player takes the turn.

Using the above rules develop a flow chart for the game.

Example 3.19

A salesman earns commission on his/her net sale as per rate given below:

Net Sale	Commission (%)
Upto 10000	5
10000 to 100000	8
100000 above	10

Flow Chart 3.18

Develop a flow chart to prepare the commission sheet for the salesman with his/her name, salesman code number, sales amount, payable commission.

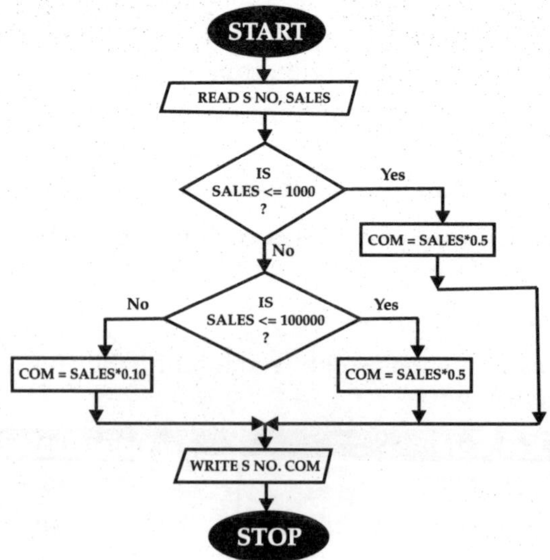

Flow Chart 3.19

Example 3.20

Draw a flow chart to calculate the sum of the series : $1^2 + 2^2 + 3^2 + \dots + N^2$

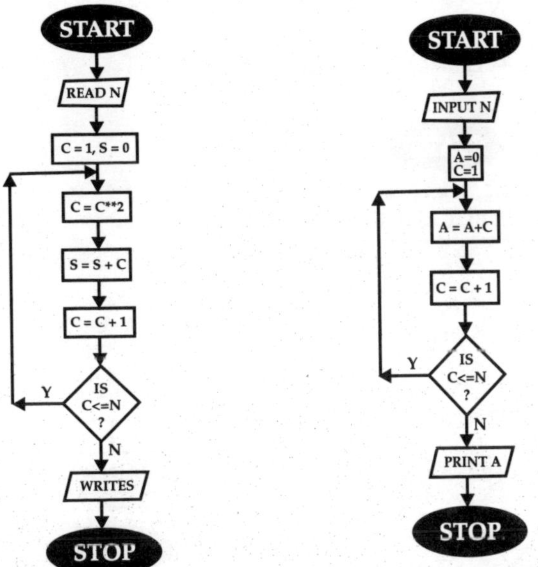

Flow Chart 3.20 *Flow Chart 3.21*

Example 3.21

DAFC to calculate the sum of a given number from 1

Algorithm

Step - 1 Input N

Step - 2 A = 0

Step - 3 C = 1

Step - 4 A = A + C

Step - 5 C = C + 1

Step - 6 If C <= N then 40

Step - 7 Print A

Step - 8 End

Develop a flow chart to calculate the value of the area of a triangle.

$$Area = \sqrt{S(S-A)(S-B)(S-C)}$$

S = (A + B > C)/2 [where A+B>C, B+C>A, C+A>B]

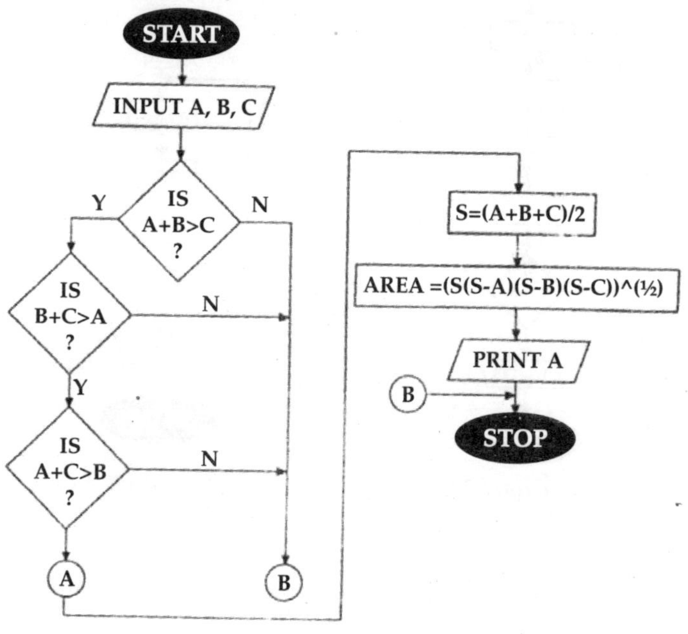

Flow Chart 3.22

Example 3.22

DAFC to calculate the sum of cube of n natural numbers.

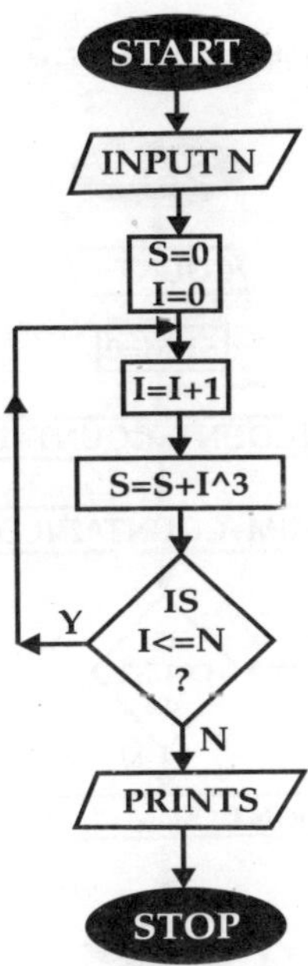

Flow Chart 3.23

Algorithm

Step - 1 REM calculation of square of N natural numbers

Step - 2 Input "Enter A Natural No." No

Step - 3 S = 0

Step - 4 I = 0

Step - 5 I = I + 1

Step - 6 S = S + I ^ 3

Step - 7 If I < N then 50

Step - 8 Print "Sum of Cube of"; No. "Natural Numbers ="; S

Step - 9 End

Example 3.23

DAFC to calculate $1^2.3^2 + 3^2.5^2 + \ldots\ldots + 98^2.100^2$

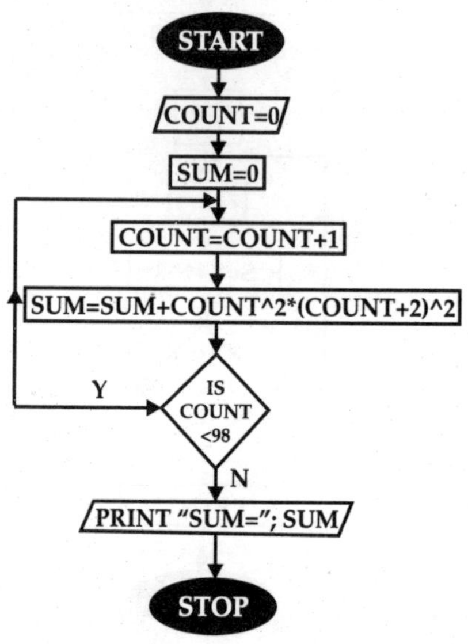

Flow Chart 3.24

Algorithm

Step - 1 Let count = 0

Step - 2 Let sum = 0

Step - 3 Let count = count + 1

Step - 4 Sum = Sum + count ^ 2* (Count + 2) ^ 2

Step - 5 If count < 98 then 30

Step - 6 Print "Sum = "; Sum

Step - 7 End

Example 3.24

DAFC to calculate the no. of electric bills in following conditions

Unit Consumed	Unit Charge
Upto 44	Rs. 66.00
Upto 88	Rs. 60 + Rs. 1.25 per unit extra
Upto 166	Rs. 115 + Rs. 1.50 per unit extra
167 and more	Rs. 232 + Rs. 2.00 per unit extra

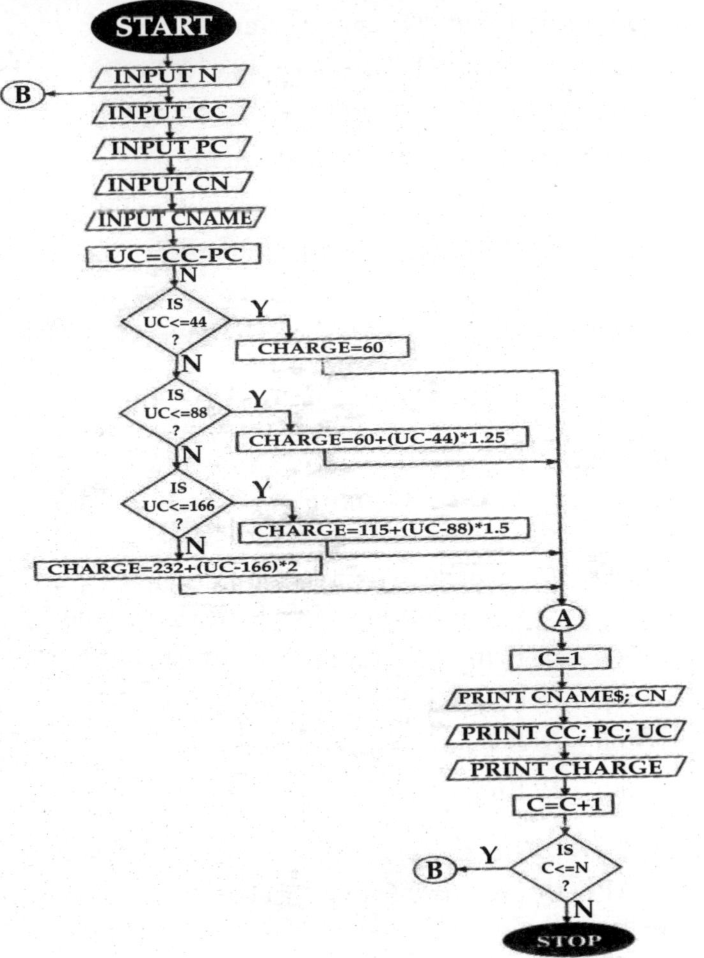

Flow Chart 3.25

Algorithm

Step - 1 REM ** Preparation of electric bill **

Step - 2 CLS

Step - 3 Input "No. of electric bills to be processed"; N

Step - 4 Input "consumption", CC

Step - 5 Input "Previous consumption", PC

Step - 6 Input "Consumer Name", CName $

Step - 7 Input "Consumer Code No.", CN

Step - 8 UC = CC - PC

Step - 9 If UC < O Then Go to 40

Step - 10 If UC < = 44 Then change = 60

Step - 11 If UC < = 88 Then charge = 60 (UC - 44) * 1.25

Step - 12 If UC < = 166 then charge = 115 + (UC - 88) * 1.50

Else charge = 232 + (UC - 166) * 2

Step - 13 C = 1

Step - 14 Print "Consumer Name"; CName E$ Consumer Code No."; CN

Step - 15 Print "Current Consumption: "CC; "Previous Consumption"; PC; Unit Consumed:"; UC

Step - 16 Print "Charge in Rs."; Charge

Step - 17 C = C + 1

Step - 18 If C < = N then 40

Step - 19 End

Example 3.25

DAFC to prepare a marksheet having the papers as English, mathematics, physics, chemistry, botany, zoology, computer studies, all are out of 100 marks declare the result as follows:

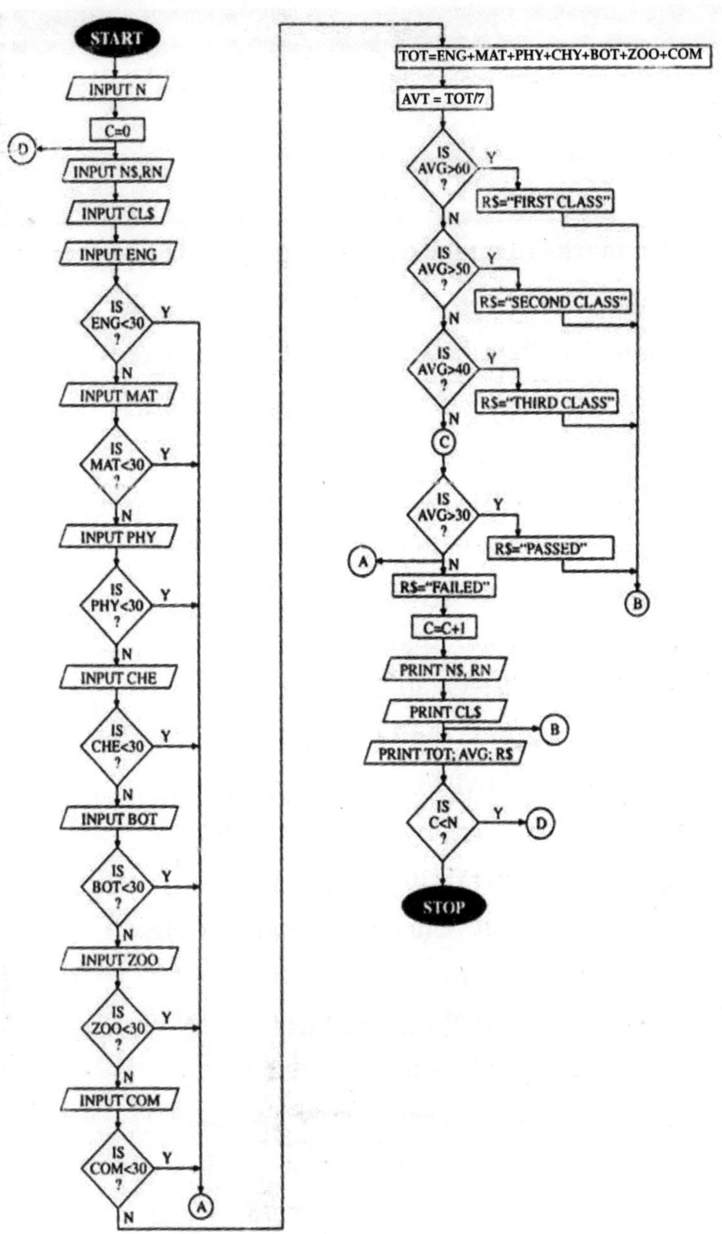

Flow Chart 3.26

Total marks	> 60First class
> 50	Second class
> 40	Third class
> 30	Pass
< 30	Fail

and also marks in an individual paper less than 30 will fail.

Algorithm

Step - 1 Rem-Preparation of mark sheet

Step - 2 Input "Enter No. of students", N

Step - 3 C = 0

Step - 4 Input "Name of the student", N$

Step - 5 Input "Roll No.", RN

Step - 6 Input "Class", CL$

Step - 7 Input "English mark", ENG

Step - 8 If ENG<30 Then 310

Step - 9 Input "Mathematics Mark", MAT

Step - 10 If MAT<30 Then 310

Step - 11 Input "Physics Mark", PHY

Step - 12 If PHY<30 Then 310

Step - 13 Input "Chemistry Mark", CHE

Step - 14 If CHE<30 Then 310

Step - 15 Input "Botany Mark", BOT

Step - 16 IF BOT<30 Then 310

Step - 17 Input "Zoology Mark", Zoo

Step - 18 If Zoo<30 Then 310

Step - 19 Input "Computer Mark", COM

Step - 20 If COM<30 Then 310

Step - 21 TOT = ENG + MAT + PHY +CHE + BOT + ZOO + COM

Step - 22 AVG = TOT/7

Step - 23 If AVG>60 Then 270

Step - 24 If AVG > 50 Then 280

Step - 25 If AVG > 40 Then 290

Step - 26 If AVG > 30 Then 300 ELSE 310

Step - 27 R$ = "FIRST CLASS"

Step - 28 R$ = "SECOND CLASS"

Step - 29 R$ = "THIRD CLASS"

Step - 30 R$ = "PASSED"

Step - 31 R$ = "FAILED"

Step - 32 C = C + 1

Step - 33 PRINT "NAME :"; N$" "ROLL No"; RN

Step - 34 PRINT "ENGLISH"; "MATH"; "PHYSICS"; "CHEMISTRY"; "BOTANY"; "ZOOLOGY"; "COMPUTER"

Step - 35 PRINT ENG; MAT; PHY; CHE; BOT; ZOO; COM

Step - 36 PRINT "TOTAL ="; TOT; "AVERAGE ="; AVG; "RESULT"; R$

Step - 37 If C < N Then 40

Step - 38 END

Example 3.26

DAFC to prepare the result of MCA Examination of DOEACC, Govt. of India, 6, CGO Complex, New Delhi - 03 of a No. of students appeared will be declared under following conditions using for next.

Marks in Total	Result in Grade
80 and above	S
70 and above	A
60 and above	B
50 and above	C
Less than 50	F

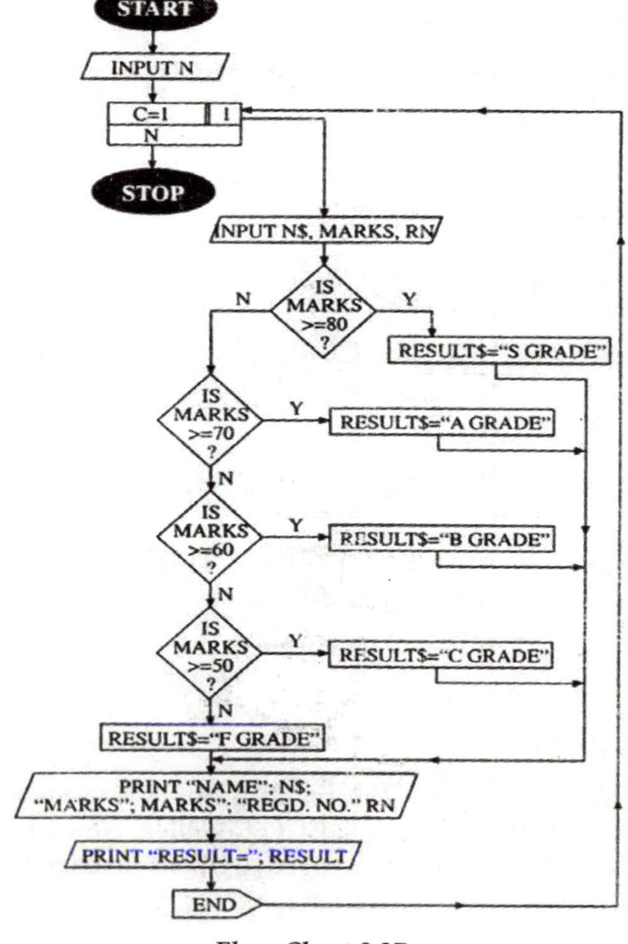

Flow Chart 3.27

Algorithm

Step - 1 Input "No. of Students"

Step - 2 For C = 1 to N

Step - 3 Input "Name"; Marks

Step - 4 Input "Marks"; Marks

Step - 5 Input "REGD. No."; RN

Step - 6 If Marks>= 80 then Result$ = "S GRADE"

Step - 7 If Marks>= 70 then Result$ = "A GRADE"

Step - 8 If Marks>= 60 then Result$ = "B GRADE"

Step - 9 If Marks>= 50 Then Result$ = "C GRADE"
ELSE RESULT$ = "F GRADE"

Step - 10 Print "Name"; N$

Step - 11 Print "REGD. NO."; RN

Step - 12 Print "MARKS"; MARKS

Step - 13 Print "RESULT"; RESULT $

Step - 14 NEXT C

Step - 15 END

Problems on Nested Loop

Example 3.27

DAFC to print the multiplication table from 2 to a specific number inputed.

Algorithm

Step - 1 REM... MULTIPLICATION TABLE

Step - 2 INPUT "ENTER A NO.", NO

Step - 3 FOR I = 2 TO NO

Step - 4 FOR J = 1 TO 10

Step - 5 PRINT I; "X"; J; "=" J

Step - 6 NEXT J

Step - 7 NEXT I

Step - 8 END

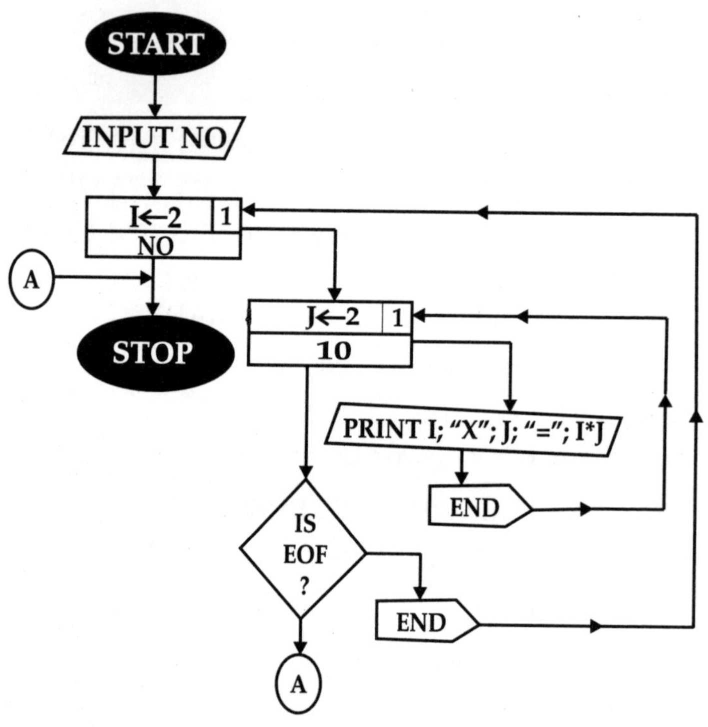

Flow Chart 3.28

Problems on User Defined Function

Example 3.28

DAFC using a defined function to plot a graph of the equation given below to the range of 1 to 10 at the interval of 0.25.

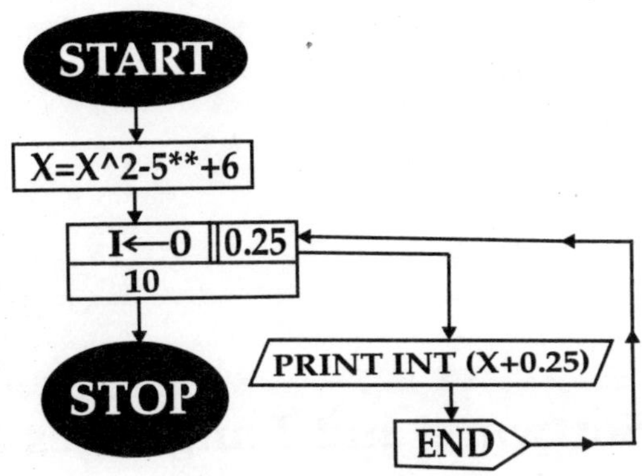

Flow Chart 3.29

Algorithm

Step - 1 REM** SOLVING OF AN EQUATION **

Step - 2 DEF FNP (X) = X^2-5** + 6

Step - 3 FOR I = 0 TO 10 STEP 0.25

Step - 4 PRINT LOCATE X, INT (FNA (X) + 0.25)

Step - 5 NEXT I

Step - 6 END

4

Software and Languages

Introduction

Computer has a vital role in the field of data processing electronic equipment. The equipment physically required for a computer system is only known as computer. But, there is an invisible part which is most essential for a computer system, otherwise the computer system is meaningless. For example, human being has not only the physical parts like his handsome body but there is the visible part i.e. his memory, intelligence, morale and logic, etc. which activates his physical structure. Without memory or remembering capacity, intelligence, logic a man or woman can not be regarded as human being. Just like, computer system consists of two elements the physical structure called hardware and the internal or logical structure which helps in the activities of hardware called software.

Hardware

The physical components of a computer is known as hardware. They are the electronic, electrical and magnetic equipments which can be visible to the common eye. For example, CPU, VDU, keyboard, mouse, internal circuits, wires, disks, etc. are belongs to hardware. These equipments are the input devices output devices, processing units, etc. used to input, output and control the computer system. When the hardware elements will be equipped to form effective working unit that may be called as computer system. Through software (SW), the hardware elements can activated effectively for specific functioning. As a TV without antenna or disk connection or video connection, TV is futile. Like wise, Computer or hardware is useless without availability of software in the system. Thus, software refers to the kind of programmes that cause the hardware effective purposefully. The hardware alone can not do any job. These programmes or instructions play a vital role in the performance of a computer.

Software

A complete set of instructions written to solve a problem on computer is called as software (SW). SW refers to the set of computer programmes which enhance the capabilities of the hardware. A programme which has a key role which is nothing but a set of sequenced programmes is called as programmer. The programmer has to know the kind of instructions a computer can understand and break up the requirements of a programme into these instructions.

Types of Software

The large variety of programmes, which are required on the computers can be classified into three categories.

Programming Language

To use a computer there is a need of software (SW). Software is a sequenced set of instructions to be given by the programmer or user to the computer for solving a required problem. As the instructions given to a servant to get any thing done, so is the case with the computer.

When ever we want to communicate some instructions to other, we need language as the medium of communication that person may understand our views. The language may apply in their daily life to communicate each other, that is the natural languages. And the programmes written with the instructions to communicate it to the computer is called as computer language or programming language. Each language has its several characteristic features suitable for a particular kind of job. So it is important to be in-depth in a specific language.

There are several programming languages available on the computers. These languages are classified as:

(a) Low Level Language

(i) Machine Level Language.

(ii) Assembly Language.

(b) High Level Language (HLL)

(i) Problem Oriented Language.

(ii) Special Purpose Language.

Low Level Language

The low level languages are more close to the working of the computer and use the basic computer instructions available on the computer. They have the several limitations that they are machine department. They also differed from one computer to another. So the programmes have no portability.

(i) **Machine Level Language** - As its name shows, the language which computer can understand i.e. binary language. Binary is the combination of only two possibilities 0 and 1 representing for OFF and ON. Thus it is called as binary numbers or binary codes. The programmer has to develop programmes in binary language by using the key digits 0 and 1.

It was very tedious. The programmer has to remember all the codes of digits, alphabets and symbols. It is a risk factor to the programmer for error in programmes. It have to take special and very careful effort to write programmes in this language. The size of programme used is very long. Debugging and testing was very difficult.

Assembly Language

In the machine level language there are the operation codes (OPCODES) used to represent the value of data. Assembly language is one step forward from the machine level language. Assembly languages used mnemonics (symbols) and macros to communicate instructions of the machine level language. To understand mnemonic it may be compared to short hand.

Mnemonics or symbols in symbolic languages are closely related to machine level languages and the internal structure of the computer on which they are working. The instructions are formed just same as the machine level languages. It is only difference that binary numbers are replaced by mnemonic codes. As computer understand only binary language, the assembly language is converted into binary language. The conversion of assembly language to binary language is made by another language i.e. assembler. It gives clear picture from the following diagram.

Assembly Language (source programme) —Input→ Assembler —Output→ Machine Level Language (object programme)

(One-to-one correspondence)

The assembly language mnemonic codes are as MPY used for multiplication, STORE to assign value of a variable, PRINT to display contents of the given variable. HLT to stop the programme, READ to input data, etc.

It is quite facilitate from the machine level language programmes, The programme size reduced. It is easy to test and debug. Most of the system software is developed in this language. The instructions used in this language are few which can be remembered by the programmer.

However, assembly language is machine dependent, writing a assembly language programme is quite difficult because there have to write a large number of statements even for a simple and small problem. Although there are the above disadvantages of assembly language, it led to the development of High Level Languages (HLLs).

High Level Language (HLL)

As there are the languages like machine level languages and assembly language, there is another language, i.e. HLL. The HLL does not require the programmer to have a detailed knowledge of computers. The HLL consists of statements that are more likely with english and mathematics. It is much easier than the machine and assembly languages.

HLL Program ⟶ Translator ⟶ Machine Language

A HLL programming language may be used on different computers. The translators are different leading to different machine language equivalent of the source programme. They are said to be machine independence:

1. It is more efficient than assembly language
2. It is easy to learn and the codes are user friendly
3. It is easy debugging and testing
4. It has greater degree of machine independent. There is no need of particular computer to execute the programme.
5. The characteristic feature and logic of programmes are more similar in all the languages.

Problem-oriented Language

The problem oriented languages are close to the type of applications, taking the user away from the intricacies of the computer. The applications of the computer may be classified as:

(a) business applications; and

(b) scientific applications.

The business applications are to be used for banking applications, financial accounts, reservation system, library management, office automation, school-college-hospital management, etc. But the scientific applications used for the purposes of animation, research and developments, mathematical-statistical applications, applications in atomic energy, automobile industry, scientific laboratories, model and infrastructure development of air craft, ship, bridges, building, satellite, space research, weather and disaster forecasting, etc.

Comparison Between Business and Scientific Applications

Both the applications played a vital role in the field of data processing. But, commonly the computer is mostly used for business purposes. An educated, trained and also in less educated even an uneducated can handle computer in business applications. The scientific applications can be done by the well trained, educated person.

Business applications handle large volume of data. For example a book has to handle all transactions, calculations of all the accounts in every month, a library keeps all records of books of the entire library updating every year, etc. For instance, an engineer designing the motor or a bridge needs to know just speed, size, model of the motor or the bridge.

Business applications have to carry out every simple and relatively lesser number of calculations on the given data. It can be used by any body with little bit familiarity. A scientific application is involved in carrying out a large number of complex calculation including trigonometric functions like SIN, COS, TAN, COT, SEC, COSEC, etc. logarithmic and anti-logarithmic functions, different formula relating to complex calculations.

Special Purpose Language

The special purpose languages are designed for a more narrow area that the problem oriented language. Each specialised area has its own requirements and peculiarities. A general purpose language may not been able to give optimal solution for such problems. Thus special purpose languages has been developed for each kind of specialised problem. Simulation problems, the application of processing alphanumeric data to determine content of a prose, generation of engineering drawing, etc. are few examples of special purpose languages.

Wide use of High Level Languages (HLLs)

There exists a few High HLLs as discussed below:

1. **FORTRAN** - FORmula TRANslation was the first HLL developed on the computer by IBM Corporation Inc, USA as a pioneer effort by J.W.Backup and his team at IBM developed this language and its translator in 1956. It is intended to be used for the scientific applications and engineering problems due to its excellent ability to handle large and complex calculations representing in the formula having the logarithmic, trigonometric functions. The version of FORTRAN was updated by American National Standard Institute (ANSI) in 1977.

2. **BASIC** - It is acronym for Beginners All Purpose Symbolic Instruction Code. It was developed by Prof. J.K. Kemeny and T.E. Kurtz at Dartmouth College of U.S.A. It was first introduced in 1964. As the name shows it was originally designed for educational environment and it is being used by the kids in the schools. It enables the beginners to start learning programming using the computers quickly. There are several versions of BASIC language like BASICA, GW-BASIC, Q-BASIC, etc. BASIC is an interpreter based language. The interpreter generally

used in micro computers which traslates information into machine language. Now, the BASIC is massively in use among the users, firms and SW developers in the new graphic user interface mode as Visual BASIC.

3. **COBOL** - It stands for Common Business Oriented Language. It was designed and work on 1959 with strong support from the US Department of Defence under the guidance of Commander Grace Murray Hopper. The maintenance and further orderly growth of the language was handed over to a group called CODASYL (Conference of DAta SYstem Language) which was endorsed by ANSI. Then it was accepted in all over the world. The first formal COBOL report was published in 1960 and then revised in 1965. The version was gradually improved. The first version of COBOL by ANSI was ANSI68 released in 1968. Then the version released to the computer world as COBOL74, COBOL85, ANSI-COBOL, etc. COBOL contains 51 character set as 0 to 9, A to Z, a to z, +, - * / < > = ( ) $,;. It is more suitable for business applications, It has more significant features for handling large volumes of data. It has english like statements. It is very close to the natural languages i.e. english and to the normal working. COBOL is compiler based language. The compiler first compiles the programme, detects error, make the error free by user then it converts to machine language.

4. **SNOBOL** - It stands for StriNg Oriented Symbolic Language. The word 'string' implies the constant set of characters to be taken into account. It was designed by a group led by Griswold in the mid 1960s. This language is intended to manipulate strings of characters i.e. for processing of text. It is used to find the frequencies of certain words and pairs of words in a text, then the required data to be processed in a text. SNOBOL provides the facilities of operations on strings

of characters such as splitting a string, combining strings, matching strings, etc. are required.

5. **LISP** - It is acronym for LISt Processing. This language was designed by McCarthy. It is suitable for non-numeric applications.

6. **ALGOL** - ALGOrithmic Language (ALGOL) had designed for scientific applications like FORTRAN. It was designed by an international group of mathematicians and developed by a group in Europe and US. ALGOL was first introduced in 1958 as the version name ALGOL85. Later it was revised in 1960 as ALGOL60. It is a block structured language which is well suited for use in a structured programming settings.

7. **PL/I** - Programming Language - I was designed in mid 1960s by IBM as general purpose language having features like COBOL for business applications and features like FORTRAN for scientific applications with the other features like string manipulation and list processing. PL/I standard was produced by ANSI committee in 1976. A subset of PL/I known as PL/I-G available for small computers. PL/I is one of the most versatile and most powerful programming language due to its combined features of COBOL and FORTRAN.

8. **PASCAL** - In accordance with the name of the well known French Mathematician Blaise Pascal, the language was named as Pascal. It was first introduced in 1971 by Prof. Nikalous Wirth of the Federal Institute of Technology in Zurich, Switzerland. Pascal has been standardised by International Standard Organisation (ISO) and American National Standard Institute (ANSI). Pascal was the first language having full embodiment of a structured language. This language is easy to learn and it allows the programmer to structure the programming problem. There are

several GOTO statements used to make the programme clumsy and unstructured. So, the language is designed in such a way that the complete Pascal programme can be written without the use of GOTO statements. The process of looping or repetition of sequence of instructions is handled automatically by special loop control instructions is handled automatically by special loop control statement. Pascal has facilities to manipulate numbers, vectors, matrices, strings of characters, sets, records, files and lists.

9. **C** - The language is becoming increasingly popular of late. It was designed by Bell Telephone Laboratories, U.S.A. Like Pascal and ALGOL. C is a block structured language. It allows the manipulation of internal processor registers of the computer. Thus, the language enjoys the advantage having some power of assembly language. It is now being used extensively used for systems programming like design of compilers and operating system. It is regarded as middle level language because it given the power of low level languages and the convenience of HLL. Most of the system software and engineering applications are being developed in this language.

10. **PROLOG** - It tends to the full form of Programming in LOGic.It is designed for complex logical operations. The language is being used to design intelligent computer system and is expected to purpose programming language, developed in 1980 at the request of the US Department of Defence (DoD) for use in military applications. The language was developed by Honeywell Computer Co. by a group of scientists headed by Ic Wriab. It was named in honour of Lady Ada Augusta Lovelace, the close friend and good assistant of Charl Babbage in the development of 'Analytical Engine'. So she is regarded as 'first programmer'.

11. **C++** - The C++ programming language was designed and developed by Bjarne Stroustripe in the Computer Science Research Centre at AT&T Bell Laboratories in Murray Hill, New Jersey. He began his work in 1980 aiming at the simulation language with the features of Object Oriented Programming (OOP) He had added the features to the well established C language. Previously C and C++ was choosen among the programmers. But, now a days, the programmers are referring more to C++ in their field of work and research. More and more developments and versions are developing day by day.

System Software

System Software is also known as system package. It is a set of one or more programmes, designed to control the operation of a acomputer system. It is a software which operates the hardware of a computer system. These programmes do not solve specific problems. These programmes written to assist human in the use of computer system by performing tasks more effectively and efficiently. In general system softwares support the running of other software, communicate with peripheral devices like printers, card readers, disks, tape, etc. The programmes used in a system software are called system programmes and the person who prepares system software is referred to as a system programmer.

The system software can be classified as:

1. Operating System (OS);
2. Translator Program;
3. Loader;
4. Linker.

Operating System (OS)

When the computer switches ON, the machine requires a set of instructions to activate the hardware, how to communicate with the user or the programmer. The set of initial programmes are essential for any computer which is called as Operating System(OS).

In other words, it is an integrated set of programmes that is used to manage the various resources and operations of a computer syste,. Like a manager of a company, Head Master of a school, Principal of a college, Director of an institution supervises and controls their firm, an OS supervises and controls all the hardware elements of a computer system. As a traffic controller OS controls all the hardware elements units in CPU, output units, I/O devices or peripherals and communicate with the user.

The OS is a set of control programmes to manage the overall functioning of the hardware. The major amount of the OS resides on the mass storage unit or secondary memory. There are two types of OS:

1. Single user OS; and
2. Multi user OS.

1. **Single User Operating System:** In single user OS, one user can operate the system at a time. There is one CPU, one monitor, one key board, one mouse. The example of single user OS may be MS-DOS, (Micro Soft Disk Operating System), DR-DOS(developed by IBM), PC-DOS (developed by ANSI), etc.
2. **Multi User Operating System:** In multi user Os. many users can operate many type of works at a time. All the computers are connected to the mian computer or server. The multi user OS are UNIX(Shell Programming and Kernel), Linux, XENIX, MS-Windows (Graphic User Interface or GUI based), OS/2, etc.

Functions of an Operating System

The OS isolates the hardware from the user. The user communicates only with the OS. The four key functions of an Os are as follows:

(a) **File and SW management**: The OS supports a large library of user programmes and files. An user wishes to use, the OS will retrieve the programme from the disk and bring it into main memory for the operator to user. These program can be created and stored in the library. Data files can also be created, stored and retrieved under the OS.

(b) **I/O and peripheral management**: The OS functions as I/O and peripheral management has specific names to use the devices through OS. These devices are divided into two broad categories as mentioned under:

  (i) Block devices; and

  (ii) Character device.

  The term block device is one that stores the information in the fixed size of blocks each one with its own address. The essential; property of block device is that a block can be read or write into independent of another block. Disks, tape, etc. are the sole example of block devices.

  A character device accepts or provides a stream of characters. Terminals, printers, network interfaces are the examples of character devices.

(c) **Memory Management**: The most significant function of the OS is to determine how much usable RAM a micro computer has. The OS also decides how RAM will be used. The transferring of programmes or data into and out of RAM takes place automatically under the control of OS.

(d) **CPU time management:** The efficiency of a computer depends upon how the CPU is kept busy. The CPU does all the processing of a computer. By OS, the CPU becomes speed processing which utilise the CPU time properly. The good OS takes less time to process. This increases the time to serve the computer many people. If the system is dedicated to one user, other CPU time is more, OS for micro computers does not schedule CPU time.

Utility Software

It may be called as an application software or system software or utility software used in the development of a programme. It is required to transfer data from one device to another. Other utility programmes like sort/merge programmes are used to sort records and merge texts in a specific sequence or order. Searching programmes used to search data, to get hard copy of the specific data or file. Such programs are normally provided by manufacturers. The programmers can also develop and keep it into their secondary memory devices for specific purposes. A few examples of utility programmes commonly available in a computer system are text editor, debugging aids, I/O routines. The common functions provided by utility software are sorting of records or files, merging several sorted files, transferring data from one I/O device to another, printing of files and contents through printer.

Translator Programmes

Translating programmes are the instructions written in human convenient form to machine language codes required by computer. These translating programmes are loaded into the computer where they control the translation process. Compilers and interpreters are used to translate programmes to machine language codes.

Translator

Translator is a programme that takes as input program written in a programming language (source programme) and produces as output of a program in another language (object program) as depicted below:

Source Program ------------> Translator ------------> Object Program

Compiler

Since, a computer hardware is capable of understanding only machine level instructions, so it is essential to convert the instructions of a program written in HLL to machine instructions before the program can be executed by the computer. As the assembly language use assembler to convert it to machine level language, in HLL it is compiler. Thus, a compiler is a translator which converts the source language (HLL) into an object language (low level or machine language).

Compiler is a translating program that translates the instructions of a HLL into machine language. It is so called, because it compiles a set of machine language instructions for every program instruction of a HLL. A program written by a programmer in a HLL is called source program. After conversion of source program into machine language by a compiler, it is referred to as an object program. The following figure illustrates the use of compiler (programmes)

HLL-------Input ------------> Compiler ------Output ------------> Machine level language
(Source program) (One to many translator (object program)

For example, in HLL like FORTRAN, COBOL, C, C++ compilers are used to translate programmes for HLL to machine for processing. A compiler can't diagnose logical errors. It diagnose only grammatical (syntax) errors in the programme. It can't know ones intension. For example, if one has wrongly punched -25 as the age of a per is 25, compiler can not diagnose it.

Interpreter

An interpreter is a translating program that appears to execute a source program as if it was machine language.

It takes one statement of a HLL and translates it into a machine instructions which is immediately executed. In other words, interpreted translates one instruction and the CU executes the resulting machine code, the next instruction translated and the CU executes the machine code instruction and so on. Interpreter differs from a compiler which merely translates the entire source programme into an object programme and is not involved in its execution. In case of a compiler, the whole source programme is translated into an equivalent machine language programme. The object programme is saved permanently for future use and is used every time the programme is to be executed. So repeated compilation is not necessary for repeated execution of a programme. However, in case of interpreter no object code is saved for future use because the translation and the execution process alternates. The advantage of interpreter over compiler is fast response to change in the source program.

The interpreter have no need for a separate compilation after each programme change to add features or necessary change. Interpreters are easy to write and they do not require large memory space in the computer as compiler requires. But the interpreter is a time consuming translation method because each statement must be translated every time while executing the source program. Thus a compiler based machine language program runs much faster than the interpreter based program. Assembler, compiler, interpreter are system software that translate a source programme written by the user to an object programme which is meaningful to the hardware of the computer.

These translator programmes like assembler, complier and interpreter are also referred as language processors since they are processing the HLL.

Loader

Once the assembler produces an object program, that programme must be placed into memory and executed. It is the purpose of the loader to assure that object programmes are placed in memory in an executable form. A loader is a programme that places programmes into memory and prepares them for execution. An significant example of loader is bootstrap loader. A bootstrap loader is a programme whose function is to start the computer when nothing meaningful is in its memory. A bootstrap performs a process similar to the initial operation involved in starting an idle engine. The loader will start functioning from the switching ON of the computer, used to load other programmes.

Linker

It refers to a service routine which converts the output of assemblers and compilers into a form which can be loaded and executed. Linkage editing is only possible if compilers are designed to produce object modules that confirm certain conventions. All the names used in a programme are placed in a table called the external symbol dictionary. It is here that the linkage editor can identify these names in order to link the various object modules together into a single address space. The following figure illustrates the clear view on the function linkage editor

Object Program----------->Linkage Editor----------->Executable Modules

Application Software

Application software are also known as application packages. They can be called as tailor made programmes, It is a set of specified applications. It is designed to handle a particular take required by the end user. These programs are written by professional programmers using different programing languages. It may be HLLs like COBOL, FORTRAN, C, C++, etc. A group of these programs are developed in the form of an application program is called as application programer. These are the few examples of application packages as inventory control, payroll, production scheduling, general accounting.

The different applications for schools, colleges, medicals, banking, institutions, insurance companies, publishing houses, manufacturing companies, science and engineering, research and development departments, etc. In fact, for the mushroom use of computers in different institutions and firms the several software development companies raise their head in the field of supplying application software. There are several types of application packages developed as follows:

(a) **Own made Application Software** - The program made by the user for specific purpose. It is most satisfactory solution. It can match the user need for business applications as per the user requirement, because the user himself is the application programmer and he is well acquainted with the application.

(b) **General purpose Application Software** - It is a set of programme special written to perform specific, commonly required task. It is designed in such a way that it can be applicable to a large number of users.

(c) **Customer Application Software** - It implies to the programmes specially written to match the exact needs of the user. It is just a ready-made cloth for a customer purposed from the shop. The quite significant advantage is that such software fulfil all the requirement for the customer. But, customer SW is much more costly than the general purpose SW. It is specially made for a particular customer.

Super HLL Application Software

As the name shows, these type of SW are written in HLLs. Some of the HLL software packages are word processor, spreadsheet, database management system, inventory control, payroll, reservation system, etc.

(a) **Word processor** - Through word processor, the user can write a text by typing through keyboard edit the text and print the document through printer with multiple copies. It works as type writer and word processor in computer i.e. in type written a key is pressed for a character to display the same character should be pressed on the paper feed in the type written on the type bar, but in word processor through computer, a text can be typed, stored, verified whether it is correctly entered and edit the text the hardcopy (printout) may be made and it can be further referred. But in type writer once a key is pressed implies it is already pressed on the paper which can be altered. In word processor, if once a text is made can be stored for future reference, print, alteration, number of copies can be printed. Mail merge can be made i.e. a same text can be printed for correspondence with several persons with address for correspondence. The word processing software are WordStar, word soft, WordPad, notepad, MS-Word, etc. There are several arts, tables, letter sizes and designs can be possible in word processing software. There are several other software used for word processing for stylus text, inserting photos, arts, etc. They are Adobe PageMaker, CorelDraw, Photoshop, SriLipi, Leap Office, Akruti, Akshyara, etc.

(b) **Database** - It is a program or a set of programs developed for collection, store data for getting required form of information on a specified subject. These software are used for keeping student record, mark sheet of students, employee record, electricity bill, telephone bill, inventory control, payroll, banking operations, hospital management, etc. Data can be stored, sorted on a specific condition, information can be found out on certain condition, data can be updated, etc. For example, a telephone exchange stores data of customer name, address, telephone number, metered calls of previous and current, call rate, etc. so that they can make the bills and send them to the concerned subscriber to collect the bill. Electric bills are similar.

In inventory control all the rate chart is fed into computer, only product name or code and number of piece or unit and name-address of the customer is to be entered, the bills will be printed and the stock data will be updated automatically. The examples of commonly used database software are dBase III+, dBase IV, FoxPro, MS-Access, Oracle, etc.

(c) **Spread Sheet** - It is a set of programs designed specially for accounting purposes. As the accounts clerk prepares accounts register by dividing columns with drawing vertical line in different register note book manuals, the spread sheet software has the same type of screen and entry of data row and column wise. There are the rows and columns. There are the facilities of calculations row wise and column wise as the clerk calculates at the last of the day to close the accounts. The examples of spreadsheet software are Lotus123, Ms-Excel, VPP, etc.

Live Ware

People develop or prepare computer programs, design computer systems, operate or maintain the hardware and software. They are the hardware engineers, involved in the manufacture or maintenance of hardware. All of them are collectively called as Liveware or peopleware or humanware. The term Liveware means all the personnel dealing with the computer system and their perform different duties in order to make a computer really worth noting while devices are listed below:

1. **Maintenance Engineer** - Look after the maintenance of the hardware components of a computer.
2. **Software Engineer** - Their task is to design and develop software such as operating system and language processors, etc.
3. **System Analyst** - Analyses the given problem and provides an efficient method of solving it with the help of a computer.

4. **Programer** - Prepare the source program to solve the given problem, according to the solution suggested by the system analysts.

5. **Computer Operators** - Operate the computer systems and possess the knowledge of the internal working of the computers.

Firmware

With the advancement of science and technology in the electronic world, software is also being made available by many computer manufacturing companies on ROM Chips. These ROM Chips can be plugged in the computer which become a part of the hardware. Such type of software are called as firmware. Thus firmware are available at hardware. Firmware refers to a sequence of program or software that is substituted for hardware and stored in ROM. Formerly, system software are supplied in the firmware, later it is supplied the application software. At last it is concluded that hardware, software and the users or the peopleware are closely related with each other. The classification of computer languages can be illustrated through the following diagram:

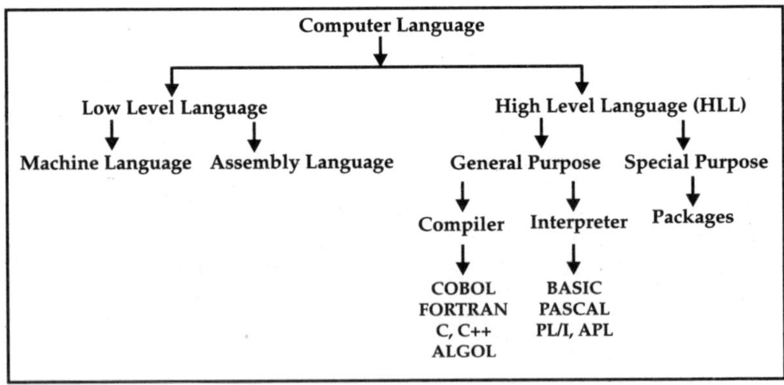

Key Points to Remember

- The physical elements of a computer is known as hardware.

- A set of instructions written to solve a specific problem on a computer is called or software (SW). Software handles hardware.
- SW consists of three types as system software, application software, programming languages.
- Programming language consists of low level language, High Level Language (HLL).
- Low level language consists of machine level language and assembly language.
- HLL consists of problem oriented language and special purpose language.
- A programme consists of a set of instructions written sequentially in a file to perform a specific task.
- Machine level language is written in machine. understandable language i.e. binary language consisting of 0s and 1s. Every input of data transforms user language to machine level language
- Assembly language used mnemonics (symbols) in opcodes (operation codes) and macros to communicate instructions into computer.
- System software is otherwise called as system package. It is a program of a set of program consisting of set of instructions in the program which performs a specific task by controlling the architecture of a computer system.

5

Representation of Information and Computer Logic

Introduction

In early days human being counted on figures, when the fingers were not adequate, stones, pebbles, sticks were used to indicate values. Science developed and the very difficulty of performing arithmetic with such a number system for representation of information come to an ease. In positional number system, there are only a few symbols are called digit and these symbols represent, different values depending the position of the number. As we know a switch is a two state device, it can be either ON or OFF.

Thus two symbols 0 and 1 are used to represent the two states of such device. These two symbols are known as BIT (binary digit). The numbers that we use in our day today life called as decimal number system because of 10 digits (0, 1, 2, . . ., 9). In this system the right most digit of a number is unity, next left most digit is tens, next left most digit is thousands, etc. One digit number system is called as unary number system(0 or 1) and two digit number system is called binary number system (0, 1).

The number system in our day-to-day life is the decimal number system consisting of 10 digits as 0, 1, 2, 3, 4, 5, 6, 7, 8, 9. In this system the weights are unity in right most digit, ten for the next left digit, hundred for the left digit of ten, thousand for the left of hundreds, like this. For example, 51754 is taken as a number, the position of its digits are as:

Lakh	Thousand	Hundred	Tens	Unity
5	1	7	5	4

Which means

$$51754 = 5 \times 10^4 + 1 \times 10^3 + 7 \times 10^2 + 5 \times 10^1 + 4 \times 10^0$$
$$= 5 \times 10000 + 1 \times 1000 + 7 \times 100 + 5 \times 10 + 4 \times 1$$
$$= 50000 + 1000 + 700 + 50 + 4.$$

From the above example we find that the positional weight of the digit is the equal to the previous (right most) weight multiplied by the base or the radix of the system. The base or radix of decimal number system is 10 (ten).

Binary Number System

The binary number system is resembles to decimal system (base 10) except the base 10 is 2. The two symbols used in the binary number system is 0 and 1 which are called as Binary Digit or in short BIT. In this system numbers are represented as strings of bits. In a binary string the right most bit is called the least significant or least important bit and the left most bit is called most significant bit. Where as in a decimal system the weight each digit increases by multiplies of 10, in a binary system the weights assigned to BIT are power of 2. The following table shows the decimal numbers up to 10 and the binary number corresponding to them.

Decimal Number	Binary Numbers
1.	1
2.	10
3.	11

(Contd...)

4.	100
5.	101
6.	110
7.	111
8.	1000
9.	1001
10.	1010

Binary to Decimal Conversion

For instance, a binary number 11101 represents 5 BITs. The right most digit is 0th position, next left digit is the 1th position, next digit is 2th position, like this. The base or radix of the binary number system is 2, so this number represents:

$$(11101)_2 = (1 \times 2^4) + (1 \times 2^3) + (1 \times 2^2) + (0 \times 2^1) + (1 \times 2^0)$$
$$= (1 \times 16) + (1 \times 8) + (1 \times 4) + (0 \times 2) + (1 \times 1)$$
$$= 16 + 8 + 4 + 0 + 1$$
$$= (29)_{10}$$

The binary number 11101 is equivalent to 29 decimal digit. It implies the data enter into computer i.e 29 is understandable by the machine as 11101 in binary digits (machine language).

Decimal to Binary Conversion

The decimal number will be converted into its equivalent binary digits dividing by 2 till the number will be 0 and the remainders will be written from the most significant digit (from the last) to upward.

Example - $(29)_{10} = (?)_2$

29

Octal Number System

We observed in the previous section that the binary numbers corresponding to large numbers are very long, to over come this disadvantage the octal number system is often used to represent binary system. The octal system has 8 digits i.e 0, 1, 2, . . ., 7, so its base is 8. So, it is easy task to convert a binary number to its octal equivalent by grouping the bits observe the table given (binary number and their octal equivalent). Three successive bits of the binary string starting from the least significant bits are grouped together to form its required octal equivalents

Decimal	Binary	Octal
0	0	0
1	1	1
2	10	2
3	11	3
4	100	4
5	101	5
6	110	6
7	111	7

Conversion of numbers from decimal to octal and vice versa. The way of conversion is same as it is done in binary except that the divisor in octal system is 8. The following example illustrates the conversion of a decimal number to its octal equivalent.

Hexadecimal Number System

Another number system is known as the hexadecimal number system. It used 16 elements for its number system as 0, 1, 2, 3, 4, 5, 6, 7, 8, 9, A, B, C, D, E, F. So, its base is 16. This system is quite suitable for big computers. Though this system represents an information in the concise form, the most commonly used micro processors having CPU chips as INTEL 808.... also prefer for this system. The base of 16 suggested choice of 16 single character digits or system. The first 10 digits are from decimal number system carrying 10 positions and remaining 6 alphabets carrying position of 11, 12, 13, 14, 15, 16. Therefore the last element of the hexadecimal number system F is 15 in decimal number.

We can convert the binary number system to decimal, hexadecimal number and vice versa as detailed in below table.

Decimal	Binary	Hexadecimal
0	0	0
1	1	1
2	10	2
3	11	3
4	100	4
5	101	5
6	110	6
7	111	7
8	1000	8
9	1001	9
10	1010	A
11	1011	B
12	1100	C
13	1101	D
14	1110	E
15	1111	F

Conversion of numbers from binary to hexadecimal and decimal equivalent is mentioned in above table.

Binary Arithmetic

Number system play a vital role in designing organization and understanding of computer. Since a computer is an electronic device, it can understand the binary language. Moreover, data processing deals with logical and arithmetic manipulation of data and the arithmetic and logic unit of the digital computer deals with it only.

Binary Addition

The addition in binary is similar to that of the decimal system. To add two binary numbers, we write the numbers one below the other with their least significant bits aligned. In the case of binary fractions we write the binary numbers, so that the binary points are vertically aligned. We add the right most column while adding two bits we will have a sum and may have a carry to the next stage of addition. Then we add the next column. An addition table for binary digits is given in the following table:

0 + 0	=	0
0 + 1	=	1
1 + 0	=	1
1 + 1	=	10
1 + 1 + 1	=	11

Binary Subtraction

Subtraction is the inverse operation of addition. Hence, when 1 is subtracted from 0, the next highest position is equal to 2 (10 in binary). These points can be depicted as rules in the below mentioned table.

0 – 0	=	0
1 – 0	=	1
0 – 1	=	1
1 – 1	=	0

Alike the decimal number system, if the subtraction lower digit is greater than the upper digit. We generally borrow immediately from the next column to the left.

Similarly while we have to subtract 1 from 0, we borrow 1 from the next column to the left. In the case of borrow from a digit which is 0, then two or more borrows must be made towards the left. We borrow from the first non-zero digit to the left and each intervening 0 becomes 1 in the process and so on.

Binary Multiplication

The multiplication of binary number is very simple and is similar to the decimal multiplication. We can multiply the multiplicand to the digits of the multiplier one by one, the first is being the least significant bit (LSB) of the multiplier. Finally the partial products thus obtained are added to get the required product. The rules for multiplying the four combinations of binary digits is given in table below:

0×0	=	0
0×1	=	0
1×0	=	0
1×1	=	1

Binary Division

We all are well known to the decimal division, It is nothing but multiplication of the division by individual digits and subtraction. Binary division is similar to decimal division.

Bit, Byte and Words

So far we have discussed the representation of numbers in the binary system, characters and special symbols are also represented as combination of 1 and 0. Generally alphabets, digits and characters are stored in a computer memory by using sequence of eight circuits. They may be in ON or OFF state. The two binary digits 0 and 1 are called as Binary Digit, in short BIT. BIT is representing the flow of electric pulses in the computer circuit through different switches as ON and OFF of the switches. Every ON is 1, Every OFF is 0.Each and every character, digit or symbol has a code from 127 standard machine understandable codes. After converting into binary number, computer stores it in as a particular arrangement of bits. The total number of characters is 94, including capital and small letters, etc.

We are clear now that a character is represented as a string of bits. Such a string of bit is known as BYTE. ASCII (American Standard Code for Information Interchange) codes uses a string of 7 bits to represent each character. A byte is a string of eight bits. In general a byte is a binary code for a character and is 8 BIT long. Even though ASCII code uses 7 bits and EBCDIC (Extended Binary Coded Decimal Interchange Code) used 8 bits for a word. A four BIT or half of the byte is called as nibble. The computer memory expresses in term of bytes. Thus a computer having 640 kilo byte memory size can accommodate 655360 bytes in its memory with fixed physical address locations. Another important term used in addition to bit and byte for the computer memory is the words.

In normal day-to-day life, we define a word means a group of characters. Similarly, a byte is a group of binary digits understood by computer from the input to its equivalent digits. To better understand, refer the ASCII code chart which indicated the position of each digit/character/ symbol. The table consists of 256 characters, which can be converted into binary value of the ASCII position. For example 'A' is in the position of 65, 'a' is in the position of 97, to get the machine code convert 65 for 'A' and 97 for 'a' into binary number. That binary number will be understandable by machine while entering data through input devices. Each byte (combination of 8 BIT) is called a word in computer. It could be a single byte word, two byte word, four byte word, etc. So we can call 8 bits, 16 bits, 24 bits computer word, rather than calling it a single byte word computer.

Integrated Circuit (IC) plays an important role in day-to-day computer field. It is twenty times faster than ENIAC and thousand times more reliable and so on. Apart from increasing the storing capacity and working speed of the computers, the chips have made the computer cheap and affordable.

BOOLEAN ALGEBRA AND COMPUTER LOGIC

Introduction

We observe that computer operate on binary information. Binary information is represented in digital systems by physical quantities called signals. In this chapter, you will learn about algebra which is widely used in designing electronics circuits of the computers. The algebra is known an Boolean Algebra. In addition to this you will also learn about the elementary logic gates that are widely used to build up circuits of different types to performs the different arithmetic operations.

In short, this chapter only teaches how to use Boolean Algebra and how it is useful in building logic circuits of arithmetic logic unit of almost all computers and etc.

Boolean Algebra

George Boole (1815-1864) an English Mathematician and logician, developed an algebra, according to his name it is known as Boolean Algebra. He developed it to examine a given set of statements and simplifying them by removing the redundant statement and later in 1938 Claude. E. Shannon a research assistant in the department of electrical engineering at the Massachusetts Institute of Technology. He submitted a thesis entitled "A Symbolic Analysis of Relay and Switching Circuits." In it, he proposed the use of Boolean algebra in the design of relay switching circuits. For this reason Boolean Algebra is also known as Switching Algebra. He used symbols to represent simple propositions. For instance, "Sumita passed the examination", let it be represented by the symbol R. This proposition may be either true or false. But is clear that it cannot be both. The proposition "Sumita did not passed the examination", it is said to be negation of symbol K. If we represent the proposition "Sumita did not passed the examination" by S, then S may be expressed as NOT R where NOT is a Boolean operator. If R is true then S is false and if R is false S is true.

In other case, "Rajesh studied hard" and "Rajesh passed the examination". Here, if proposition "Rajesh studied hard" is represent by the symbol B and C for another proposition, then the compound proposition may be expressed as "B AND C" when "AND" is a Boolean operator. The expression can be written as below :

A = B AND C

Here, A will be true if both B and C is true. Follow the given below table:

Table 5.1

B	C	A
FALSE	FALSE	FALSE
FALSE	TRUE	FALSE
TRUE	FALSE	FALSE
TRUE	TRUE	TRUE

Another Boolean Operator is known as OR operator. Let we take two proposition i.e. "Simran loves Sumita" represented by the symbol A, and "Sumita loves Simran" in this proposition let we take B as a symbol, then the compound proposition may be expressed as A OR B if A is true or, B is true or if both are true. We can write as K = A OR B. Observe the true table.

Table 5.2

A	B	K
TRUE	FALSE	TRUE
FALSE	TRUE	TRUE
TRUE	TRUE	TRUE
FALSE	FALSE	FALSE

In our day-to-day life we come across so many situations where we make use of Boolean Algebra. For instance, suppose you have three phones at different places in you home (such as in bed room, study room, and in T.V. room) if your friend rang the phone you may receive if you are in bed room or in study room or in TV room. This situation is called OR operation, because you may talk with you friend if you are in any of these three rooms.

For AND operation take one examples, when you want to start your computer, you have to turn on power supply switch first of all, then switch on you stabilizer which is connected to the power supply, at last switch on your computer system. In this case you have to follow these three respective steps or you have to turn on these respective switches one after another. If you turned on power supply switch and before switch on your computer system, make sure that stabilizer switch already turned on, until and unless your computer system will not start. This situation is known as AND operation, where all the conditions should be true to get output as a true.

We use the symbol "0" and "1" to represent the above states, here one has to noticed that "0" and "1" is only symbols and they have no any arithmetic significance. Thus the variable which can assume only two value either "0" or "1" is known as BOOLEAN VARIABLE. The OR operation represented the symbol "+" and AND operation represented the symbol "." (similar to multiplication symbol).

In short, it is clear that if all given conditions are true output will be true in AND operation. But in the other hand if any one given condition is true, the output will be true in OR operation.

GATES/Computer Logic

All operations within a computer are carried out by means of combinations of signals passing through standard blocks of built in circuits that are known as Gates. In other, words, the manipulation of binary information are only possible by the help of logic circuit (in the form of 0's and 1"s or true and false) these are known as Logic gates. They have their distinct graphic symbols and applications.

Truth Table

The manipulation of the binary codes are represented in a tabular form is known as Truth Table.

Boolean Functions

As we know, the Boolean function can be expressed in the terms of O's and 1's, in addition to that three another binary operators such as AND OR, and unary operator NOT. Generally Boolean expression formed with binary variables, the logic operation symbols, parenthesis and equal sign. For instance, observe the following Boolean function.

$$K = X + Y - Z$$

Here, the variable K is a function of X, Y and Z. This can be written in other form i.e. K = f(X, Y, Z), the right side equation f(X, Y, Z) is known as expression.

Postulates of Boolean Algebra

To manipulate any boolean expression the basic rules are highly essential or the user has to know about them. The rules and regulations also the definitions are used for combine boolean expression are called as Postulates of Boolean Algebra. Since, 0's and 1's here, has no arithmetic significance, but boolean algebra follows the following laws.

OR Operator:

(i) 0 + 0 = 0

It is clearly shows that if both conditions are false, the output is also false.

(ii) (a) 0 + 1 = 1

Here, it states that if any one of the condition is satisfy the output will be true.

(b) 1 + 0 = 1

(iii) 1 + 1 = 1

If both the condition is true then the output is true.

6. 2. AND Operator

(i) 0.0 = 0

If both the condition is false then the result is also false,

(ii) (a) 0 . 1 = 0

If any one value is false then the output is also false.

(b) 1 . 0 = 0

(iii) 1.1 = 1

If both the value is true the final result is also true or 1.

6. 3. NOT Operator

(i) 0 = 1

The complement of false is true and vice versa.

(ii) 1 = 0

Different Types of Gates

As we discussed earlier there are different types of logic gates to perform the necessary operations. But we shall consider here only some of the most significant ones. They are as follow:

(i) AND

(ii) OR

(iii) NOT

(iv) NAND or Universal NAND

(v) NOR or Universal NOR

(vi) XOR or eXculsive OR

(vii) XNOR or eXculsive NOR AND Gate.

In this gate the result will be true if all inputted signals or conditions are true. The AND operation is represented by ".". The "." is resemble to the multiplication sign of arithmetic, but it has no such importance. For instance, we have two switches A and B which are normally open, they are connected in series with a battery and a bulb. The bulb (C) will turn on if both the conditions or both the switches are closed to each other, means an output signal will be one or true if both the conditions or signals are true or 1. Observe the following two propositions:

Example 1

A = Sujata loves Ramesh

B = Ramesh loves Sujata

C = A . B (it means if both loves the output will be true or 1)

Table 5.3

A	B	C = A.B
1	0	0
0	1	0
0	0	0
1	1	1

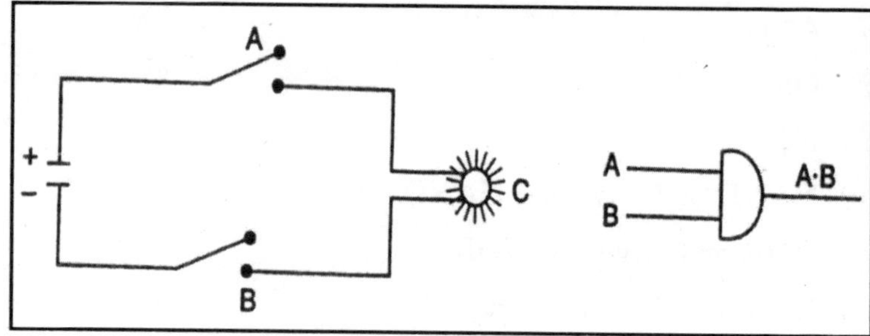

Fig. 5.1

OR Gates

The OR gate is the physical realisation of the logical addition operation. The output will be 1 or true if any one of the condition is true or 1. Otherwise the output will be false or 0. Observe the following truth table, logic circuit, and circuit diagram also two propositions.

Example 2

A = Rajsheker will purchase a Computer system.

B = Rajsheker will purchase a motor car.

C = A + B (it means Rajesheker will purchase a computer system or a car).

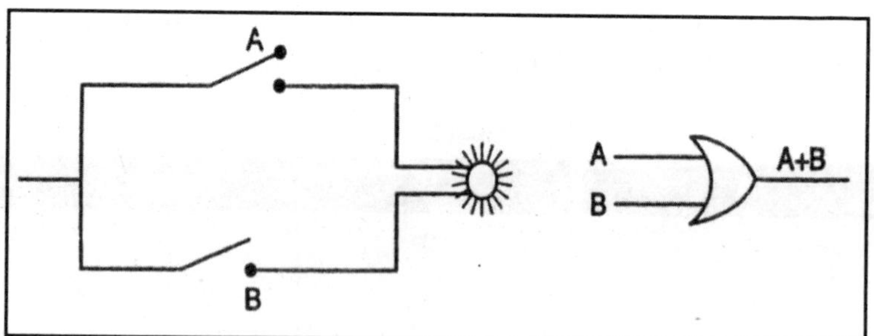

Fig. 5.2

Table 5.4

A	B	C=A+B
0	0	0
1	0	1
0	1	1
1	1	1

NOT Gates

It is also called an inverter, it has only one input and also one output signal. It can be said that opposite of the input state, or binary operation. Thus, if input is 1 or true the output will be false or 0 and vice versa e.g. if a boolean variable A = 0 than NOT A = 1. The negation is also known as complementation. The output is as follow:

$$X = X \text{ and } X = X$$

In this case, if we have a switch P connected to a battery and a bulb, the bulb will be turn on when P is open and will be off and P is closed. Observe the following truth table, logic circuit and switch diagram also given two propositions.

Example 3

A = Rosalene is a beautiful girl.

B = Rosalene is not a beautiful girl.

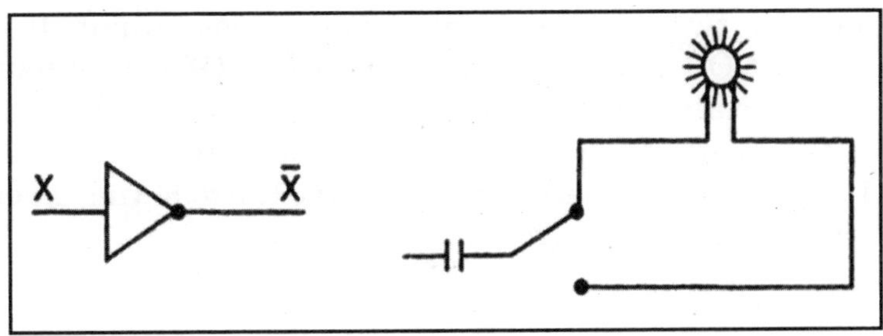

Fig. 5.3

Table 5.5

X	$\overline{X}$
0	1
1	0

NOT and NAND or Universal NAND

The NAND Gate is basically an inverted of AND gate (NOT AND). That is the output of NAND gate will be 1 or true if any of the input is 0 or false and will be 0 only when all the inputs are 1 or true. The operation of a NAND gate can be analysed using the equivalent block diagram, and truth table as given below:

Table 5.6

A	B	A.B	A.B
0	0	0	1
0	1	0	1
1	0	0	1
1	1	1	0

The AND function A.B is complemented giving A.B, this gate also indicates the complementary function with bubble in front of the logic diagram.

NOT or (NOR) or Universal NOR

The NOR Gate is always complement of OR function. It has also two or more inputs but only one output. It is clear that NOR gate output is opposite of the OR gate output. Hence logically a NOR gate output is an OR gate followed by a NOT gate. All inputs must be false or 0 to get a true or 1 as a output and vice versa. Observe the following given truth table and logic circuit.

Table 5.7

A	B	A+B	A+B
0	0	0	1
1	0	1	0
0	1	1	0
1	1	1	0

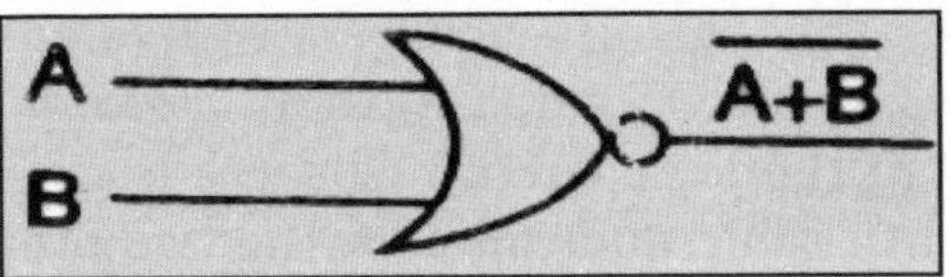

Fig. 5.4

Exclusive OR (XOR)

XOR Gate has an output of 1 or true if any input is 1 or true, but excludes the combination when both inputs are 1 or true. The XOR operation is represented by X symbol, e.g. X = A + B. Observe the circuit diagram and truth table given below also given two propositions:

Example 4

A = Shahida will be a Doctor.

B = Shahida will be a Engineer.

C = A + B (It means she will be any one, but not both)

Table 5.8

A	B	C=A+B
0	0	0
0	1	1
1	0	1
1	1	0

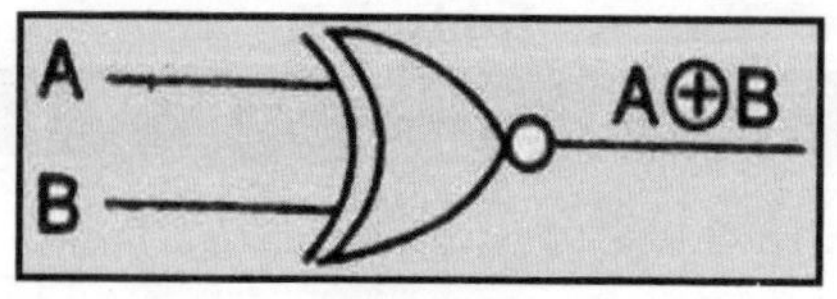

Fig. 5.5

Exclusive NOR (XNOR)

This is the complement of the exclusive OR (XOR). The output is 1 or true only when the both input have the same value. Hence the logically XNOR is equivalent to an XOR gate followed by a NOT gate i.e. A + B, it states with bubble in the front of the logic circuit. Observe the following logic network, truth table and compare the two proposition:

Example 5

A = Bhupati passed M.C.A degree.

B = He will be a software engineer.

C = A + B (It means he should complete his M.C.A then only he will be a software engineer, both should be true).

Table 5.9

A	B	C=A+B
0	0	1
0	1	0
1	0	0
1	1	1

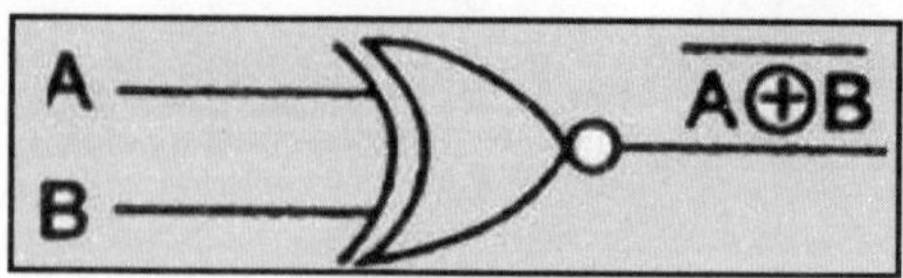

Fig. 5.6

Application of Logic Circuit

The following three logic circuit show the application methods of logic gates. They are as follow:

(a) Decoder Circuit;

(b) Half Adder Circuit; and

(c) Full Adder Circuit.

(a) *Decoder Circuit*

It is used to convert binary numbers to equivalent decimal number. For instance, 0001 (binary) is equal to 1 in decimal, generally binary digits are in four digits forms. Observe the following decoder circuit.

Table 5.10

Input Combination	Binary Form	Decimal Form
W . X . V . Z	0000	0
W . X . V . Z	0001	1
W . X . Y .Z	0010	2
W . X . Y . Z	0011	3

(b) *Half Adder Circuit*

By the help of this logic circuits simple arithmetic operations are made. The below table shows that the addition of two bits. The first and second columns represents input bits, the 3rd column gives the sum of these two bits and the last (fourth) column stands for carry the bit. This table is called a half adder truth tables.

Table 5.11

INPUTS		OUTPUTS	
A	B	S	C
0	0	0	0
0	1	1	0
1	0	1	0
1	1	0	1

In short, we can say a half adder circuit is used to add two binary bits without previous bits. Here, "S" stands for Sum and as we know the higher significant bit of this result is called carry (C). The Boolean expression will be:

$S = A . B + A . B$ and $C = A . B$.

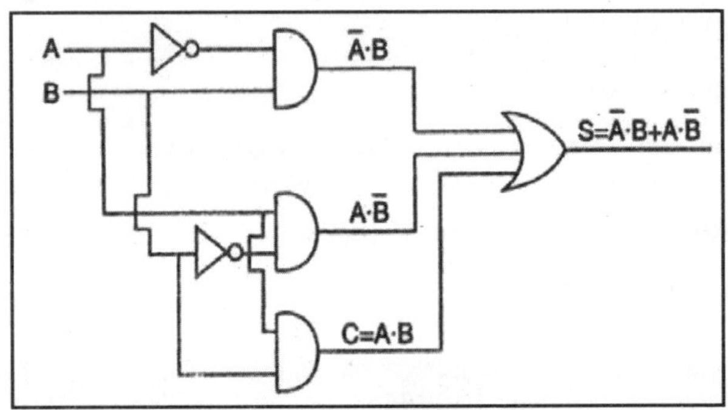

Fig. 5.7

Full Adder Circuit or Three Bits Adder

The Full Adder Circuits otherwise known as three bits adder, because it performs the addition of three bits (two significant bits and one previous carry digit). Observe the given example.

Table 5.12

1	0	1	1	1					→ Carry bits
0	1	0	1	0	1	1	0	0	→ Input bits
0	1	0	0	1	1	0	1	0	
1	0	1	0	0	0	1	1	0	→ Sum

INPUTS			OUTPUTS	
O	p	Q	S	C
0	0	0	0	0
0	0	1	1	0
0	1	0	1	0

(Contd...)

0	1	1	0	1
1	0	0	1	0
1	0	1	0	1
1	1	0	0	1
1	1	1	1	1

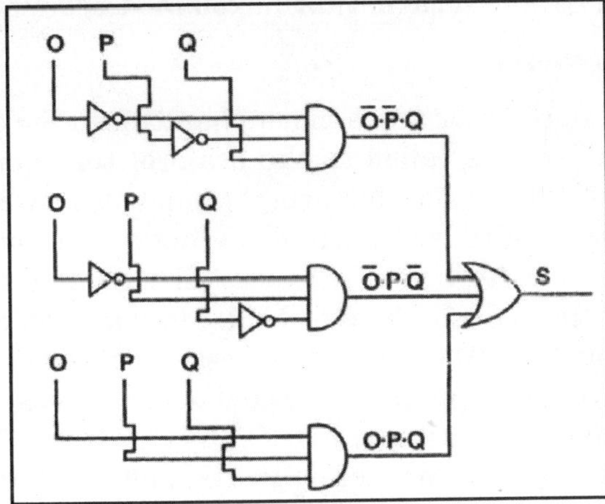

Fig. 5.8

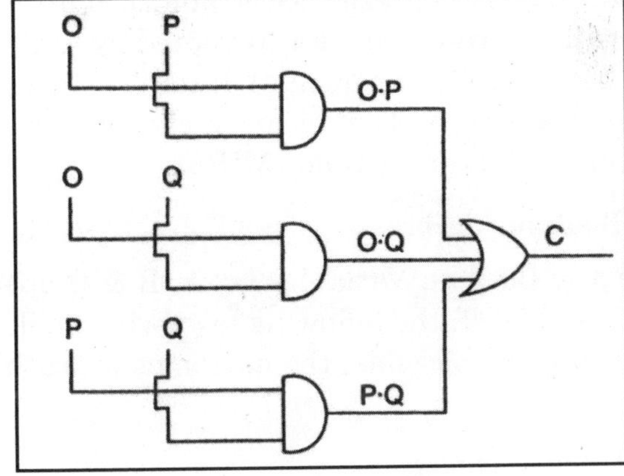

Fig. 5.9

Here, one point has to remember that two half adders can be employed to implement a full adder. Hence, the boolean expression is as given below:

S = O.P.Q + O.P.Q + O.P.Q + O.P.Q

C = O.P + O.Q + P.Q

Observe the logic network explained below.

How Chip Works

Micro-processor acts a major character in the computer system, often it is called as the brain of the computer. It doles out instructions for every component. A computer consists of hundreds of parts including a monitor, mouse, disk drives and keyboard. It houses all sorts of micro chips, including those for ROM and RAM. Mounting on a printed circuit board (PCB) is a micro processor, which is housed in a protective container and connected to rows and gold plated pins. In side the micro package is the chip itself. This tiny square of silicon is packed with transistors that process instructions and data for the computer. Silicon is replaced by Gallium Arsenide, it is cheaper and faster. Recently, in 1997 INTEL'S (INTegrated Electronics) Pentium II (686) has came into market, which is invented by Andrew Steven Grove, CEO and Chairperson of Intel. This chip contains 7.5 million transistors. That means it can process 500 million instructions per every second (MIPS).

Laws of Boolean Algebra

For any Boolean Variables i.e. A, B & C operators i.e. AND, OR and NOT, the following laws which hold good and to keep it up, the possible, the outcomes of truth table are as follow:

Laws of Complementary

(a) A + A = 1

Table 5.13

A	A	A+A
1	0	1
0	1	1

(b) A. A = 0

Table 5.14

A	A	A.A
0	1	0
1	0	0

0.2 Law of Commutative

(a) A + B = B + A

Table 5.15

A	B	A+B	B+A
1	1	1	1
1	0	1	1
0	1	1	1
0	0	0	0

(b) A. B = B.A

Table 5.16

A	B	A.B	B.A
1	1	1	1
1	0	0	0
0	1	0	0
0	0	0	0

1. Distributive Laws

(a) A. (B + C) = A.B + A.C

Table 5.17

A	B	C	B+C	A.(B+C)	A.B	A.C	A-B+A.C
1	1	1	1	1	1	1	1
1	1	0	1	1	1	0	1
1	0	1	1	1	0	1	1
1	0	0	0	0	0	0	0

Thus, the value of Therefore, A. (B + C)

(b) A + (B . C) = (A + B). (A + C)

B + Q is equal to the value ol A. B + A. C same as (I, 1, 1, 0), A. B + A. C

Table 5.18

A	B	C	B.C	A+(B.C)	A+B	A+C	(A+B).(A+C)
1	1	1	1	1	1	1	1
1	1	0	0	1	1	1	1
1	0	1	0	1	1	1	1
1	0	0	0	1	1	1	1
0	1	1	1	1	1	1	1
0	1	0	0	0	1	0	0
0	0	1	0	0	0	1	0
0	0	0	0	0	0	0	0

Thus, the value of A. (B + C) is equal to the value of (A + B) . (A + C) same as (1, 1, 1, 1, 1, 0, 0, 0). Therefore A. (B + C) = (A + B). (A + C)

Laws of Complementary

(a) A + A″ = 1

Table 5.19

A	A	A+A
1	0	1
0	1	1

(b) A. A = 0

Table 5.20

A	A	A.A
1	0	0
0	1	0

Thus, the value of A + A = 1 and the value of A. A = 0, hence it is proved.

Laws of Identity Elements

(a) A + O = A

Table 5.21

A	O	A+O
0	0	0
1	0	1

(b) A. I = A

Table 5.22

A	1	A.1
0	1	0
1	1	1

Idempotent Laws

(a) A + A = A

Table 5.23

A	A+A
1	1
0	0

(b) A. A = A

Table 5.24

A	A-A
1	1
0	0

Associative Laws

(a) (X + Y) + Z = X + (Y + Z)

Table 5.25

X	Y	Z	X+Y	(X+Y)+Z	Y+Z	X+(Y+Z)
1	1	1	1	1	1	1
1	1	0	1	1	1	1
1	0	1	1	1	1	1
0	1	1	1	1	1	1
0	1	0	1	1	1	1
0	0	1	0	1	1	1
0	0	0	0	0	0	0

(b) (A. B). C = A. (B. C)

Law of Involution

Table 5.26

A	B	C	A.B	(A.B).C	B.C	A.(B.C)
1	1	1	1	1	1	1
1	1	0	1	0	0	0
1	0	1	0	0	0	0
1	0	0	0	0	0	0
0	1	1	0	0	1	0
0	1	0	0	0	0	0
0	0	0	0	0	0	0

(a) (A) = A

Table 5.27

A	A	(A)
0	1	0
1	0	1

De Morgan's Laws

(a) A + B = A.B (i)

Table 5.28

A	B	A+B	A	B	A+B	A.B	A.B
0	0	0	1	1	1	0	1
0	1	1	1	0	0	1	0
1	0	1	0	1	0	1	0
1	1	1	0	0	0	1	0

(b) A.B = A + B (ii)

Table 5.29

A	B	AB	A.B	A	B	A+B
0	0	0	1	1	1	1
0	1	0	1	1	0	1
1	0	0	1	0	1	1
1	1	1	0	0	0	0

These above two theorem are similar to the De Morgan laws in set theory. Typically, they are used to"simplify the expression, and the final value will be either 0 or 1.

Theorem 1

A + B = A.B

Here, it states that the complement of the sum of two variable in equal to the product.

Proof: As we know that

X. X = 0 and X + X = 1 (Law of Complementary)

Or

We can say that

(X + Y).(X + Y) = 0 *(i)*

(X + Y) + (X + Y) = 1 *(ii)*

If we can show that

$(X + Y).(X.Y) = 0$ *(iii)*

$(X + Y) + (X.Y) = 1$ *(iv)*

The above (X + Y).(X.Y) = 0, is both (X + Y) and (X. Y) are complementary to each other. If we can prove the (X + Y).(X.Y) = 0, then it also will complement to the (X + Y). (X + Y)

The equation (i) and equation (iii), are complementary to each other and right side value is 0, then if we show

(X + Y).(X.Y) = 0 and (X + Y) + (X.Y) = 1,
then easily we can prove that

(X + Y) = X.Y

Equation (iii)

$(X + Y).(X.Y) = 0$

L.H.S. : $(X + Y).(X.Y) = f(X.X) + (Y.X)).Y$

$= Y.X.Y$ (distribution law)

$= (X.Y).Y = X.(Y.Y)$

$= X.0 = 0$ R.H.S.

Equation (iv)

$(X + Y) + (X.Y) = 1$

L.H.S.: $(X + Y) + (X.Y) \Rightarrow (X + Y + X).(X + Y + Y)$

$\Rightarrow (X + X + Y).(X + Y + Y)$

$\Rightarrow (1 + Y).(X.1)$ [where X + X = l and Y + Y = 1]

$\Rightarrow 1.1 = 1$ R.H.S.

As the two relational equations are proved hence the main theorem is proved i.e. (X + Y) = (X.Y).

Theorem 2

If the complement of the product of the two variables is equal to the sum of the complements of the variables. That is (X. Y) = (X.Y)

Proof

As we : X.X = 0

If we show

(X.Y). (X.Y) = 0 *(i)*

(X.Y).(X + Y) = 0 *(ii)*

Then we can prove : (X. Y) = X + Y

The above equations are complementary to each and both, and the right side value is 0.

So we can easily prove that, (X. Y) = X + Y. But first of all we have to show that equation (1, 2) are true, they are true, then it is solved.

Equation (ii)

(X.Y).(X +Y) = 0 L.H.S. (X.Y).(X + Y)

⇒ {(X.X).(X.Y)}.Y =>(0).X.Y.Y [where X.X = 0]

⇒ 0.X.Y.Y [here Y.Y = 0]

⇒ 0.X.0 [here X.0=0]

⇒ 0 R.H.S. (Proved)

X.Y.(X.Y) = 0 *(i)*

Table 5.30

X	Y	X	Y	X.Y	X.Y	(X.Y).(X.Y)
0	0	1	1	0	1	0
1	0	0	1	0	1	0
0	1	1	0	0	1	0
1	1	0	0	0	1	0

(X.Y).(X +Y) = 0 *(ii)*

Table 5.31

X	Y	X	Y	X.Y	X+Y	(X.Y).(X+Y)
0	0	1	1	0	1	O
1	0	0	1	0	1	0
0	1	1	0	0	1	0
1	1	0	0	0	0	0

Here, equation (ii), i.e. (X.Y).(X + Y) = 0 is proved once again it is complementary to equation (i), i.e. (X. Y). (X. Y) = 0. Therefore equation (i), (ii) both and each are complementary to each other.

Hence, it is proved that X. Y = X + Y.

Dual Theorem

These above methods of proving theorems through truth table is called method of exhaustive enumeration. In addition to that the Boolean Algebra also follows some duality between the operations (AND) and (OR), and the digit 0 and 1. That means, the theorem obtained by interchanging "." with "+" and "0" with "1", this important property is known as the principle of duality in Boolea'n algebra. Observe the table closely.

Theorem	Dual Theorem
(a) A + 0 = A	(a) A.0 = A
(b) A + B = B + A	(b) A.B = B.A
(c) A.(B + C) = (A.B) + (A.C)	(c) A + (B.C) = (A + B).(A + C)
(d) A + A = 1	(d) A.A = 1
(e) A + A = A	(e) A. A = A
(f) A + 1 = 1	(f) A.1 = 1
(g) A + (A.B) = A	(g) A.(A + B) = A
(h) A + (A.B) = A + B	(h) A.(A + B) = A.B
(i) A + B = A.B	(i) A. B - A + B
(j) A + (B + C) = (A + B) + C	(j) A.(B.C) = (A.B).C

In other way we can also prove these two theorems.

First Theorem

The complement of a sum (OR) is equals to the product (AND) of the complements, i.e. (A + B) = A.B.

Proof

The left hand side it represents a NOR-gate and right side stands for an AND gate along with inverted input, (see fig. 5.11). From the truth table two circuits are logically equivalent to each other.

Table 5.32

A	B	A+B	A+B	A.B	A	A	B	B
1	1	1	0	0	1	0	1	0
1	0	1	0	0	1	0	0	1
0	1	1	0	0	0	1	1	0
0	0	0	1	1	0	1	0	1

Hence, from the above truth table, it is proved that A + B = A.B

Second Theorem

The complement of a product (AND) is equal to the sum (OR) of the complement i.e. A. B = A + B.

The left hand side represents a NAND gate and the right side shows OR gate with inverted input. The truth table indicates the logical equivalent to each other.

Table 5.33

A	B	A-B	A-B	A+B	A	B	A	B
0	0	0	1	1	0	0	1	1
1	0	0	1	1	1	0	0	1
0	1	0	1	1	0	1	1	0
1	1	1	0	0	1	1	0	0

Hence, from the above cited two tables, it is clear that A. B = A + B. Simplify the following Boolean Expression

Example 6

X.Y(X.Y + X.Z)

Solution

X.Y(X.Y + X.Z)

⇒ X . Y. X. Y + X. Y. (X. Z)

⇒ (X. X).(Y. Y) + (X.X).(Y.Z)
[Here X.X = X.Y.Y = Y and X.X = 0]

⇒ X.Y + 0=>X.Y

Example 7

X.(X + Y).(X + Y)

Solution

⇒ X(X.X + X. Y + Y.X + Y. Y)

⇒ X(X + X.Y + Y.X + 0) [Here X.X = X and Y.Y = 0]

⇒ X.X + X.X.Y + Y.X.X + 0 . X

⇒ 0 + O.Y + Y.O + O.X [Here X.X = 0, X.X = 0 and O.X = 0]

⇒ 0 + 0 + 0 + 0 [Here 0.Y = 0,Y.0 = 0]

⇒ 0 Ans.

Example 8

Find the complement of the following:

(i) A + B

(ii) (A + B).(A.C)

Solution

(i) A + B= A.B = A.B

(ii) (A + B)(A.C)⇒A + B + A.C ⇒A.B +A.(C)
(here A + B = A.B and C = C]

⇒A(B + C)

Prove the following Boolean Expression

(i) X.(X + Y) = X

L.H.S. X.(X + Y)

⇒ X. X + X. Y ⇒X + X. Y ⇒X. 1 + X. Y

= X(1 + Y) ⇒X.1 = X R.H.S.

(ii) X.(X + Y) = X.Y

L.H.S. X.(X + Y)

⇒ X.(X + Y)

⇒ (X.X) + (X.Y) [Here X.X = 0]

⇒ 0 + X . Y [Here 0 + X.Y=X.Y]

⇒ X.Y R.H.S.

L.H.S. = R.H.S. (Proved)

Draw the truth table for the following Expressions

(a) X.Y+ X.Y.Z = M

Table 5.34

X	Y	Z	Y	X.Y	X.Y.Z	M
0	0	0	1	0	0	0
0	0	1	1	0	0	0
0	1	0	0	0	0	0
1	0	0	1	1	0	1

(b) X.(Y + Z) + (X.Y) =K

Table 5.35

X	Y	Z	Y	Y+Z	X.(Y+Z)	X.Y	K
0	0	0	1	0	0	0	0
0	0	1	1	1	0	0	0
0	1	0	0	1	0	0	0
1	0	0	1	0	0	1	1

Example 9

For selection of actor, the following conditions has been fixed.

Condition 1

The candidate must be age group 20-25 years and should be at least intermediate.

Or

Condition 2

The candidate must have proved his/her skill in stage performance or he/she should pass one year relevant course.

Assign the variables P, Q, R, T & E

P = 1, if the candidate must be age group 20-25 years.

P = 0, If not so.

Q = 1, If the candidate is intermediate in qualification.

Q = 0, If not so.

R = 1, If stage performance is good.

R = 0, If not so.

T = 1, If the candidate passed one year relevant course.

T = 0, If not so.

E = 1, If the candidate is selected.

E = 0, If not so.

(a) Construct the logic network for the above problem.

(b) Draw the truth table.

Solution

(a) E – (P.Q) + (R + T)

Table 5.36

P	Q	R	T	P.Q	R+T	(P.Q)+(R+T)=E
1	1	1	1	1	1	1
1	1	1	0	1	1	i
1	1	0	1	1	1	1
1	0	1	1	0	1	1
0	1	1	1	0	1	1
0	0	1	0	0	1	1

Key Points to Remember

- Every input through input devices are the electric pulses as a bult has two functions ON and OFF while data transfrers to computer. The presencc of pulses is ON represents 1, absence of pulses represent 0 for OFF.
- Every data transfrred into the computer with only two numbers i.e 0 and 1, so it is called as binary number system.
- In decimal number system, any number consists of its digits from 10 digits, so its radix or base is 10.
- In binary number system, the base or radix is 2.
- In octal number system, any number can be consisting of 8 digits, so its base is 8.
- In hexadecimal number system, the number can be for the set of 10 digits and/or from 6 alphabets, so its base is 16.
- BIT represents Binary Digit i.e 0 or 1.
- Combination of 8 BITs is 1 Byte. 1024 Bytes is 1 Kilo Byte (KB), 1024 KB is 1 Mega Byte (MB), 1024 MB=1 Giga Byte (GB)
- ASCII code uses a string of 7 bits to represent each character.

- EBCDIC uses a string of 8 bits to represent each character.
- George Boole is the inventor of Boolean Algebra
- The manipulation of binary information are only possible by the help of logic circuit are known as gates.
- The relationship between binary codes are represented in a tabular form is known as truth table.
- The Boolean function can be expressed in the terms of 0 and 1.
- In OR gate any one given condition should satisfy.
- In AND gate both or all given conditions should satisfy.
- NOT gate is unary because it has only one input and one output.
- NOR (NOT OR) is otherwise known as Universal NOR.
- In half adder circuit, addition of two bits can be possible.
- In full adder circuit, three bits addition or any other arithmetic functions can be possible.
- Silicon is replaced by Gallium Arsenide, it is cheaper and faster.
- De Morgan's theorem is similar to set theory.
- Boolean algebra also follows some duality between the operation such as AND & OR.
- The complement of a sum (OR) is equal to the product (AND) of the components.
- The complement of a product (AND) is equal to the sum (OR) of the complements.

6

Operating Systems

Introduction

Computer is classified into two as Hardware and Software. Software is the programme(s) which operate the hardware. Hardware is the physical components of a computer system. Without software, hardware is futile. Further software is divided into two system software and application software. System Software implies that the programme(s) activates the hardware equipments. Application or programme software is the programme(s) written for specific applications.

But system software is applicable for activating the system only.

It is a set of instruction used to manage the various resources and operations of a computer system. Like a principal manage a school or a college, a manager manages an industry or a firm, a traffic police manages traffic, a system software supervises and controls all over the hardware elements of a computer system. It acts a traffic police controls the moving traffic around his/her area. Thus system software is otherwise called as operating system.

MS-DOS

Operating System (OS) is an organised collection of software that controls the overall operation of a computer.

The OS enables the system's hardware to work with the users application programmes.

Disk Operating System (DOS) is an OS, a system software which controls the overall operation of hardware elements of a computer system like input devices, output devices and CPU. The operating system DOS is stored on a separate disk and controls the entire computer system and the same disk also. Hence, it is called as Disk Operating System, shortly DOS. It is the most familiar OS in the world of Personal Computers (PCs). In spite of various OS, DOS gathered a momentum in the PC world as an OS i.e. MS-DOS (Micro Sort-Disk Operating System) which is compatible for IBM PCs.

Different Names of DOS

Different flavours of DOS are available in the market as follows:

- MS-DOS from Micro Soft Inc., U.S.A.
- PC-DOS from IBM Corporation Inc., U.S.A.
- Novel DOS from Novel.
- DR-DOS from Digital Research, U.S.A.

History of MS-DOS

With the success of home computers in U.S.A, International Business Machine Corporation Inc. (IBM) planned to introduce personal computers (PCs) into the market. At the same time they were looking for an operating system (OS). MS-DOS 1.00 was the first version, which was available with every purchase of PCs, compatible with IBM PCs. In 1981 MS-DOS 1.00 was came into market. From that day onwards, MS-DOS is functioning with its forward steps by developing its version 6.22 in 1995 onwards.

Getting Started with MS-DOS

MS-DOS is so popular in the IT field as an OS, because Micro Soft Inc. has developed many user friendly software with continuous developments. So, we will read about MS-DOS.

Each time the user switch on the computer, it checks its memory and all its devices working properly or not, it will display message if any error occurs. The system beeps after it has made sure that a device well functioning, the drive light will flash. This process of checking is called as POST (Power On Self Test), then computer will load DOS into memory. On the system without Hard Disk, a DOS system disk should be inserted into Floppy Disk Drive before it is switched on. If DOS system disk is not inserted in Floppy Disk Drive (FDD), an error message will occur. In the system there is the system transferred to a disk, there will be the presence of COMMAND.COM file. Otherwise, it will get the error message like:

- Non-System disk or disk error.
- Replace and strike any key when ready.

But, in hard disk, there will be the system file already transferred, otherwise, computer will not boot automatically through hard disk. The same message will occur when the computer will ON. When, it is switched on, the DOS system file will load on the computer and computer will work.

Booting

Loading DOS into memory on POST is called as "Booting" the computer system. The disk through which booting is made called as Bootable disk. The term is borrowed from the phrase "pulling yourself up by your bootstrap", because DOS essentially pull itself up by its bootstraps loading from disk into memory. The booting is possible with the availability of a file viz. COMMAND.COM on the disk through which booting is made. It is a system file.

There are the other system files like AUTOEXEC.BAT, CONFIG.SYS will function as COMMAND.COM functions at the time of getting switched on the computer. COMMAND.COM made up two hidden system files IO.SYS and MSDOS.SYS in it for interfacing the computer. DOS kennel is made up by these two system files. It will read the information stored in some special files and changes the internal configuration or internal settings according to the need or wishes of the user. By booting through the disk, the system prompt will appear as:

A:\>

If booting is through hard disk, the DOS prompt will be

C:\>

Col Boot

To load system files on the memory by switching on the computer is called as cold booting. Some times when computer is on use, some error occurs or halts, then the proper procedure of switching off is followed and after few minutes of switch off, the switch to be on.

Warm Boot

To load system files again by discarding the operations while the computer is working because of error occurred or halt the machine, the RESET button to be pressed or ALT+CTRL+DEL to be pressed which will disconnect the power on to the mother board and will supply power to the board immediately to run the function to load system files immediately. At that time the power is in the CPU, but the memory cells are only vacated by disconnecting the power from that cells. It is called as warm boot.

Keyboard Familiarity

Keyboard (KB) is the key example of input device. There are 101 keys on the KB. After all the new KBs having 105 keys as windows keyboard, 120 keys called as multi media and internet keyboard, etc. in which 15 keys are for multimedia keys, 3 keys are for mouse operations, 3 are specified for Mouse operations.

Types of Keys

The keys on the KB are classified into 6 types:

1. **Alphabetic Keys:** The keys contain on the keyboard of alphabets are 26 in number. These keys are used for alphabets A to Z (upper case) and a to z (lower case) letters.
2. **Numeric Keys:** There are 10 keys on the keyboard labelled as 1, 2, 3, 4, 5, 6, 7, 8, 9, 0. These keys are on the 2nd row of the KB, before the alphabetic keys and there are separate key pad on the right side of the KB i.e. numeric key paid which activates only when the Numeric Lock (Num Lock key) on. When the Num Lock light is off the symbols written on the keys will function.
3. **Function Keys:** The keys labelled as Fl, F2, ..., F12 on the top most row of the KB. The function keys are otherwise called as programmable keys. It has several functions in several software or applications.
4. **Special Character or Symbolic Keys:** The keys labelled as ' ! @ $ % A & * () _- + = {}[ ]:; '"<>,.?/ \ I.
5. **Edit or Cursor Control Keys:** There are only four keys indicating arrows to four sides. It is used to edit or control the cursor only. Hence, it is called so.
6. **Special Keys:** The keys labelled as Ctrl, Pause, Alt, Delete, Shift, Shift Lock, Caps Lock, Tab, Num Lock, Scroll Lock, Print Screen, Insert, End, Home, Page Up, Page Down, Backspace, Enter/Return, Alt and Space Bar (the largest key on last row of the KB).

Some Important Keys on the Keyboard

1. **Enter/Return**: There is a key on the KB written ENTER or RETURN or an arrow mark (↵) differing from manufacturing company of the KBs. This key marks the end of line or instructions. Usually DOS has

to be informed with the pressing of this key, a command is entered.

2. **Shift:** It will shift the characters to upper case or to lower case letters. The uppercase letters are A to Z and the lower case letters are from a to z. Other than these letters there are some keys having two characters written on the same key. The upper character written on the key should got by pressing Shift and that key at-a-time. If lower case letter is required simply press the required key. But when you are using the Shift key please confirm that the Shift Lock is ON or OFF. If Shift Lock is On, the upper case letters will appear, for other characters like symbols and numbers it has no function. But the Shift key will be effective for giving the both upper and lower case letters.

3. **Esc (Escape):** This key cancels a current line or command in has typed. It displays reverse of slash symbol (\) to indicate that cancellation. It will not give any prompt in DOS. In other software or application it will return the control from the current position to another position. But it will indicate still it is ready to do some job.

4. **Ctrl (Control):** This key is generally labelled as Ctrl, have no effect on its own. But when it is used in combination with some other keys give desired effect.

5. **Backspace (←):** This keys is labelled a long left arrow key. It is used to erase the left most characters from the position of the cursor.

6. **Num Lock:** It is the Numeric Lock key which have a light, will born by pressing the Num Lock key. When the light will born, the numeric keys on the numeric key pad will work, otherwise the lowercase letters will functions.

7. **Break:** This key is labelled as Pause. The same work will be done by the Scroll Lock by boring a light as

Shift Lock and Num Lock. It cancels the current command or it stops the execution of the programme which is performed by the current command entered in it.

8. **Alt (Alternate):** It is labelled as Alt. Alt key has specific functions in various applications and software pre-defined by the manufacturing company. For example in DOS Alt+Ctrl+Delete will reset the computer which is the same thing to press the switch ON the computer currently or pressing of Reset switch.
9. **Delete (Del):** This key is labelled as Delete or Del varying from manufacturing company of the KBs. Delete key will delete the characters right from the current position of the when the key is user to delete the characters to right. Hence, before pressing the Delete key, the cursor have to move to the particular character from which the characters have to delete to right most characters.
10. **Cancelling a command:** If one command is used recently for an execution further the decision is made not to use that command Ctrl+C should be used to cancel the command. It is mostly effective in DOS.

File

It is a collection of related information to perform a specific task. It is group of organised data, which assembled for one particular purpose and consider as one unit. The data is in permanent off-line storage like a disk drive, tape, a disk. For example, a programme file contains a set of instruction organised to perform a certain task, a database file contains related data.

Rules of Naming a File

1. The file name should exceed eight characters and the extension name should not exceed three characters. If more than the specific number of characters used the

first eight and three character will be taken as file name and extension names by the computer and the rest characters should be truncated.

2. There should be a period or dot as separator between primary name and extension names.
3. First character of a file should be an alphabet. Any numeric or special character should not be allowed as first character of a valid file name.
4. Space is not allowed between characters of a file name.
5. Hyphen (-) is not allowed as a character of a file name, but underscore (_) is allowed as a character of a file name.

Numeric File

The file names are divided into two parts as a primary name or file name and the other name is extension name. The primary name or file name should not exceed 8 characters. The extension name should not exceed 3 characters. Between file name and extension name, there appears a dot or period.

Example 6.1

PRY_NAME.EXT

(File name) (dot) (Extension name)

DOS shell allow the characters of a file naming as alphabets, numeric as well as the special characters or symbols as follows:

_ ! @ $ A & ( ) ~ f } ' % #

There are the specific characters will not be accepted by the computer as valid characters as follows:

* . ?/\ I :;,[]<> + = and blank space.

Example 6.2

Valid name Invalid names Error in file names

ITEM98.TAX ITEM 98.TAX Space is not allowed

TRIAL1.DOC 1TRIAL.DOC First character should be an alphabet

PHONE#1.TBL #1PHONE.TBL First character should not be a symbol

Internal Command

COMMAND.COM file consists of instructions for executing some commands which the users common issue. These instructions are called internal command. Internal commands are possible only with the availabilities of COMMAND.COM file in a disk i.e. booting. After booting all the internal commands will function.

Creating a Text File

A text file can be used by using COPY command of DOS. The format is:

COPY CON <FILE NAME> (PRESS ENTER)

Example 6.3

A: \>COPY CON ABBRVIAT.TXT

It will display a screen. It that screen any text can be typed as follows:

- DOS stands for Disk Operating System
- LAN stands for Local Area Network
- OS stands for Operating System
- SW stands for Soft Ware
- IBM stands for International Business Machine Corp. Inc., USA
- ANSI stands for American National Standard Institute, USA press Ctrl+Z or AZ (A implies Ctrl) When type is complete, press Ctrl and Z simultaneously, then press ENTER/RETURN.

This process will close other file. It will return the control to DOS prompt from that file and store that text in the ABBRVIAT.TXT file. Then the DOS prompt will appear as

A:\>1 FILE(S) COPIED

Display a File

TYPE command is used to display the contents of a file. It's format is

[D:] TYPE <FILE NAME> <ENTER>

Example 6.4

A:\>TYPE ABBRVIAT.TXT (PRESS ENTER)

It will display the content of the file typed on COPY CON command in 6.9.1 on the VDU screen.

But for display on the paper through printer if printer is connected to computer, the format is

[D:] TYPE <FILE NAME> >PRN

Example 6.5

A:\>TYPE ABBRVIAT.TXT>PRN (PRESS ENER)

If printer is connected this computer and it is on, immediately after pressing the ENTER key, it will begin to print the content of the file.

Copying a File

It is used to copy the content of a file to another file or directory. It's format is:

[D:] COPY <SOURCE FILE> <TARGET FILE> (PRESS ENTER)

Example 6.6

A:\>COPY ABBRVIAT.TXT SAMPLE (ENTER)

After this process the message will display for user self reliance that the command has functioned as:

A:\>1 FILE(S) COPIED

It will copy the content of the ABBRVIAT.TXT file to SAMPLE file. But, be cautious about the file you want to copy, if the file is an existing one, after copying the content of a file to it, it will lost the previous content. For example, if the file SAMPLE has some content previously, after copying the ABBRVIAT.TXT, the SAMPLE file will be the same as the content of ABBRVIAT.TXT. For your confirmation, TYPE the SAMPLE file, you will get the same content of ABBRVIAT.TXT file.

To See the Version of DOS

VER is the command to see the version of the DOS working in the computer. It's format is:

[D:] VER (PRESS ENTER)

Example 6.7

A:\>VER (PRESS ENTER)

Rename a File

REN command is used to rename a file. This process will change the name an old file into a new file name. Its format is

[D:] REN <OLD FILE NAME> <NEW FILE NAME> (PRESS ENTER) |

Example 6.8

A:\>REN ALLIED.CAL INFOTECH.DAT

It will change the ALLIED.CAL file as INFOTECH.DAT. Here only the file name will change and the content of the file should be same.

Delete a File

DELETE or DEL will be used to delete one existing file in the disk. It's format is:

[D:] DEL <FILE NAME> (PRESS ENER)

Example 6.9

A:\>DEL ABBRVIAT.TXT (PRESS ENTER)

After this process the said file ABBRVIAT.TXT will be deleted from the disk.

To Display/Change the Current Date

DATE command is used to see the date of a day in the computer screen. There is one calendar and a clock inside the computer. After closing of Off the computer that clock will not stop. Internally there is an battery self charged in the current flow when the computer is On. Hence, that clock is updating the time and date of the day. At any time the date and time can be seen. The 'date' command will show the date the current day. It's format is [D:] DATE (PRESS ENTER)

Example 6.10

A:\> DATE (PRESS ENTER)

It will show the current date in the format of mm-dd-yy or mm-dd-yyyy.

mm stand for month, it is form the range of 01 to 12. dd stands for date, it's range is from 01 to 31. yy or yyyy stands for the year in two digits (dd) as 98 or four digits as 1998. The message will appear as

Current date is Tue 06-23-1998 Enter new date (mm/dd/yy):

To display/change the Time

TIME command will show the time of the present moment at which the user uses the computer. It's format is

[D:] TIME (PRESS ENTER)

Example 6.11

A:\>TIME (PRESS ENTER)

It will immediately show the message Current time 7:37:49.lip Enter new time.

It will show the time in the format of hh:mm:ss.xx as ll:23:43.50a.hh stand for hour in the range of 01 to 11. mm stands for minute in the range of 01 to 59. ss stands for second in the range of 01 to 59. xx is the sixtyth part of a second in the range 01 to 59. p stands for PM. For indicating AM, a will appear as p appears for indicating P.M.

Clear the Screen on the VDU

CLS is the command to clear the screen of the VDU. If the screen of the VDU is in descent looking by many figures, letters/symbols or sentences, to clear the screen CLS command is required. It's format is:

[D:] CLS (PRESS ENTER)

Example 6.12

A:\>CLS (PRESS ENTER)

To See the List of Files and Directories

List of files and Sub-directories DIR command is used to see the list of files and Sub-directories of the current drive or directory. It will display the list of files and sub-directories in the current disk as file names with its extension names, the date and time of its creations, the directories. Its format is

[D:] DIR (PRESS ENTER)

Example 6.13

A:\>DIR (PRESS ENTER) It will display the message as Volume in drive a is RAJIB Directory of A:\

RAJIB 19,580 04.02.09 18.05p

TRIAL TXT 14,480 08.02.98 12.00a

ABBRVIAT TXT 20,345 20.05.98 09.23a

SAMPLE 18,840 20.05.98 09.25a

MANGLAM <DIR>

COMMAND COM 58,657 03-11.97 01.24p

6 file(s) 1,31,902 bytes 4,95,862 bytes free.

In the above example MANGLAM is a directory name and the others are the file names with their extension names. In that directory some files can be stored. To separate some files such directories are created.

Directory is a set of files. In the directory there are certain files. If a person want to store his/her files in the computer, he/she would feel to make separate directory, naming as his/ her convenient to remember or as per the purpose of files to be stored.

Other Applications of DIR Command

DIR/P	–	It will display the files and directories page wise with size, date, time of file.
DIR/W	–	Display only files and directories widely on the screen
DIR/W/P	–	Display files, directories widely page wise.
DIR/B	–	Display only file name one per line
DIR/S	–	Display only file names one per line
DIR/O: N or ON	–	Display files. directories in ascending order i.e. a to z.
DIR/O:-N	–	Display files, directories in descending order i.e. z to a.
DIR/O:E or OE	–	Display files in ascending order of extension names.
DIR/O:-E	–	Display files in descending order of extension names.

DIR/O:D or OD	–	Display files from lower date to higher date
DIR/O:-D	–	Display the files from higher date to lower.
DIR/S	–	Display the directories and subdirectories in tree structure.
DIR/OS	–	Display the files in ascending order in size.
DIR/O:-S	–	Display the files in descending order in size.
DIR/AH	–	Display all hidden files only.
DIR/A:-H	–	Display all unhidden files.
DIR/AR	–	Display all read only files.
DIR/A:-R	–	Display all non-read only files.
DIR/AS	–	Display all system files.
DIR/A:-S	–	Display all non-system files.

Making a Directory

MKDIR or MD command will allow the create a sub-directory. The format is

[D:] MKDIR <DIRECTORY NAME> (PRESS ENTER)

or

[D:] MD <DIRECTORYNAME> (PRESS ENTER)

Example 6.14

MD RAJARAM <press Enter>

It will make the directory in the name of rajaram. If you will use the DIR command, it will display the directory as

C:\RAJARAM <DIR>

Change the Directory

CHDIR or CD command will change the directory i.e. RAJARAM, which implies that it will ready or open the directory for the operation of files inside the directory. After making a directory a directory, directory should be changed by CD command. It's format is

[D:] CD <SUB-DIRECTORY NAME> (PRESS ENTER)

Example 6.15

A: \>CD RAJARAM (PRESS ENTER)

It will display the format as follows:

A:\RAJARAM>

Here the control (cursor) will move after the DOS prompt. Now, if you will put DIR command, it will display the file(s) stored in the directory. If there will no files in the existing directory, then this command will display as

Volume in drive a is RAJIB Volume Serial Number is IF4E-12E3 Directory of A:\RAJARAM . <DIR> 10-06-98 6.40p

<DIR> 10-06-98 6.40p 2 file(s) 0 bytes

627,746 bytes free

Close the Directory

CD... command will close the directory opened by CD or CHDIR command. It will transfer the control from the directory to the DOS prompt. It's format is

[D:] \DIRECTORY NAME>CD... (PRESS ENTER)

Example 7.16

A: \RAJARAM>CD... (PRESS ENTER)

It will display as

A:\>

It close the directory and transfer the control to the DOS prompt.

Remove the Directory

RMDIR or RD command will be used to remove a directory which has been made previously. It's format is

[D:] RD <DIRECTORY NAME> (PRESS ENTER)

Example 6.17

A:\> RD RAJARAM (PRESS ENTER)

Now, it has removed the RAJARAM directory from the existing disk.

Difference Between Internal Command and External Command

These commands (6.9.1 to 6.9.15) are the internal commands. Whenever, computer is boot, which implies the presence of COMMAND.COM file in the system, internal commands will function in anywhere in the computer. But, external commands will not function. Every external command will require the presence of certain .EXE or .COM files in the disk. In case of external command the commands will function through DOS only where the external files are available.

For instance, FORMAT is an external command. It will format the diskette to allocate the tracks and sectors for memory location, when it is newly used or any error found in the diskette. For performing the task FORMAT.COM file should be required. If the FORMAT.COM file is available in the DOS directory, to format a diskette the control should be transferred to DOS. From DOS directory only, FORMAT command is entered. The external commands are DISKCOPY, XCOPY, CHKDSK, DISKCOMP, SYS, TREE, COMP, MODE, FIND, etc.

External Commands

1. **Move:** This command requires move.exe file to be available in the disk where the command is working. This command will move a file/specific files from source

location to destination. MOVE command will be used to transfer the content of source file to target file. After transferring the Target file will be same as the source file, the source file will be empty. For your confirmation, you can TYPE the target file and also the source file. The target file will display the content, but the source file will display nothing.

Syntax: MOVE <source> <destination> (Press Enter)

Example 6.18

A:\> MOVE SAMPLE ALLIED.CAL (PRESS ENTER)

But, remember COPY command will copy the content of the source file to target file. The source file and the target file will show the same content, if both will type. (This command will function in DOS 6.x versions. So, you have to see the version of the DOS.)

2. **Edit:** It requires edit.com file in the disk. Through this command, an existing file can be edited i.e changed, typed, and also a new file can be made through this command. Edit command will work as a type writer/ word processing in DOS. In Windows to open EDIT screen, go to SRART->RUN - press Enter, one screen will appear with a writing bar to open, type 'command' or 'cmd' then press ENTER. It will open the edit screen.

In MS-DOS, its syntax is EDIT <FILE NAME> to edit the specific file, to create a new file through EDIT command, just type EDIT, then the edit screen will be opened and make type the required text, then save the file by pressing ALT+F+S, the system will ask the file name, enter the file name and press ENTER. It will save the text typed in the file name given. In the EDIT screen there are three menus on the task bar (upper bar of the screen) as FILE, EDIT, SEARCH, VIEW, OPTIONS, HELP which has the bus-menu as:

Command	Description	Shortcut Key
File:		
1. **New**	To create a new file.	ALT+F+N
2. **Open**	To open an existing file	ALT+F+O
3. **Save**	To save the current file	ALT+F+S
4. **Save As**	Save the current in another duplicate name	ALT+F+A
5. **Close**	Close the current file	ALT+F+C
6. **Print**	Print the current file or selected area of text	ALT+F+P
(To select a selected are of text, locate the cursor at the text from which to be selected, press the SHIFT key and move the cursor in the direction which to be selected, then left the SHIFT key. The specific text to be highlighted.)		
7. **Exit**	To exit EDIT screen	ALT+F+X

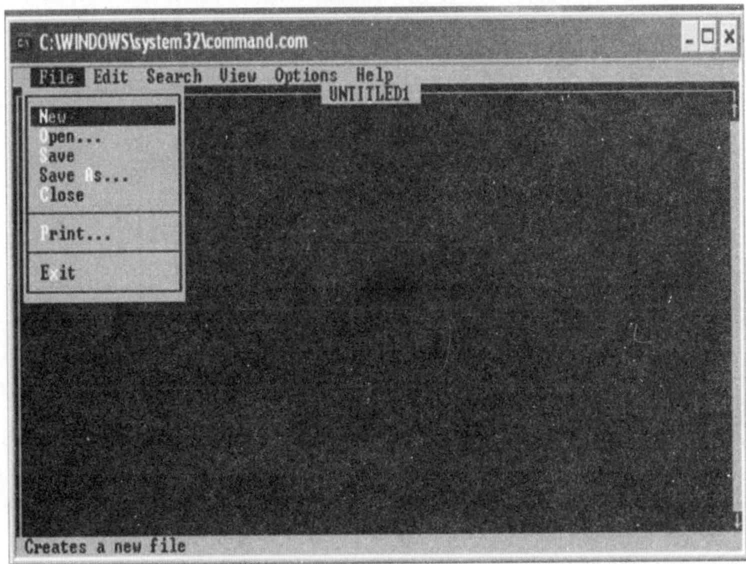

Fig. 6.1: **MS-DOS Edit Screen & File Menu on it**

Edit

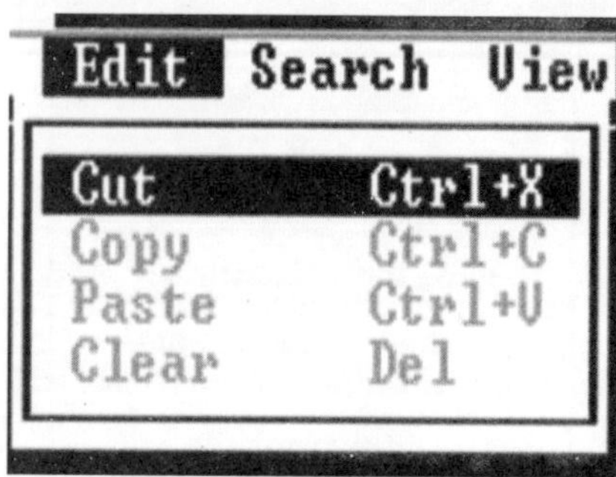

Fig. 6.2

1.	Cut	To cut a selected text (the text will be deleted and kept in the memory for paste/replace)	ALT+E+T/CTRL+X
2.	Copy	To copy a selected text	ALT+E+C/CRTL+C
3.	Paste	To paste the cutting of the text	ALT+E+P/CTRL+V
4.	Clear	To clear the delete selected text	press DELETE key

Search

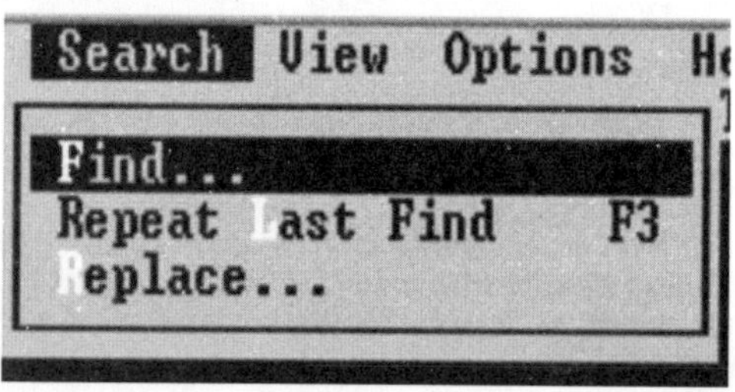

Fig. 6.3

1.	Find: To find word(s) in the current text	ALT+S+F
2.	Repeat Last Find	ALT+S+L pressing of F3 key
3.	Replace: Replace word(s) against word(s) (... menu has again another screen of action)	ALT+S+R

In Edit command there are cursor movement commands/short cuts keys

HOME	–	To go to beginning of the line where cursor is present
END	–	to goto the end of the line
CTRL+up arrow	–	To move the cursor up one line
CTRL+down arrow	–	To move the cursor down one line
CTRL+left arrow	–	To move one word left
CTRL+right arro	–	To move one word right
CTRL+HOME	–	To move the cursor beginning of the file
CTRL+END	–	To move the cursor end the file
PgUP	–	Scroll the cursor up one page
PgDn	–	Scroll the cursor down one page
CTRL+PgUP	–	Scroll left one screen
CTRL+PgDn	–	Scroll right one screen
DELETE	–	To delete the forward/right side characters of the cursor
Backspace	–	To delete left side/back characters of the cursor
TAB	–	Move the cursor to the next tabular stop on the text line
INSERT	–	It will do insert ON/OFF. It is switch between insert(ON) and overwrite (OFF) modes.
CTRL+Y	–	Delete current line
CTRL+U	–	Paste buffer contents into file
CTRL+P	–	Allows special characters to be inserted
Caps Lock	–	It will allow for capital letter typing and it will light the caps lock indicator, to off CapsLock, again press the key.
SHIFT	–	Hold and type will be uppercase letters capital letters, otherwise small letters, when CapsLock is on, it will act reverse.
SHIFT+Tab	–	It will unindent the selected lines

3. **ATTRIB** - To hide files and unhide hidden files, ATTRIB command is applicable which needs ATTRIB.EXE file to be available in the machine.

   Its syntax is: ATTRIB (parameters) <file name> press ENTER

Parameters

+R Makes the file read only.

- R Makes the protected file free from read only mode.

+A Sets the archieved attribute of a file turn into one.

- A Sets the archieved byte of the archieved file turn into one.

+H Hide the files from the directory where DIR command will not display

- H Unhide the hidden files where DIR command can display the files

4. **MEM** - To display the memory of the disk this command is used which requires MEM.EXE file to be available in the disk.

   Its syntax is: MEM (press ENTER)

5. **TREE** - To display the tree structure of the directories and sub-directories.

   Its syntax: TREE (press ENTER)

It will display the tree structure of the directories and sub-directories from the current location of the command entered.

6. **UNDELETE** - It will undelete the deleted files immediately delete/del/erase command. . It requires UNDELETE.EXE file to be available in the disk.

   Syntax: UNDELETE <wild card characters as entered in the del command> ENTER

7. **SCANDISK/CHKDSK** - This command requires availability of SCANDISK.EXE file in the current disk.

This command check and repairs the cross linked files and physical errors. It will check the lost clusters of the disk. Physically errors including the surface flaws. In stead of using SCANDISK, we can use CHKDSK. CHKDSK requires CHKDSK.EXE file availability in the disk. It repairs the disk by checking errors in clusters/locations of tracks and sectors.

Syntax: SCANDISK <destination to scan> press ENTER

MS-WINDOWS

MS-Windows has been developed as the superior system software in the PC world as an multi-application operating system. MS-DOS is the subset of MS-WINDOWS and MS-WINDOWS is the superset of MS-DOS. MS-WINDOWS is enhanced by a group of programmes. All MS-DOS operations can be performed in MS-WINDOWS and more special applications can be done in it. At a time many applications can be run in MS-WINDOWS, but in MS-DOS one command or operation at a time. So, MS-DOS operations are sequential and Ms-WIDOWS applications can be used randomly and can be simultaneous. Every application have its own screen. Each screen is called a window. So, its name is called as Windows. Though it is developed by Micro Soft Inc. it is named as MS-WINDOWS. MS-WINDOWS has one advantage is that every thing is on graphic mode and mouse is the main operating device which indicated the descriptions when the pointer goes on any item on the screen/window, so it is more user friendly and have no need to remember any application. So, it is called as Graphic User Interface (GUI). In MS-DOS, for any application, the command to be remembers how it will work and that requires specific files to be available in the disk. DOS is General User Interface. MS-Windows is WYSIWYG (What You See Is What You Get).

Advantage of MS-Windows

1. Graphic User Interface.
2. No need to remember commands.
3. Inclusive of Ms-DOS applicable in graphic mode.
4. Executable files are available.
5. Clip board where the cut and paste of files, documents, texts can be possible.
6. OLE (Object Linking & Embedding) applications are possible.
7. Multitasking which allows many applications at a time.
8. WYSIWYG which is graphic presentation with description of application.
9. Easy application of operations of files, folders (directories).
10. No need to remember syntax of the commands.
11. Multi media applications.
12. Networking applications and internet.
13. Multi user applications can be possible.

1. **Desktop** - The screen in windows displayed on the Monitor is called as desktop as appeared above.
2. **Icon** - The small objects on the desktop is called icon. These are the picture elements containing programmes/ files in it. An icon may be called as folder (directory). But, icon has some specific identity which are generally developed for specific purposes or by developed by company.
3. **Folder** - A picture element of directory which contains files/programmes. A folder may be called as an icon but an icon may not be called as a folder. Folder is user defined, icon is company made.

Parts of MS-WINDOWS Screen

Fig. 6.4: **MS-Windows Screen/Desktop**

4. **Task Bar** - Task bar is positioned at the bottom of the desktop containing start button, open folders (if any), tool bars, notification area, etc.

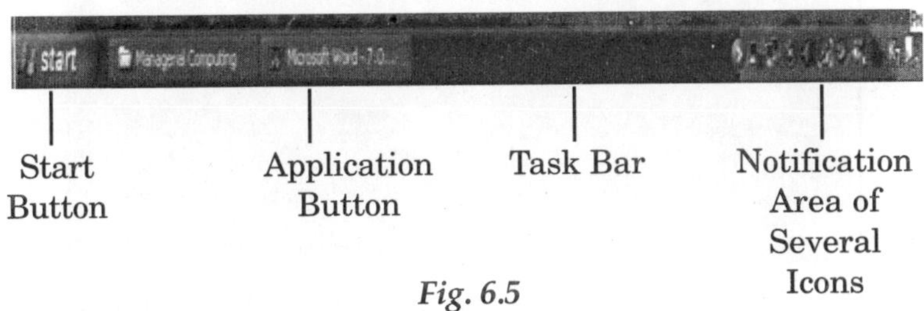

Fig. 6.5

START Menu Options

Left most item of the task bar is START button which contains items like documents, my pictures, my music, my computer, control panel, connect to, printer and Faxes, help and support, search, run, email, media player, all programmes, etc. The applications on the following screen should be pointer by mouse pointer and click the left mouse button for its application, the menu which as right arrow symbol will consist of another menu which has its own applications. START button has one vital operation of log off, turn off computer.

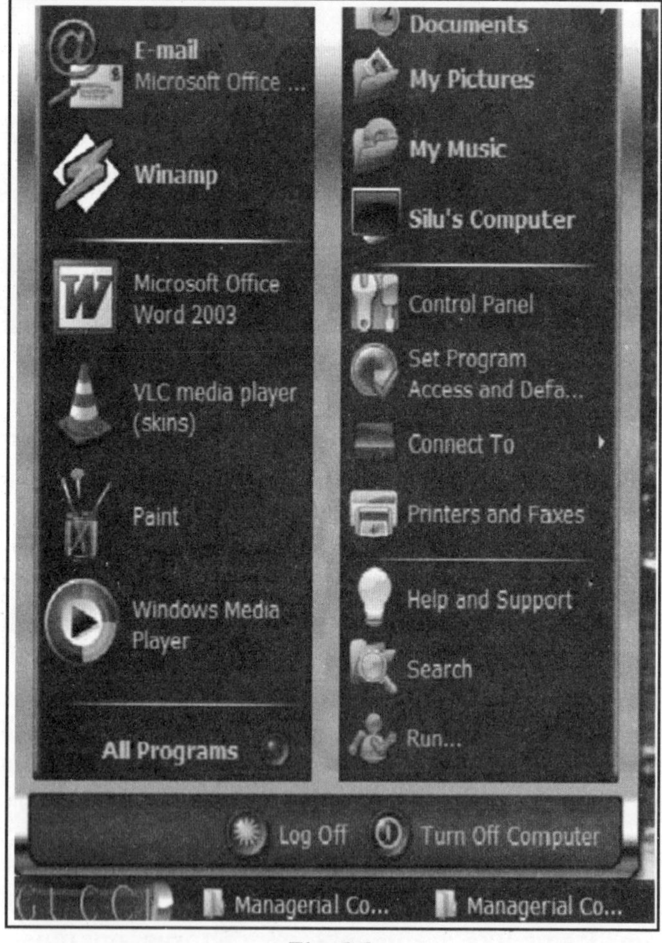

Fig. 6.6

Turn off Computer

It is the menu which have another menu as displayed under consisting of standby, turn off, restart options. Turn off will switch off the computer by closing all the windows open in the operation. Restart will shut down the computer and again will start the computer for operation. It is called as cold booting. Stand by is the option of stopping operation of the computer temporarily.

Fig. 6.7: **System Icons on Desktop**

My Computer

It contains computer's drive icons and the drives, external disks, pen driver, mobile devices, camera, control panel, printers, dialup networking and scheduled tasks system folders.

Internet Explorer

When the folder/application opened windows will dial up/connect to the internet, if there is a set of account with an internet provider to the PC. Internet Explorer is developed by Micro Soft Inc. which is an supplement of MS-Windows.

Network Neighbourhood

A system which contains icons of network computers that the user can use any of the shared computers in that network.

Recycle Bin

It stores the files and folders which have been deleted by the user. Till the items are available in this icon which can be restored back to the source from where the file(s)/ folder(s) deleted. To delete file(s)/folder(s) in the recycle bin, press delete on that. But, note when the file(s)/folder(s) deleted from recycle bin, which can not be reverted/restored back. The file(s)/folder(s) will be deleted permanently. Recycle bin is just as dust bin.

My Documents

It stores the document (text) files of the computer developed by the user. It is the default storage location of the text files.

KEY POINTS TO REMEMBER FOR MS-DOS

- DOS is acronym for Disk Operating System developed by Micro Soft Inc.
- MS-DOS is a single user operating system. It is general user interface.
- Operating System (OS) is a set of instructions used to manage the several resources and operations of a computer system. DOS is OS, UNIX is an OS.
- MS-DOS was developed by Micro Soft Inc. delivered in 1981.
- PC-DOS was developed by IBM (International Business Machine) Inc., U.S.A.
- a Loading DOS into memory is called as Booting. After Power On Self Test (POST), after switch ON, Booting

will activate the compute system. It is the initial stage of function a computer.

- There are 6 types of keys on the Keyboard of a computer as Alphabetic, Numeric, Function, Symbolic, Edit and Special Keys.
- Space Bar is the longest key on the Keyboard.
- File is a collection of released information to perform a specific task. It is a group of organised data, assembled for on particular purpose and considered as one unit.
- A file name is divided into two parts: primary name or file name and extension name.
- Primary name or file name should not exceed 8 characters following specific rules.
- Extension name should not exceed 3 characters following specific rules.
- One dot(.) or period is used as the separator between primary name and extension name of a file.
- Internal commands are those instructions used commonly any where in the computer on DOS prompt i.e. in root directory or in sub-directory.
- External commands are the commands function in the directory where the specific DOS file with extension names like .EXE, .COM currently available.
- a DIR command (internal) is used to display the list of files with sub-directory in root directory or in current sub-directory.
- MKDIR or MD command (internal) can create a sub-directory. O CHDIR or CD command (internal) can change a sub-directory.
- RMDIR or RD will remove a sub-directory from the current sub-directory, but the sub-directory should have no files.

- REN command (internal) will rename a file.
- DATE command (internal) will show the current date.
- TIME command (internal) will show the current time.
- CLS command (internal) will clear the screen.
- MS-Windows has been developed as the superior system software in the PC world as an multi-application operating system.
- MS-WINDOWS has one advantage is that every thing is on graphic mode i.e Graphic User Interface (GUI).
- MS-Windows is WYSIWYG (What You See Is What You Get)

Word Processing

Introduction

Through word processor, the user can write a text by typing through keyboard edit the text and print the document through printer with multiple copies. It works as type writer and word processor in computer, i.e. in type written a key is pressed for a character to display the same character should be pressed on the paper feed in the type written on the type bar, but in word processor through computer, a text can be typed, stored, verified whether it is correctly entered and edit the text the hardcopy (printout) may be made and it can be further referred. But in type writer once a key is pressed implies it is already pressed on the paper which can be altered. In word processor, if once a text is made can be stored for future reference, print, alteration, number of copies can be printed. Mail merge can be made i.e. a same text can be printed for correspondence with several persons with address for correspondence. The word processing software are WordStar, word soft, WordPad, notepad, MS-Word, etc. There are several arts, tables, letter sizes and designs can be possible in word processing software. There are several other softwares used for word processing for stylus text, inserting photos, arts, etc. They are Adobe PageMaker, CorelDraw, Photoshop, SriLipi, iLeap, Leap Office, Akruti, Akshyara, etc.

MS-WORD

MS-Word has the opening screen as displayed below (Fig. 7.1). After MS-Word opening, when the new document to be opened from the menu File->Open or Alt+O as shortcut key, the following screen will appear to open what type of document viz. Blank document, XML document, web page, E-mail message, from existing documents. Generally, blank document to be choosen. Then the text to be entered into the new file which can be saved by pressing Alt+F+S or Ctrl+S.

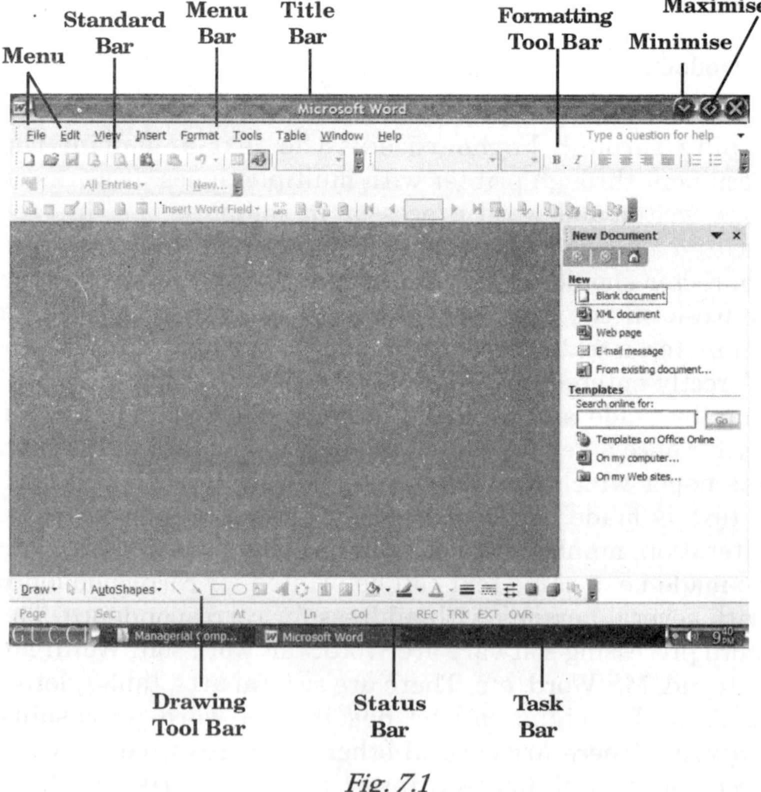

Fig. 7.1

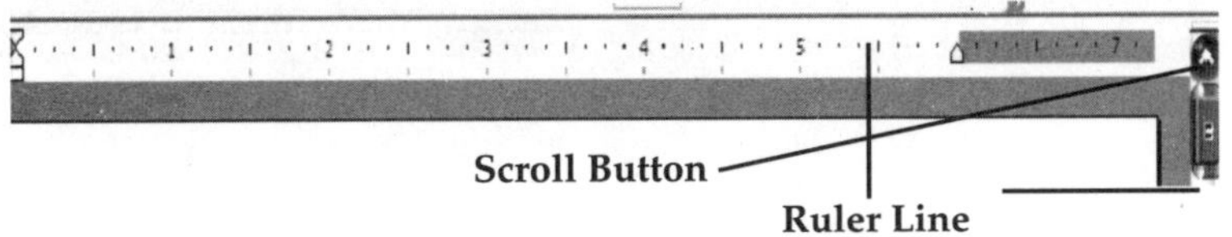

Fig. 7.2

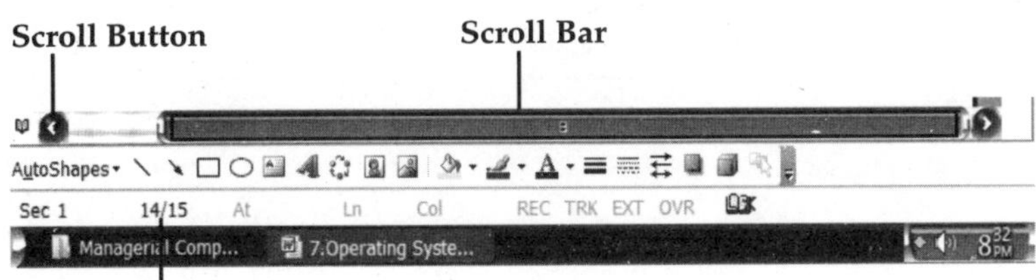

14th Page of the text in the file 7. *Operating System* where insertion point present now

Fig. 7.3

Insertion Point - It is the vertical line which indicates the position of the user in the text where the text to be inserted.

Menu in MS-Word

Menu		Short Cut Key to get the sub-menu	Function of the menu
1.	**File**	**Alt+F**	**To open File menu**
(i)	New	Alt+F+N or Ctrl+N	New Document File
(ii)	Open	Alt+F+O or Ctrl+O	Open an existing file
(iii)	Close	Alt+F+C	Close the recent file
(iv)	Save	Alt+F+S or Ctrl+S	Save the current file
(v)	Save As	Alt+F+A or F12	Save the current file in other name
(vi)	Page Setup...	Alt+F+U	Set the space of the document page
(vii)	Print	Alt+F+P or Ctrl+P	Print the current document
(viii)	Print Preview	Alt+F+V	Display the preview of the document on printing

1.	File	Alt+F	To open File menu
(ix)	Send to	Alt+F+D	Send the file to email or FAX
(x)	Properties	Alt+F+I	Properties of the current file
(xi)	Exit	Alt+F+X	Close the MS-Word

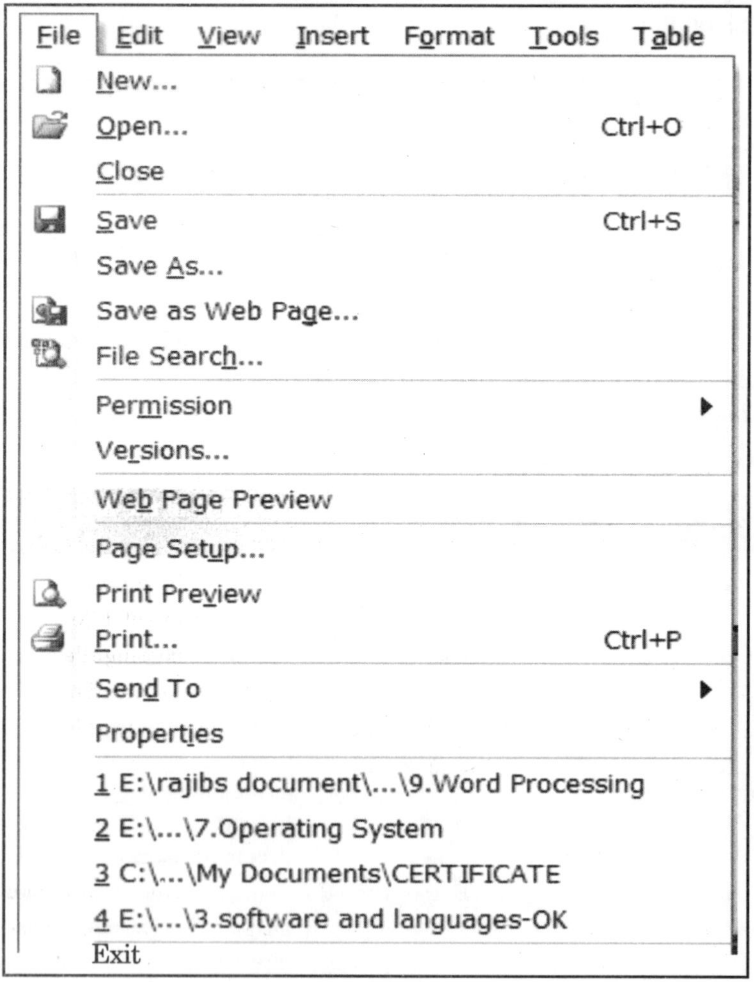

File Edit View Insert Format Tools Table

New...	
Open...	Ctrl+O
Close	
Save	Ctrl+S
Save As...	
Save as Web Page...	
File Search...	
Permission	▶
Versions...	
Web Page Preview	
Page Setup...	
Print Preview	
Print...	Ctrl+P
Send To	▶
Properties	
1 E:\rajibs document\...\9.Word Processing	
2 E:\...\7.Operating System	
3 C:\...\My Documents\CERTIFICATE	
4 E:\...\3.software and languages-OK	
Exit	

Fig. 7.4

2.	Edit	Alt+E	To open Edit Menu
(i)	Undo Typing	Alt+E+U or Ctrl+Z	Undo the current change in text
(ii)	Repeated Typing	Alt+E+R or Ctrl+Y	Redo the current change in text
(iii)	Cut	Alt+E+T or Ctrl+X	Cut the selected text
(iv)	Copy	Alt+E+C or Ctrl+C	Copy the selected text
(v)	Paste	Alt+E+P or Ctrl+V	Paste the text in clipboard
(vi)	Paste Special	Alt+E+S	Paste the clipboard data into OLE
(vii)	Clear	Ctrl+C	Clear the setting/ delete text
(viii)	Select All	Ctrl+A	Selects entire text of the file
(ix)	Find...	Alt+E+F or Ctrl+F	Find the given text
(x)	Replace...	Alt+E+E or Ctrl+H	Replace a text against another text
(xi)	Go to...	Alt+E+G or Ctrl+G	Go to a page no, line no., etc.
(xii)	Links	Alt+E+K	Paste the clipboard data to HTML purpose
(xiii)	Object	Alt+E+O	

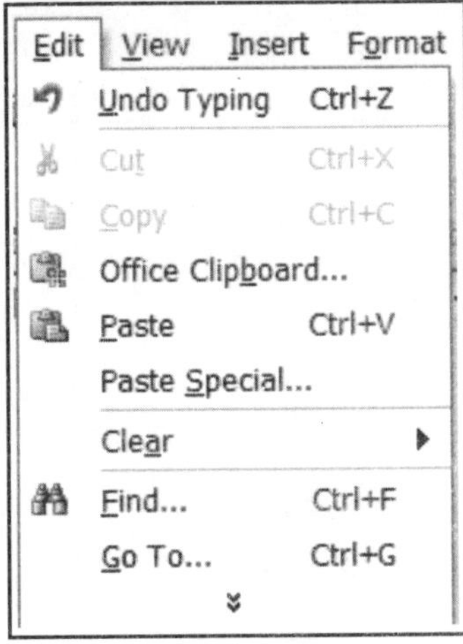

Fig. 7.5

3.	View	Alt+V	To open View Menu
(i)	Normal	Alt+V+N	Set the normal page layout
(ii)	Web Layout	Alt+V+W	Set the page layout as web page form
(iii)	Print Layout	Alt+V+P	Shows the layout as the page will print
(iv)	Reading Layout	Alt+V+R	Shows two part page layout for reading
(v)	Outline	Alt+V+O	Shows the page outline view
(vi)	Task Pane	Alt+V+K/Ctrl+F1	Shows the help menu in rightside
(vii)	Toolbars	Alt+V+T	Shows tool bars and to enable/disable
(viii)	Ruler	Alt+V+L	Ruler line on/off
(ix)	Document Map	Alt+V+D	Shows document headings in left side
(x)	Thumbnail	Alt+V+B	Shows pages in small view in left side
(xi)	Header and Footer	Alt+V+H	Gives header/footer of the document
(xii)	Footnotes	Alt+V+F	Gives foot note of the document
(xiii)	Markup	Alt+V+A	
(xiv)	Full Screen	Alt+V+U	Makes full screen for the document
(xv)	Zoom...	Alt+V+Z	Zooms up the document

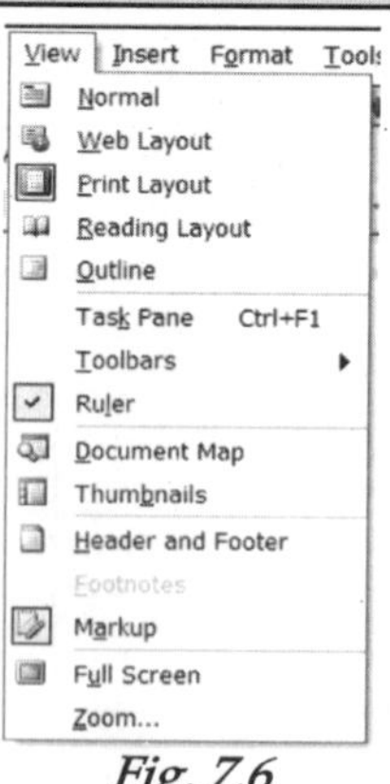

Fig. 7.6

4.	Insert	Alt+I	
(i)	Break...	Alt+I+B	Inserts breaks
(ii)	Page Numbers...	Alt+I+U	Page Numbering of document
(iii)	Date and Time...	Alt+I+T	Inserting system Data and Time
(iv)	Auto Text	Alt+I+A	Types of text available in autotext box
(v)	Field...	Alt+I+F	Special field of assistance for document
(vi)	Symbols...	Alt+I+S	Special symbols to insert in document
(vii)	Comments	Alt+I+M	Comments for text
(viii)	References	Alt+I+N	References for text
(ix)	Web Components...	Alt+I+W	Web based comments to insert
(x)	Picture	Alt+I+P	Pictures available in disk to insert
(xi)	Diagram...	Alt+I+G	Diagrams available to insert
(xii)	Text Box	Alt+I+X	Text box for drawing insertion
(xiii)	File	Alt+I+L	Insert a file in specific location of disk
(xiv)	Object...	Alt+I+O	Special applications to be inserted
(xv)	Book Mark...	Alt+I+K	Book mark to be inserted
(xvi)	Hyperlink...	Alt+I+I/Ctrl+K	Shows current directory contents

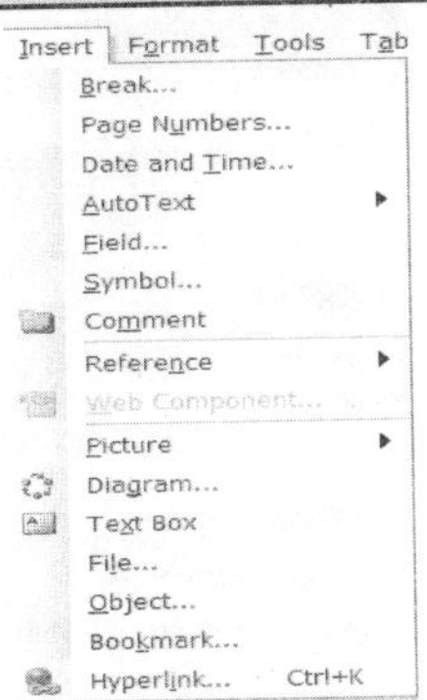

Fig. 7.7

5. Format	Alt+O	
(i) Font...	Alt+O+F	Changes font by showing preview
(ii) Paragraph...	Alt+O+P	Changes paragraph in specific spacing
(iii) Bullet and Numbering...	Alt+O+N	Bullet and numbering can be given
(iv) Boarders and Shading...	Alt+O+B	Boarders and shading can be given
(v) Columns...	Alt+O+C	Columns can be made in a text
(vi) Tabs...	Alt+O+T	It makes tab setting
(vii) Drop Cap...	Alt+O+D	
(viii) Text Direction...	Alt+O+X	
(ix) Change Case...	Alt+O+E	Changes cases of letters
(x) Background	Alt+O+K	Colour of the background to be made
(xi) Themes		Alt+O+H
(xii) Frames		Alt+O+R
(xiii) Autoformat	Alt+O+A	
(xiv) Styles and Formatting...	Alt+O+S	
(xv) Reveal Formatting...	Alt+O+V	
(xvi) Objects...	Alt+O+O	

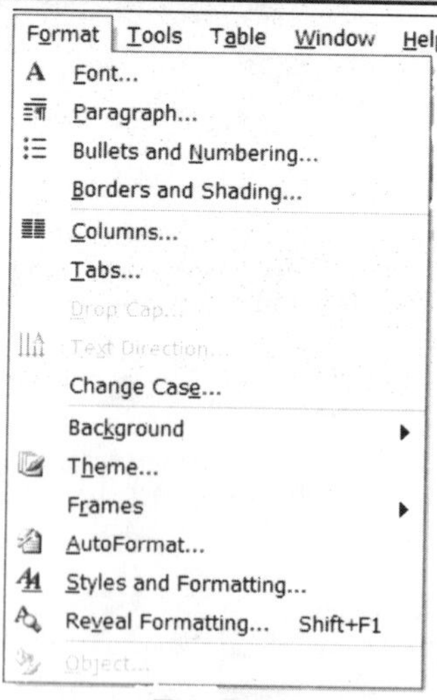

Fig. 7.8

6.	Tools	Alt+T
(i)	Spelling and Grammar	Alt+T+S/F7
(ii)	Research...	Alt+T+R/Alt+Click
(iii)	Language	Alt+T+L
(iv)	Word Count...	Alt+T+W
(v)	Auto Summarise,,,	Alt+T+U
(vi)	Speech	Alt+T+H
(vii)	Shared Workspace...	Alt+T+K
(viii)	Trace Changes	Alt+T+T/Ctrl+Shift+E
(ix)	Compare and Merge Documents	Alt+T+D
(x)	Protect Document	Alt+T+P
(xi)	Online Collaboration	Alt+T+N
(xii)	Letters and Mailings	Alt+T+E
(xiii)	Macro	Alt+T+M
(xiv)	Templates and Add Ins...	Alt+T+I
(xv)	Auto Correct Options	Alt+T+A
(xvi)	Customise	Alt+T+C
(xvii)	Options	Alt+T+O

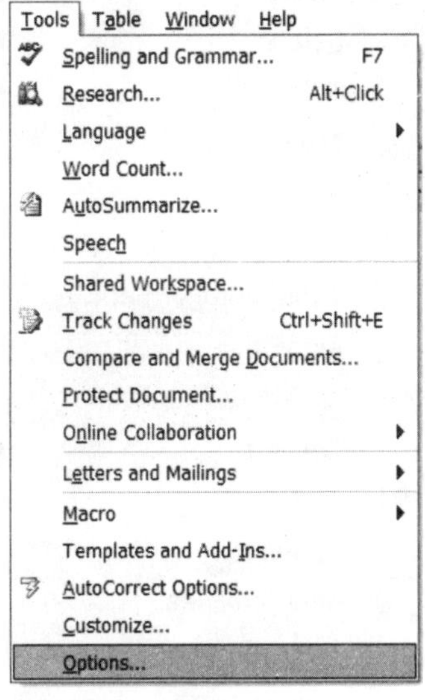

Fig. 7.9

7.	Table	Alt+A
(i)	Draw Table	Alt+A+W
(ii)	Insert	Alt+A+I
(iii)	Delete	Alt+A+D
(iv)	Select	Alt+A+C
(v)	Merge Cells	Alt+A+M
(vi)	Split Cell	Alt+A+P
(vii)	Split Table	Alt+A+T
(viii)	Table Auto correct Format	Alt+A+F
(ix)	Autofit	Alt+A+A
(x)	Heading Rows Repeat	Alt+A+H
(xi)	Convert	Alt+A+V
(xii)	Sort...	Alt+A+S
(xiii)	Formula...	Alt+A+O
(xiv)	Hide Gridlines	Alt+A+G
(xv)	Table Properties	Alt+A+R

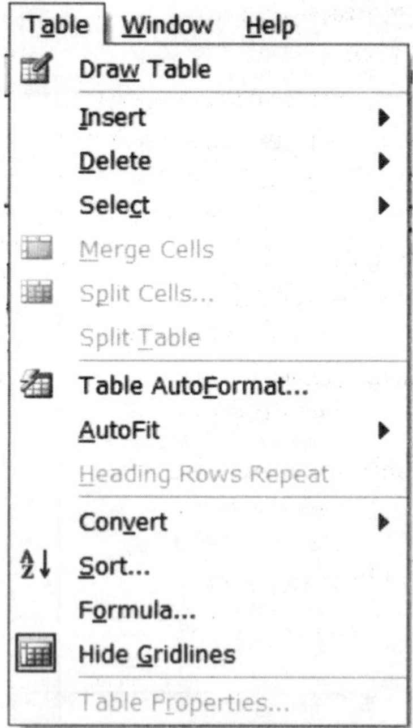

Fig. 7.10

8.	Window	Alt+W
(i)	New Window	Alt+W+N
(ii)	Arrange All	Alt+W+A
(iii)	Compare side by side with...	Alt+W+C
(iv)	Split	Alt+W+S

Last option in this menu is the current document file in use.

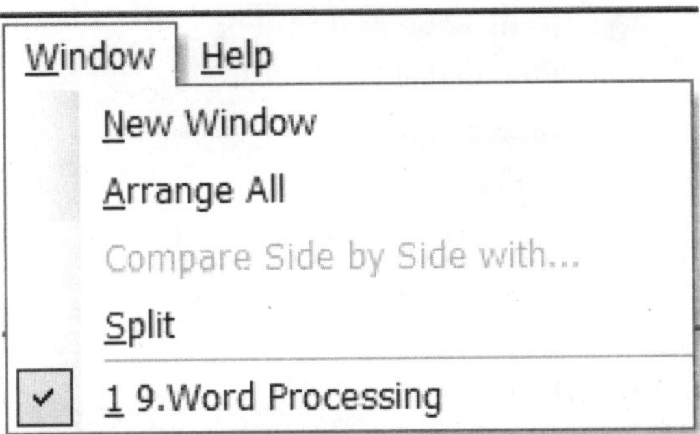

Fig. 7.11

9.	Help	Alt+H

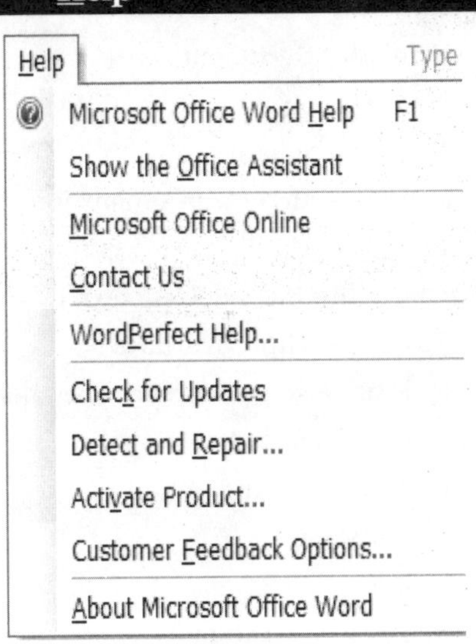

Fig. 7.12

Shortcut Keys from A to Z

Short cut Key	Function
Ctrl+A	Select All
Ctrl+B	Bold selected text
Ctrl+C	Copy the selected text
Ctrl+D	Appear Font dialog box
Ctrl+E	Centre alignment of the line where insertion point is present
Ctrl+F	Find dialog box
Ctrl+G	Goto dialog box
Ctrl+H	Replace dialog box
Ctrl+I	To make selected text to be italic
Ctrl+J	Justify Alignment
Ctrl+K	Insert hyperlink
Ctrl+L	Left Alignment
Ctrl+M	To move one tab
Ctrl+N	Create New Document
Ctrl+O	Open an existing document file
Ctrl+P	Print the Document
Ctrl+Q	Nill
Ctrl+R	Right Alignment
Ctrl+S	Save the current document file
Ctrl+T	Indent setting
Ctrl+U	Underline the selected text
Ctrl+V	Paste the clipboard data
Ctrl+W	Quit or close the current document
Ctrl+X	Cut the selected text
Ctrl+Y	Repeating typing
Ctrl+Z	Undo typing
F1	Help
F7	Spelling & Grammar

Ctrl+2	Double spacing the lines
Ctrl+5	1.5 spacing the lines
Ctrl+=	Subscript
Ctrl+Shift	Super Script
Ctrl+Shift+>	Increase the font size of the selected text
Ctrl+Shift+<	Decrease the font size of the selected text

MS-Word has a very effective tool for office communication is mail merge. It implies, a communication to more than one person is possible to print by specifying each name in the same communication. One data file to be made by storing each name and address. Through mailmerge operation, a common text to be printed specifying each name and address while printing each page of document.

8

Spread Sheet

Introduction

It is a set of programmes designed specially for accounting purposes. As the accounts clerk prepares accounts register by dividing columns with drawing vertical line in different register note book manuals, the spread sheet software has the same type of screen and entry of data row and column wise. There are the rows and columns. There are the facilities of calculations row wise and column wise as the clerk calculates at the last of the day to close the accounts. The examples of spreadsheet software are Lotus123, MS-Excel, VPP, etc.

MS-EXCEL

MS-Excel is the spread sheet application of MS-Office which is developed by Micro Soft Inc. for numerical data for accounting purposes and to be printed. It is a graphic user accounting application software used for numerical calculations with presentation of data in charts and figures of spread sheet. Following is the screen layout of the excel spreadsheet.

Cell

It is the location where data can be stored. Position of the cell is indicated by the row and column number of the

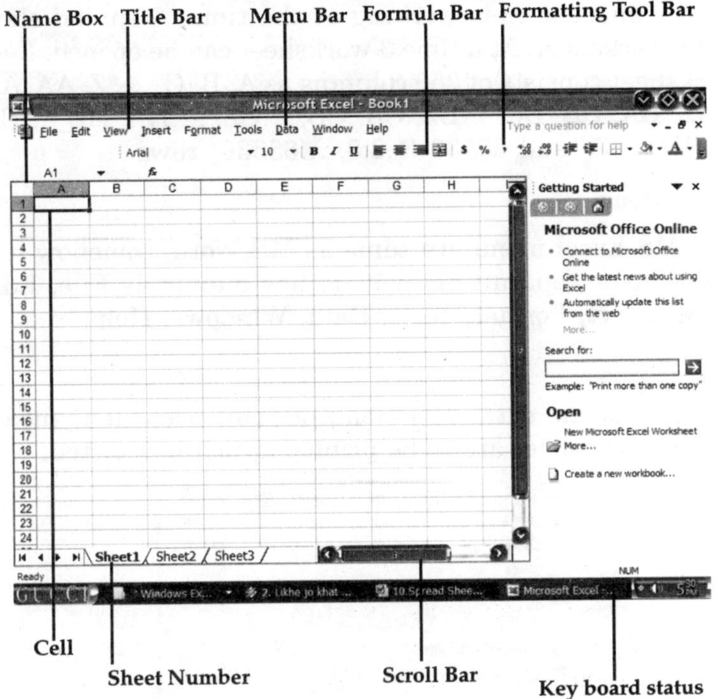

Fig. 8.1

worksheet sheet. The work sheet is indicated as Sheet 1, Sheet 2, Sheet 3, etc. The cell is defined by the instruction of a row and column as F23, which implies the cell position is 'F' number of column and 23rd row. So the cell has the cell reference as F23 for call address. User can enter alphabetic, numeric data and formula in cells. Each cell can store 32000 characters. To write in a cell position the mouse pointer and click, if not possible press F2 as edit option to enter in the cell with insertion point.

Work Sheet

Each sheet of the spread in MS-Excel is called as work sheet. The work sheet is indicated as Sheet 1, Sheet 2, etc. in the button of the spread sheet indicating the highlighted for the sheet user is working at the time. A spread sheet has 8 worksheet. At a time 3 worksheet can be opened. Each worksheet consists of 256 columns as A, B, C, ..., Z, AA, AB, ...AZ, BA, BB, BC, ...BZ, CA, CB, ...CZ, ...,HA, HB, ...HZ, IA, IB, ...IV and 65536 (1,2,3, ...65536) rows.

Excel Menu

MS-Excel menu are same as MS-Word, somehow it is different or separate from it. It has menus as File, Edit, View, Insert, Format, Tools, Data, Windows, Help.

File

It has the extra sub-menu of print area. It is meant for the worksheet are to be printed which is selected.

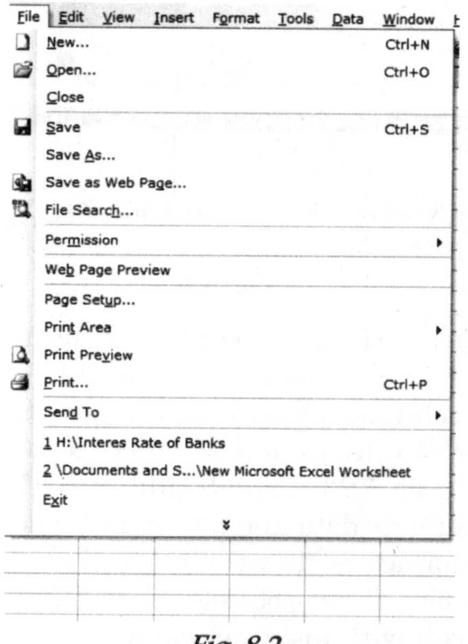

Fig. 8.2

Edit

It has the sub-menu Fill, Delete..., Delete Sheet, Clear, Move or Copy Sheet are extra from MS-Word which is for deleting the current sheet.

Fill Alt+I+E+F

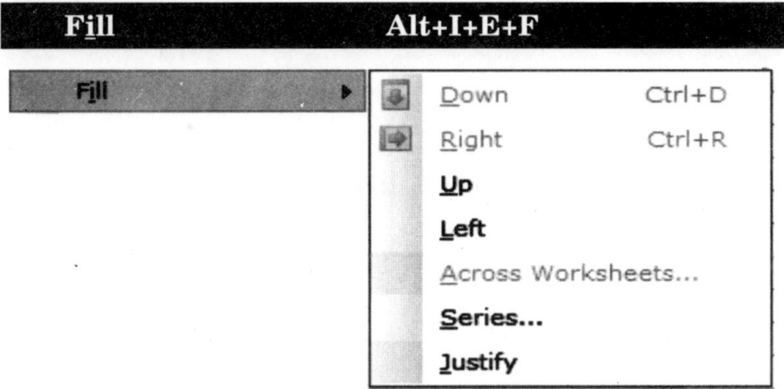

Fig. 8.3

Clear Alt+I+E+A

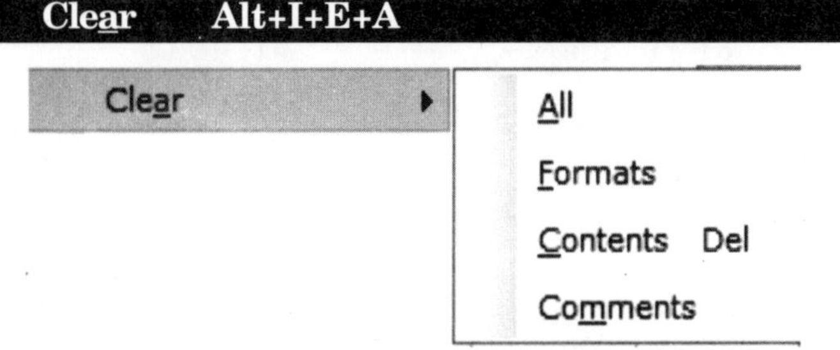

Fig. 8.4

Delete... Alt+I+E+D

It will delete the data in the cells of area as the menu selected

Fig. 8.5

Delete Sheet Alt+I+E+L

It will delete the current sheet, Please take care before use.

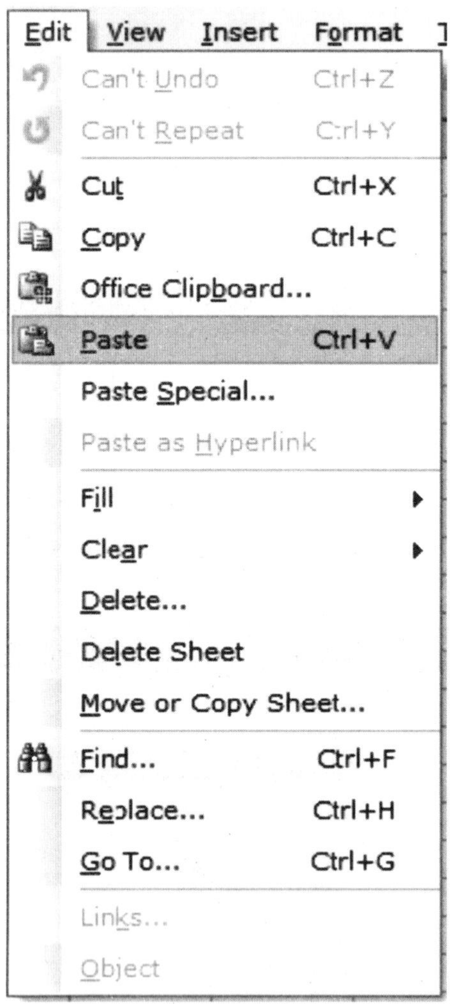

Fig. 8.6

View: It is same as MS-Word.

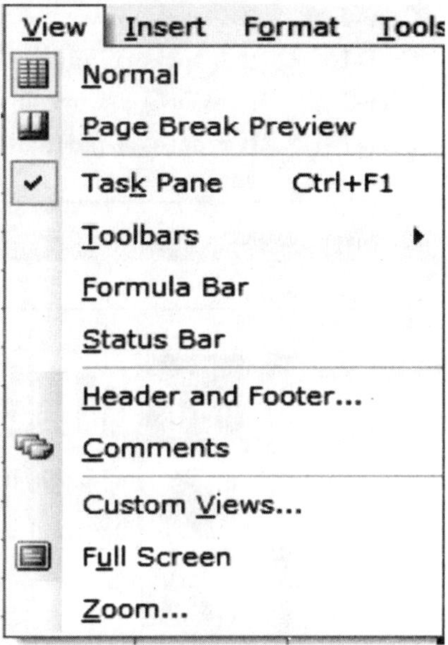

Fig. 8.7

Insert: Insert menu has the new sub-menu of Cells, Rows, Columns, Worksheet, Chart, Function, Name, Comment, Diagram other than Ms-Word.

Fig. 8.8

Cells	Ctrl+I+E	It inserts cell.
Rows	Ctrl+I+R	It inserts row.
Columns	Ctrl+I+C	It inserts column.
Worksheet	Ctrl+I+W	It inserts a worksheet
Chart	Ctrl+I+H	It creates a particular charts of the data selected.

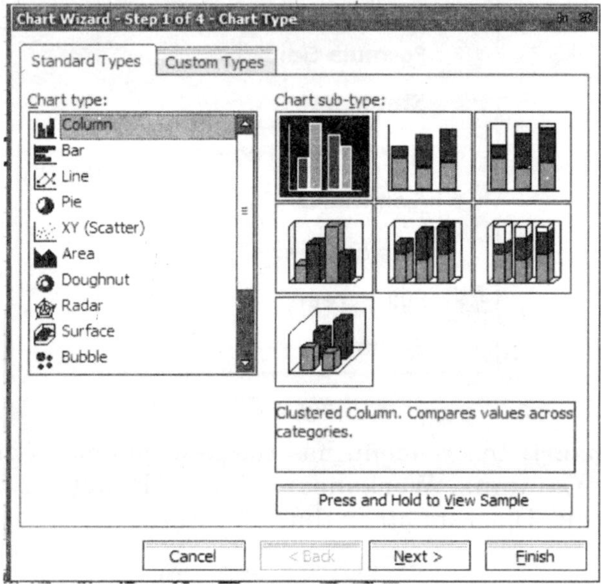

Fig. 8.9

It will make the of the selected cells of data on the worksheet as the chart selected and made next and finish or in some MS-Excel software make OK.

There are 14 types of charts as:

1. Column Chart
2. Bar Chart
3. Pie Chart
4. Bubble Chart

5. Line Chart
6. Pyramid Chart
7. Scatter Chart
8. Area Chart
9. Doughnut Chart
10. Radder Chart
11. Surface Chart
12. Cone Chart
13. Cylinder Chart
14. Stock Chart

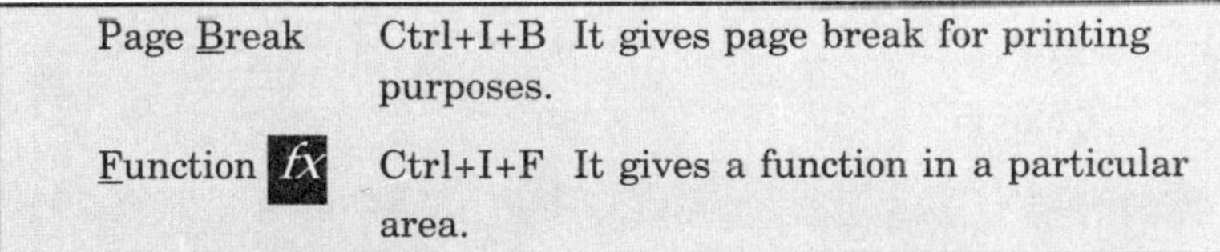

Page Break	Ctrl+I+B	It gives page break for printing purposes.
Function	Ctrl+I+F	It gives a function in a particular area.

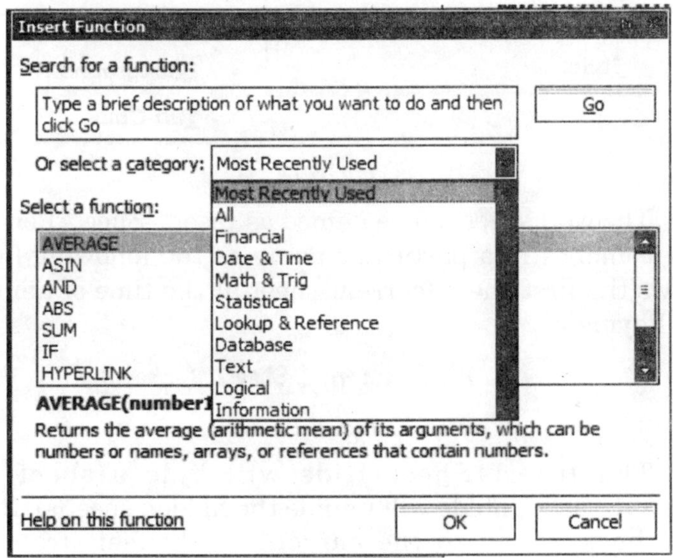

Fig. 8.10

It will insert a function as Average, ASIN, etc. out of 11 functions and can insert the function from the selected category as Financial, Date & Time, etc.

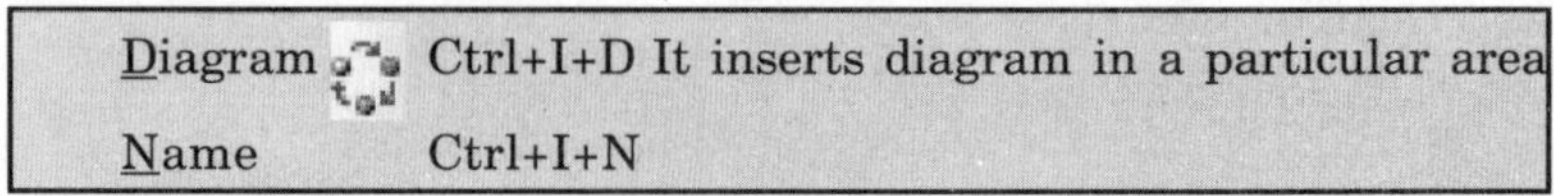

Diagram	Ctrl+I+D	It inserts diagram in a particular area
Name	Ctrl+I+N	

Format

It will format cells, rows, columns and sheets, auto-formatting, conditional formatting, stylus of the selected area.

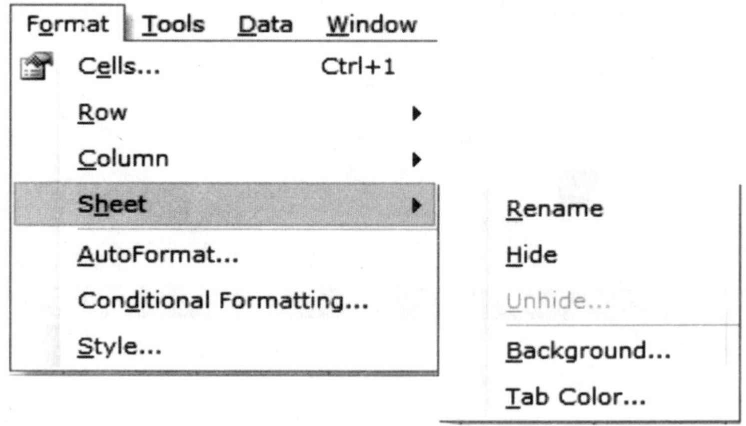

Fig. 8.11

The worksheet can be named as Insert+Sheet+Rename, it will names in a particular name as the following figure shows the first sheet (current sheet at the time of naming) as "Payment".

Payment / Sheet2 / Sheet3

Fig. 8.12

The Insert+Sheet+Hide will hide a sheet and Insert+Sheet+Unhide will unhide the hidden sheet(s). It can give background to the current worksheet (from the background figures available which will opt for selection).

To delete background in the place of "Background" sub-menu of the background availed worksheet, the sub-menu will be “Delete Background”. Its option will be Insert+Sheet+Delete Background.

Tools

It is same as MS-Word. Only the following sub-menu separate than MS-Word.

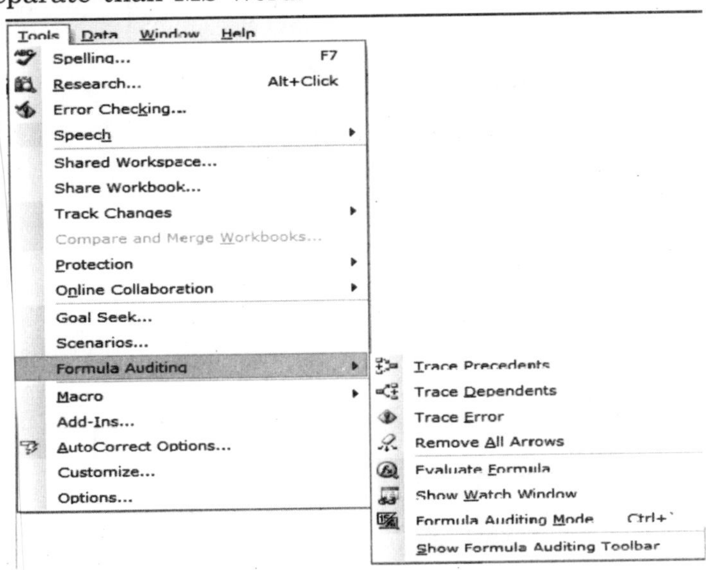

Fig. 8.13

Data: It is a new menu in MS-Excel.

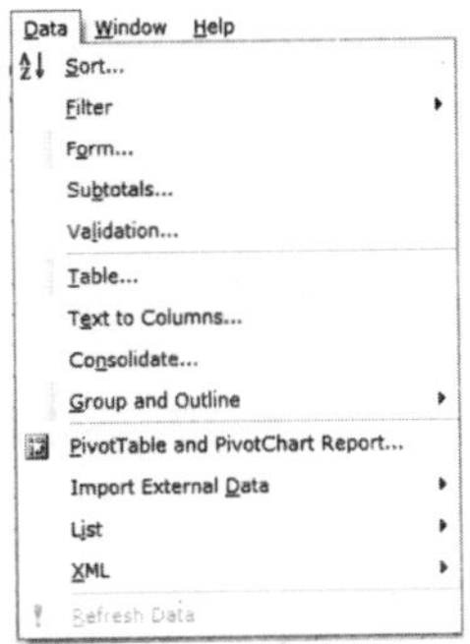

Fig. 8.14

Windows

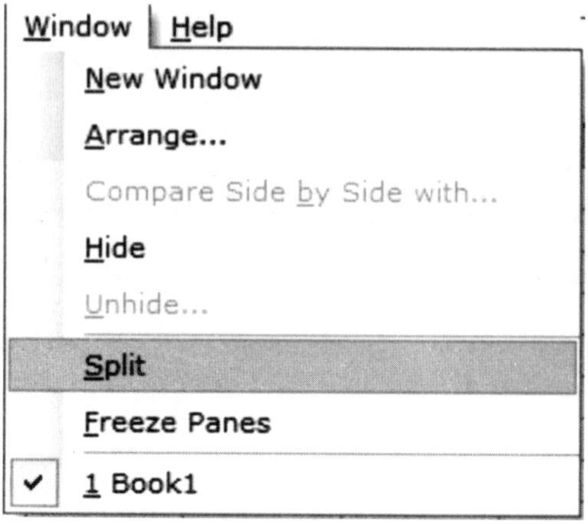

Window | Help

New Window
Arrange...
Compare Side by Side with...
Hide
Unhide...
Split
Freeze Panes
✔ 1 Book1

Fig. 8.15

Help

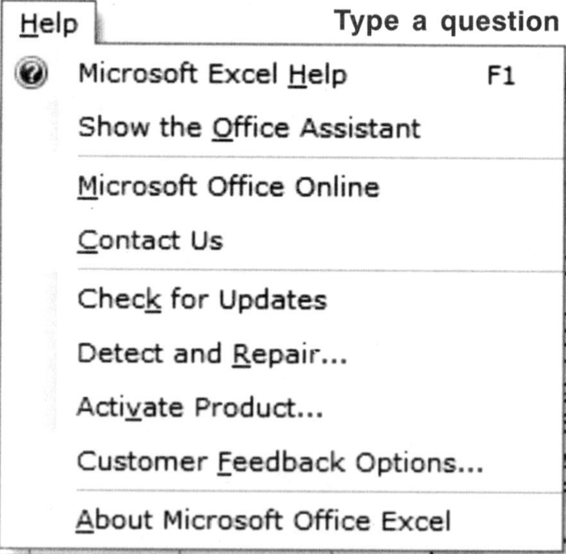

Fig. 8.16

9

Power Point

Introduction

Micro Soft Inc. has emerged the IT field for presentation of any matter for teaching, training, research in class room, seminar, conference, workshops in graphic mode with overhead projectors for easy and attractive understanding by the beneficiaries and easy taught by the presented. This credit goes to Micro Soft Inc. for their development for effectiveness of the presentation in graphic mode through IT. It uses multimedia technology including photographs, graphs, tables, texts, video clips, audio records, web pages, clip arts, drawings, figures, for presentation/ lecture in class room teaching or seminar/workshops. The management and other technical students and teachers are using their easy and effective interaction with power point presentation of slides. Each page of the presentation is called as slide. It can automatically be shown which is called as slide show. This is very effective tool for managers.

Power Point Screen

It is the opening screen of the MS-Powerpoint for slide preparation. The default slide name is presentation1.ppt.

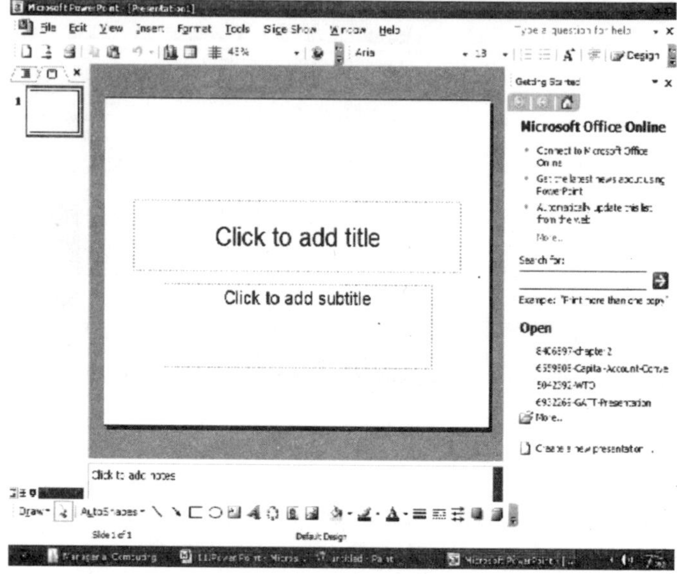

Fig. 9.1: Power Point Screen

New/Add Slide

To make a new slide, the menu option is File+New or Insert+New Slide or click on **New Slide** button on Formatting tool bar or press Ctrl+M. The following screen will appear with slide/adding new slides with the view of slide layouts in which design you are interested to do slide, you have to choose it. After choosing the slide layout, that will give the message to add text. To duplicate slide Edit+Duplicate Slide or press Ctrl+D (Fig. 9.2).

Delete Slide

To delete the current slide Edit+Delete Slide.

Show Slide

To present the slides, View+Slide Show or press F5, View Show will present the slides (Fig. 9.3). Before presenting slide, slide can be set up by the help of this dialog box.

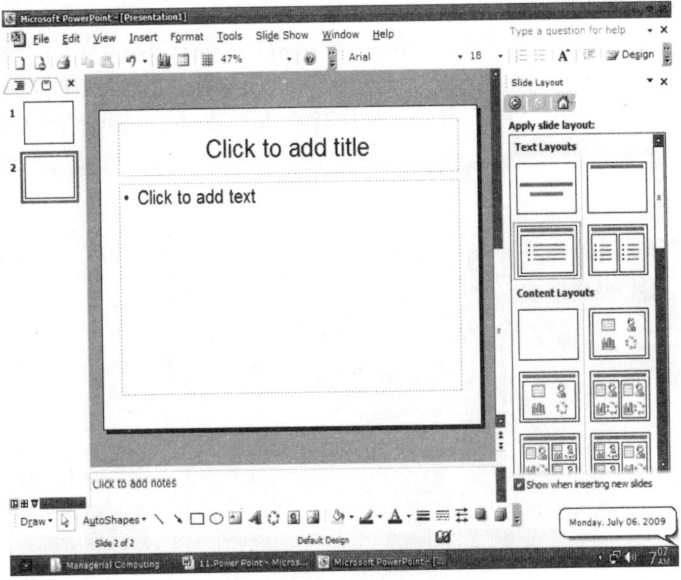

Fig. 9.2: New Slide

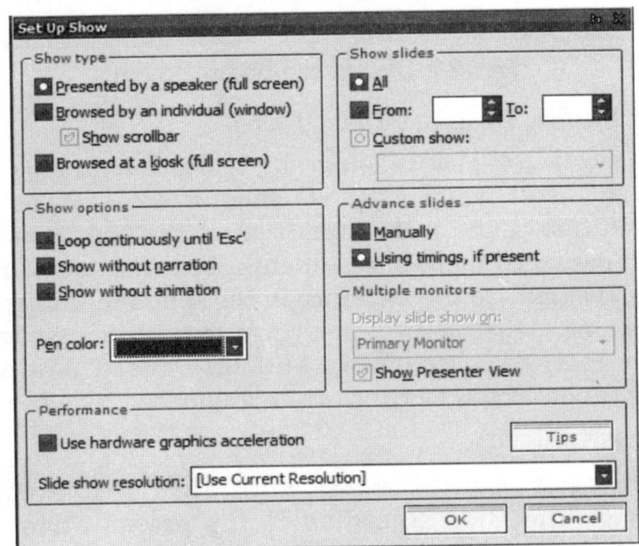

Fig. 9.3: Show Slide

Design the Slides

To make the slide more lucrative with background and other slide designs available in the computer, goto Format+Slide Design. It will the design the slide as under.

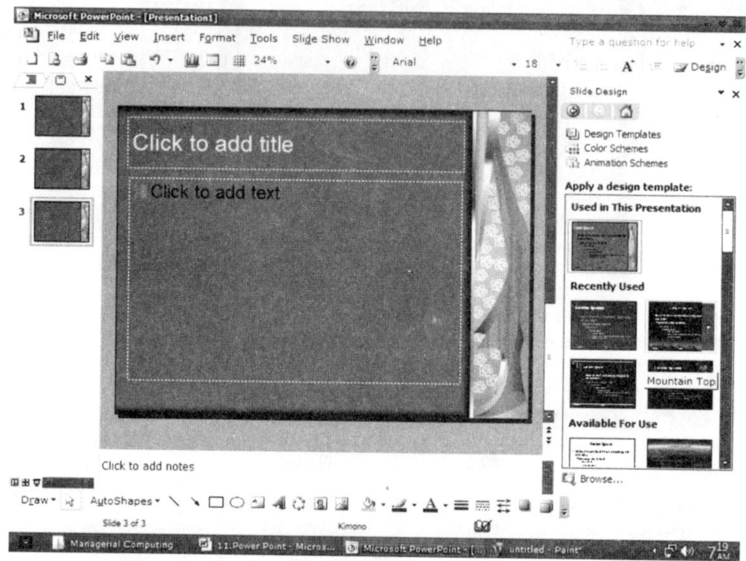

Fig. 9.4: Design the Slides Screen

Insert Picture, Diagram, Table, Chart

Inserting of picture, diagram, table, chart can be made through Insert menu. Because slide show or power point presentation is the main attraction of the presentation of subjective teaching to the students, presentation of ideas, views, thoughts to the audience in the seminar. Conference, workshops, sensitisation meetings, etc. It will show the better method of teaching and integrated method of presentation of the subject to the audience.

Insert Picture

To insert picture, Insert+Picture (Fig. 9.5). It is required to design the slide according to the presentation to be attractive and integrated. Figure 9.6 is the screen of inserting picture in the slide.

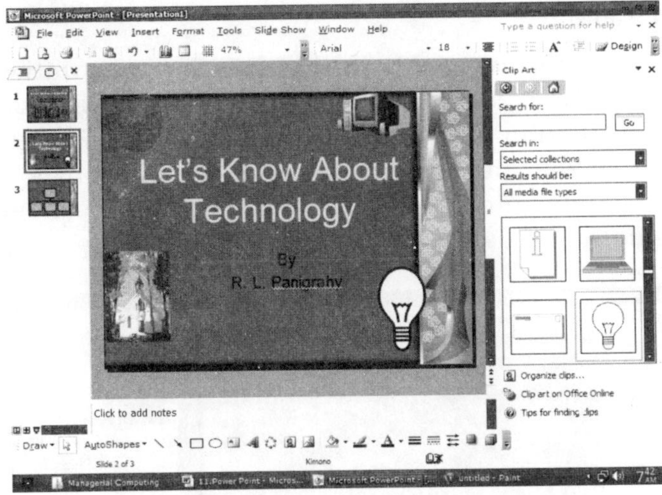

Fig. 9.5: Insert Picture Screen

Insert Diagram

It will insert diagram in the slide by Insert+Diagram which will appear Diagram Gallary from which diagram can be choosen for preparation of slide design as under Fig. 9.6.

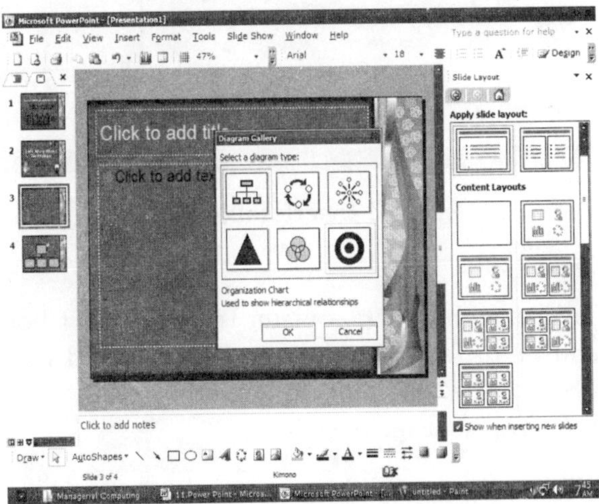

Fig. 9.6: Insert Diagram Screen

Insert Table

It will insert a table in the slide for presentation by Insert+Table as the screen depicted below. It will ask the row and column of the table to be inserted. After giving number of row and column press OK. It will draw a table on the slide and fill the table according to need of presentation of data (Fig. 9.7).

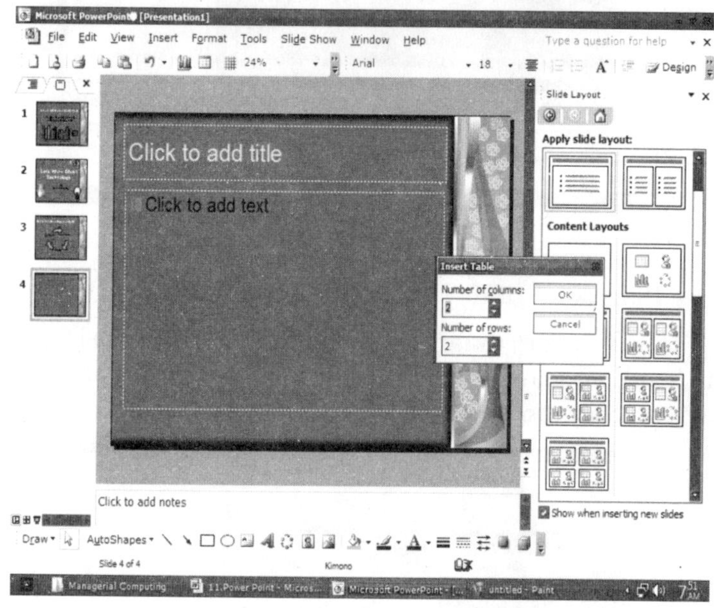

Fig. 9.7: Insert Table Screen

Insert Chart

To insert a chart, the option Insert+Chart has allowed the presenter to feed the data to be prepared in the chart in the MS-Excel worksheet on the slide, then it will do the chart accordingly (Fig. 9.8).

Background

The slide background is required to make the slide more lucrative to the audience. To give background in the slide

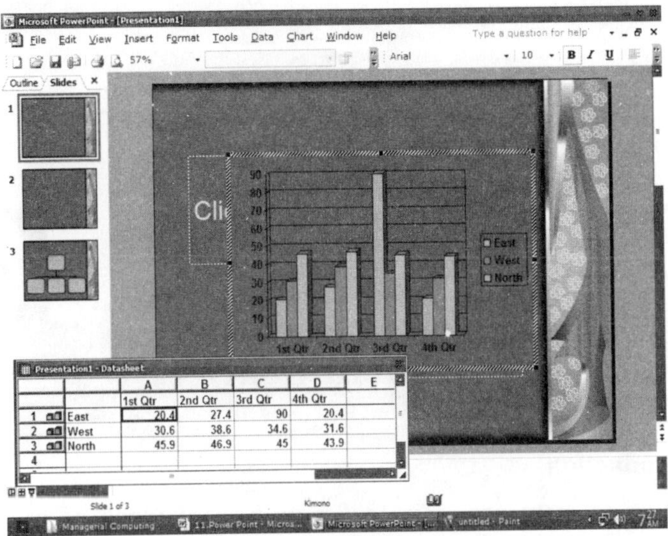

Fig. 9.8: Insert Chart Screen

Insert+Background which will appear the back ground dialog box to choose the slide colour and gradients (Fig. 9.9).

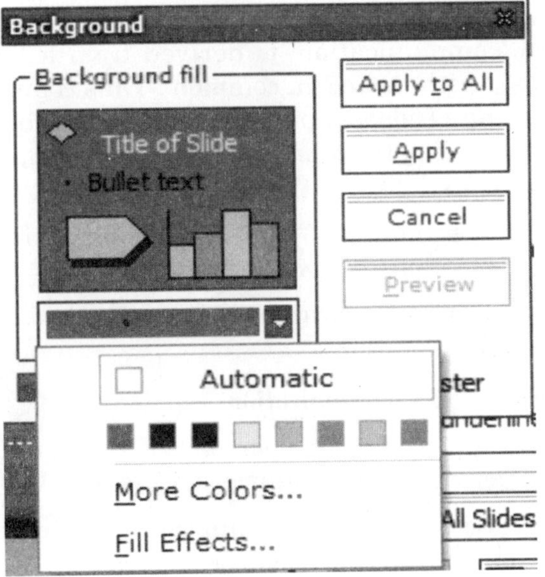

Fig. 9.9: Background Screen

10

Communication

Introduction

Communication is a fundamental work of an office work. For individuals also it is required. It is the connection for handling information. Its main function is to receive, send, transmit ideas, information, documents, facts, opinions, etc. Handling of information is called communication and transmitting it is called as communication system. The word 'communication' is derived from a Latin word 'communis' which means 'in common'. Thus communication is the sharing of ideas, opinions, facts and information in common. According to *Oxford Dictionary*, "communication is imparting or exchanging thoughts or information."

Neuman & Summer, "It is an exchange of facts, ideas, opinions or emotions by two or more person".

Shurter, "Communication is imparting or exchanging thoughts or information".

Characteristics of Communication

1. It involves at least two persons. There must be two or more persons in communication system.
2. Message is a must in communication, either in writing, voice of order, instructions or suggestions, documents. So, a communication must convey some message.

3. Communication may be written, oral or gestural - communication should be commonly understandable by the persons communicated either in writing or oral speaking or wink of eye or wave of hands.
4. Communication is a two way process understanding is the end way of communication. Communication should consist of information which is understandable b the communicated person.
5. Communication to motivate a person commutation is a way to motivate a person and not an end in itself by good drafting of message, proper timing and situation of communication which will create good understanding.
6. Communication may be formal or informal - Formal communication leads to organisational structure which is within an organisation from higher official subordinate and vice-versa. Informal communication does not need organisational structure. The communication develops among personal contacts.

Essential Elements of Communication

The basic elements required or communication are:

1. **Communicator** - One person is required to communicate message.
2. **Communicatee** - One or more person required to receive the communication made by communicator.
3. **Message** - One message is required to send or communicate by communicator to communicatee.
4. **Media of communication** - A method through communication to be made to link between communicator and communicatee.
5. **Response** - There should be an effect through reaction, reply, understanding of message by communicatee. Every communication seeks positive communication.

So, communication process depicts the transmission of message towards response as illustrated in Fig. 10.1.

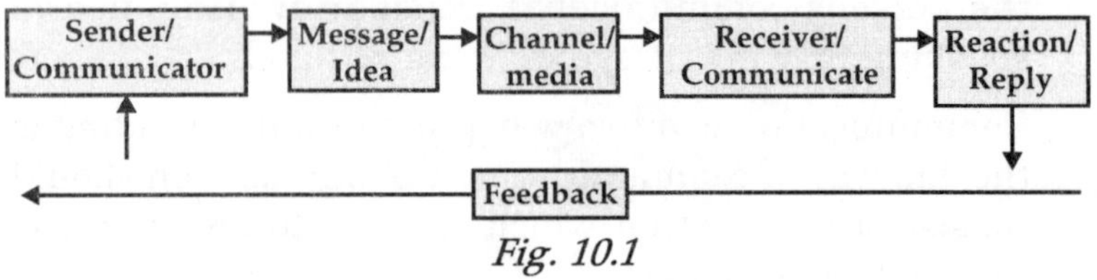

Fig. 10.1

Importance of Communication

Communication is a basic kind of office work. It is an indispensable work of a business enterprise. The first executive function is to develop and maintain a system of communication. Communication is a foundation of all office activities. According to G.R.Terry, "Communication is a lubricant fostering for the smooth operations of management process". So, the following points are the importance of communication.

1. It is essential for decision making and planning. Effective communication helps in proper implementation of plans and policies of the management.
2. It makes possible to smooth and efficient working of an enterprise. Communication regulates changes in management and action of the subordinates in the desired direction.
3. It facilitates coordination between the people in the organisation.
4. Effective communication increases managerial efficiency. Through communication, management conveys its goals, desires, responsibilities, evaluations, job description and performance to subordinates.
5. It promotes cooperation and industrial peace. Effective communication creates cooperation, coordination among employees and increases trust towards organisation. They can communicate their performances, pleasures, grievances, suggestions, etc.

6. Effective communication helps in establishing effective leadership communication is essential for maintaining better relationship among management (leader) and worker (led) and workers in the organisation.

7. Effective communication is helpful for motivation among workers in an organisation to achieve organisational goal and can increase and maintain good morale as a tool of HRD activity.

8. Effective communication increases managerial capacity by saving time, energy and can delegate authority, responsibility.

9. Effective communication controls managerial function. It is an effective tool for communication of organisational data from management to top management and management to low level up to workers who made it effective.

10. Effective communication creates job satisfaction among workers.

11. Effective communication is essential to achieve workers participation in management b involving workers in the process of decision making. It is the democratic form of management.

12. Effective communication increases productivity, reduces cost, maintains good relation in the organisation.

Principles of Communication

1. Clarity
2. Objectivity
3. Adequacy
4. Consistency
5. Timeliness
6. Feedback or follow up

7. Attentiveness
8. Appropriateness of publicity
9. Consultation on Planning
10. Proper Environment
11. Mutual Trust and confidence

Media of Communications

A basic function of an organisation is communication service. The communication service signifies the organisation or management quality. Every organisation that is big or small, government or non-government, profit oriented or not for profit making has the process of communication and exchange of information. Hence, there is a communication department or section in ever organisation with responsible person of effective communication. Communication may be oral or written, internal or external. Method used in communication is manual or mechanical depending on the effectiveness, safety, secrecy, economy, speed and easy to deliver.

Internal Communication

Media of internal communication:

1. Letter
2. Memos
3. Notification
4. Instructions
5. Orders
6. Circulars
7. Reports
8. Announcements
9. Opinions/feedback

10. Suggestions
11. Periodicals/bulletins
12. Manuals

External Communication

1. Acknowledgements
2. Enquiries
3. Quotations & Tenders
4. Order Placement
5. Reminders
6. Confirmations
7. Adjustments
8. Meetings
9. Greetings
10. Complains
11. Notice
12. Seminar/Conference

These may be made through personal, postal/courier service, telephonic/SMS service/eMail. Selection of Communication media for both internal and external communications, keeping in view of speed, safety, secrecy, accuracy, impression, cost effectiveness.

Communication is of two types:

- Manual; and
- Mechanical

Manual Communication

Manual Communication leads oral, messaging through internal and external communication media.

Mechanical Communication

Mechanical communication is made through mechanical devices for both internal and external communications.

Now-a-days, mechanical communication become more effective reliable, speed, cost effective, overall effectiveness of communication.

Mechanical Devices of Communication

1. *Telephonic Conversation*:
   (i) Telephone with/without extension
   (ii) PBX (Private branch Exchange)
   (iii) Intercom system
2. *Telegram*
3. L*aud speaker system* - Office, institutions, railways, air ports used laud speakers for communication of message to a particular person or group of persons.
4. *Wireless / Radio Phonic* - It is used in works departments where person working in scattered areas.
5. *Recorded message* - It is through cassette, disks, tapes, etc.
6. *Pager* - It is used for communication to executives, department heads, leaders, etc.
7. *Speaking tubes* - It is very old method of communication. In a noisy area, one room to another, one work place to another, a rubber or metallic pipe connected to communicate message through the pipes.
8. *SMS service* - In mobile technology from mobile to mobile communication can be made through message, organisation can message to any person to group of persons through SMS service. Now-a-days, SMS is ver good tool for communication. The organisation doing

their marketing communication through SMS to general mobile subscribers. So, through SMS service, marketing communication became effective.

9. *E-Mail* - It has paved a dominant role in the field of office works and communication. Internet is very effective tool of communication in forward and downward. Email is a good tool of communication.

Computer Networking

Introduction

The management of computers with data communications is one of the most exciting development in data processing today. The main goal of this chapter is to introduce various aspects of communications technology and examine how this technology can be used along with computer technology to provide powerful networks of computers. A network allows many users to share a common pathway to communicate with each other. Whereas computer network is a number of computers interconnected by one or more transmission paths.

Data transmission facilities deal with the hardware required to transmit the data from one place to another. There are various kinds of such facilities i.e simple cables, telephone lines, satellite link, etc. In short we can say that two or more computers are said to be interconnected if they are able to exchange information and the network components may be located at remote locations or within the same office or the boundary.

As we know communication is the process of transferring messages from one point to another, the three basic elements of any communications are as:

1. A sender (source) which creates the message to be transmitted to another place.
2. A medium which carries the message.
3. A receiver (sink) which receives the message from the sender.

For instance when you speak to your friend on phone, you are the sender (source) and the telephone line is the medium, which carries the message, at last your friend is the receiver.

Importance of Networking

There are many ways to achieve a network goals and each of this has reasons why it is desirable ? So many question arises in our mind, how the network will be used, by whom, for what applications, with what expected performances, for what distances and at what cost ? So, it is worth pointing out why people are interested in computer networks and they can be used for.

Resource Sharing

Many company has a substantial number of computers at each location to keep track of inventories, monitor productivity and do the local payroll. Initially, these may have worked in isolated from the others, but at some point they may have plans to connect them and to be able to extract and correlate information about the entire company. Here we can clear that the main aim of resources sharing is to make all programmes, data and equipment available to anyone on the network without regard to the physical location of the resource and the user.

High Reliability

The second and foremost goal is to provide high reliability by having alternative sources of supply. For instance, all the files could be replicated on two or three machines, so if one of them is unavailable, the other copies could be used. Networking also provides the critical function of backup, which is especially useful in systems like air traffic control.

Money Saving

It also saves money, because one can use small computer instead of mainframe.

Powerful Communication Medium

It also provides powerful communication medium among widely separated people. When one makes a change to the document the others can see the change immediately.

Applications of Networks

Some of the new applications may have important effects on the society as a whole. To give an idea about some important uses of networks, ti can be categorised into three tier, as below

1. **Access to Remote Programmes** - Remote time sharing terminals are most useful for programme development. A user who has a personal computer at home would use it for most of his work and connect the video terminal of the PC to a big computer for solving larger programmes, to access specialised library programmes, databases, languages and special facilities available in the big computer. For instance, a model developed company which simulates the reservation of air tickets world-wide, allows the customer to just log into the network and see how many seats are reserved so far and how many has not been reserved and get his booking done. Here we came to the conclusion that it can access remote programmes which already stored in the system.

2. **Access to Remote Databases** - Access to Remote Databases is one among the major are of network application. It is very easy for the average person

sitting at home to make reservation for airplanes, boats, restaurants and son on, any where in the world with instant confirmation. Home banking, the automated news paper also comes under this category.

3. **Communication Medium or Facilities** - Another important remote terminal application is for information retrieval. A user requiring to send electronic mail from his terminal to his colleagues anywhere in the world is possible through this medium.

4. **Distributed Data Processing** - In banks, airlines, railways, etc. are used distributed data processing system to access common business information to each one. In this system each site has its own small processing facultics linked to the central site. When a request is made to the central site (computer) through the terminal provided at a branch, the centralised computer process the data and provides meaningful information at the branch. This complete processing is known as distributed data processing.

In this case of on-line processing, one computer may be performing tasks for hundreds of users at individual terminals. But, if the computer fails, the whole line grinds to a halt. To avoid such problems distributed data processing provides several alternative arrangements consisting of a number of computers and peripherals. In addition to that it needs large interactive installation with high degree of reliability and the development of mini computers made it economic to use more than one computer in a network. The advantage of the distributed data processing are such as if the failure of a computer at any one site would not effect any other sites and computer failure at head quarters doesn't effect branch operations.

Network Topologies

The term topology in the context of a communication and network refers to the way in which the end points or work stations of a network are linked together. In a computer network as discussed earlier, there are two main type of networks as:

1. Local Area Network (LAN)
2. Wide Area Network (WAN):
   - *(i)* Metro Area Network (MAN)
   - *(ii)* Very Metro Area Network (VMAN)

Local Area Network (LAN)

In a LAN, there are various data communication devices which are inter connected, so that information could be communicated across these devises. All these devices are connected physically with in a local site e.g. in a room, building, campus, actor, institution, university, etc. It seems a small network having 3 to 50 nodes. The maximum distance between the various devices may be of the order of 1 or 2 KM.

It also supports a very large number of systems, quite simple to use, has a reasonably low error rate, loss cost and quite stable. LANs are characterised by communication rates between 1 to 10 mbps (million bits per second). It has also its own and specific Network Operation System (NOS), which ties all the devices together and make operations transparent to the user. The LANs are connected various hardware devices, printers, plotters, tape devices, communication equipments, etc. LAN is being used for a large number of applications, such as:

(a) File transfer from one to another node

(b) Electronic mail (email)

(c) Applications of Data base- creation, updating, access

(d) General business data processing

(e) CAD/CAM applications.

There are various methods in which the various physical systems can be inter connected. They are:

(a) Bus or Multi drop topology

(b) Star topology

(c) Loop or ring topology

(d) Point to point topology

(a) **Bus Topology** - It is otherwise called as multipoint or multi drop topology. It is very popular as it is not expensive, standardised and supported by all computer vendors, It is also known as Ethernet cable. 'Ether' was originally thought of the medium through which electro-magnetic waves are propagated. It allows data transmission at the rate of 10 mbps.

As shown in the figure, in a bus structure there is a single data bus which carries the data traffic in the complete network. Various devices can be connected to the same bus such as processors, main memory, I/O devices, disk or tape controller, etc. The bus can span a large distance and it is quite reliable in operation. Since, all the computers are attached to the same line. When a particular computer wants to send any message to another, it appends the destination address to the message and checks whether the communication line is free or not, then it broadcasts the message on the communication line. That means messages are broadcasting along the whole bus order to receive a transmission to work station must be recognised their own addresses. It is also known as a 'broadcasting network'.

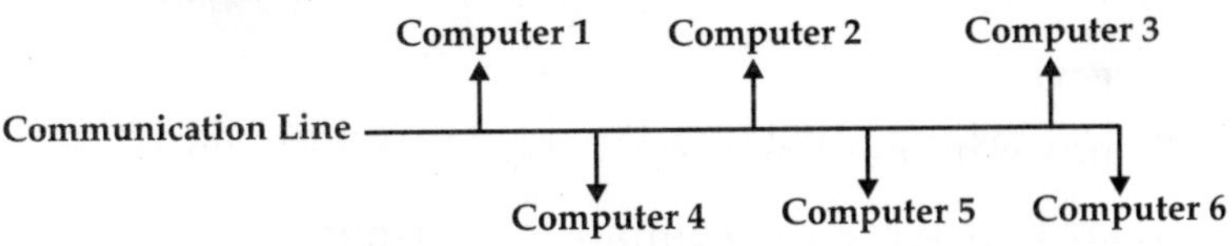

Fig 11.1: Bus/Multi drop/Multi point Topology

Advantages

1. The main and important advantages of a broadcasting network is the reduction in physical lines. It is quire easy to set up.
2. The reliability is high because the failure of a computer does not effect the network functioning for other computer.
3. Easy to add new computer to the network line
4. Any workstation can be moved to another in office as the bus moves any where.

Disadvantages

1. If the communication line fails, the entire system will collapse.
2. Each and every connected computer must have possess good communication.

(b) **Star Topology** - Among these, the star topology used a local telephone exchange to connect the computers. In other words all the data device are connected to a single parent node. The host computer (parent node 1) plays a vital node because each computer is connected with it, through a dedicated point to point channel. Any data transmission from one computer to the other has to be routed through the host computer. Because local computers are not linked directly to each other and can communicate only via the host computer. Since the parent node 1 or host computer controls all the operations, good security can be built around such system.

Advantages

1. It has minimal line cost
2. If any other local computer will out of order, the remaining portion of the communication is unaffected.

Disadvantages

1. Though the whole system crucially depends on the host computer or parent node 1, if it is of order the entire network will collapse.

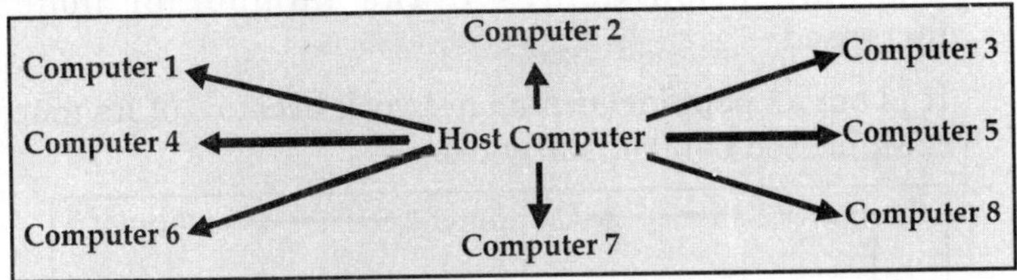

Fig 11.2: Star Topology

(c) **Ring Topology** - In a ring or circular arrangement all the nodes are connected in the form of ring. There is no main or controlling computer, as in the star system to control the other nodes. It uses Fibre Optical Cables (FOC) as transmission medium. All the nodes (computers) have simple communication capacity. The data flows from one node to another in the form of ring. This data flow is in a single direction only.

A node will receive that data from one of its neighbours. The only decision the nodes has to take is whether the received data is for its use or not. If the data is addressed to it, it utilises it. Otherwise, it merely passes it on to its other neighbours and so on till it reaches its destination node. Thus, if computer 4 receives the data from computer 3, it examines whether it is addressed to itself, it is so then it uses the data else it passes the data to the computer 5.

Advantage

1. Since there is no central site computer system, it is really distributed data processing system.
2. It is more reliable than a star network because communication is not dependant on a single computer. If one line between any two computers breaks down or if one of the computers breaks down, alternate routing is possible.

Disadvantages

1. It is difficult to add computers.
2. The main disadvantage of a ring is larger communication delays if the number of nodes increased.
3. It is not as popular as star network because of its more complicated control software.

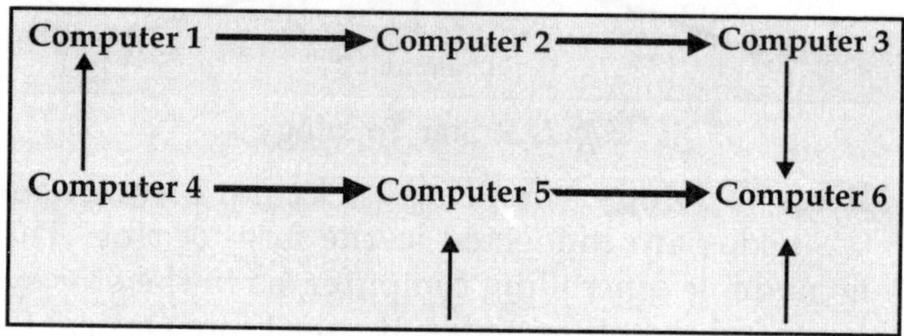

Fig 11.3: Ring Topology

(d) **Point to Point Topology** - It is completely connected network. It has a separate physical connection for connecting each node to any other node. Thus, each computer has a direct dedicated link, called a point to point link with all other computers of the network. It is most expensive from point of view of lines, as shown in figure. The control is distributed with each computer deciding its communication priorities.

Advantages

1. It is however, very reliable as any lone break down will effect only communication between the connected.
2. Each nodes need not have individual mounting capacity.
3. Communication is very fast between any two nodes.

Disadvantages

It is most expensive from the point of view of line costs, Thus, the cost of linking the system grows with the square of the number of nodes.

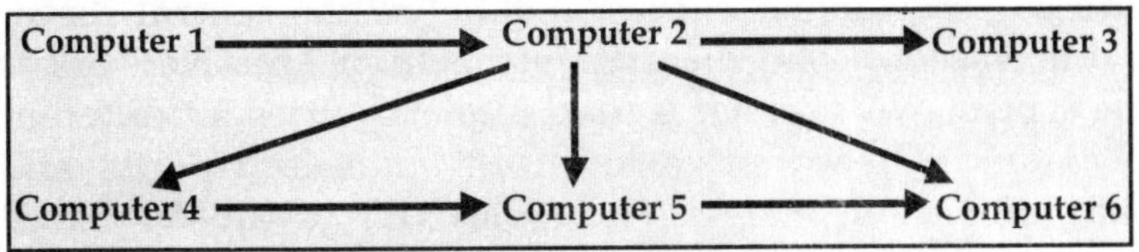

Fig. 11.4: Point to Point Topology

(e) **Hybrid Topology** - An organisation will use some sort of hybrid network, which is simply a combination network. Different networks have their own advantages and limitations. Hence, in reality a particular network is rarely used. In some cases, the hybrid networks may have components of star, ring as well as point to point networks. Hybrid network is as follows:

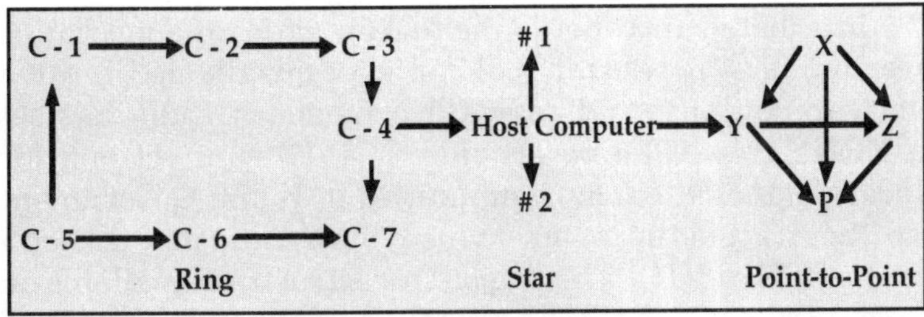

Fig 11.5: Hybrid Topology

Wide Area Network (WAN)

WAN is also called a Long Haul Network. It is digital communication system which interconnects different cities and towns. This type of communication network may be developed to operate nationwide or worldwide. The transmission medium used are normally public system such as telephone lines or VSAT(Very Short Aperture Terminal) looking line dish antenna, through a micro wave on particular satellite space reserved for it. The financial institutions, companies with its branches in different places of the country, university colleges, etc. setting up of WAN for their own contact in which no public contact is there. Their own communication and downloading of necessary data or programmes can be updated in the central server and accessed by the clients. Metropolitan Area Network is one type of WAN which is used in metro cities for different locations. These networks often span continents and communication is slow. The ARPANET of the Advanced Research Project Agency of the US Department Defence is an good example of WAN. Another example of a WAN is the INDONET which is being planned by the Computer Maintenance Corporation(CMC) of India. It links three IBM-4361 systems one each at Mumbai, Kolkata, Chennai and PDPII/44 system at Delhi. It is a public or private network used to connect various locations including suburbs of in a metropolitan city. And in the other hand Very Wide Area Network (VWAN). It is a public network connecting different continents and countries.

Internet or intranet is the tool for wide area networks. Internet is a potential tool for every walk of life at a relatively low cost and easy. Government of India has set up ERNET in 1986 to provide TCP/IP connections for education and research communities in India. Government also facilitated the users to use WAN/Internet through VSNL, BSNL, NIC. The major infrastructure available in the country has two types of WAN - Terrestrial WAN, VSAT WAN. The following are the different options for setting of connecting WAN/Internet/Intranet - Leased Line, Dial-up connection, VSAT, Radio Link.

Transmission Media

The data signal travels through transmission media. The transmission media are of two types as bounded and unbounded. The bounded(guided) transmission is the transmission of network through twisted pairs, coaxial cable, fibre optics. The data signal travels within the boundaries is called unbounded media or unguided media. And the microwave and satellite transmissions travel through air which has no boundaries which ahs also called unbounded transmission.

Hub

The Hub receives data pockets and send them to other computers connected to it. The network hub is a centralised distribution point for all data transmissions in a network. Hub may also be referred to as a concentrator. It does not know the destination of a received data packet. Hence, it is required to send the data packets to all the hubs connected. Hubs are classified in different types as:

- Stackable and non-stackable hubs - Stackable hubs are the stackable or interconnected hubs to make a single hub appearance. Non-stackable hubs can not be interconnected which provides fixed number of connections.
- Active and passive hubs - The hubs that connect to the network are known as active hubs. The hubs which are connected only to active hubs is called as passive hub.
- Intelligent and non-intelligent hubs - Intelligent hub contain a special firmware that can be accessed by remote workstations. The firmware is known as simple network management protocol (SNMP). The network performance and network status data are read from SNMP. The hub which has no special firmware called as non-intelligent hub.

Repeater

It is a connection device that connects between two segments of the network cable. The repeater is also used to extent the cable length or enlarge the LAN. WAN has many repeaters

Bridge

A bridge interconnects two networks using the same technology. Bridge is more sophisticated than the repeater. A bridge reads the destination address for the received data pocket whether the address is on the same segment, if from the other side, the bridge transmits the packet into the traffic on the cable segment. Network administration often used bridges to split the big network into number of small networks.

Routers

A router transfers data between networks. It is also possible for a router to transfer data between different compatible network technologies. A router has the address on the network, a bridge does not have an address. Router also bridges networks. The router transfers data packets to other networks. The bridge must examine all the packets that which will transmit between networks but the router examines a packet only if it contains router's address. Router also called as brouter which receives the packet and examines whether it supports the protocol used by the packet.

TCP/IP

Transfer Control Protocol(TCP)/Internet Protocol(IP) is that the protocols capable of providing transparent communications interoperability services between computers irrespective of computers, hardware, operating system. TCP/IP became popular because of public availability of protocols specifications. It gives open system where users rely for the purpose of file transfer, electronic mail(email), login services, etc.

FTP

File Transfer Protocol (FTP) is the oldest protocol used in internet/intranet. FTP is used in almost all operating system platforms. FTP is a file server access protocol that enables a user to transfer files between two hosts across the network or access from a host by the client. This is also established through FTP. FTP sites requires the user must have the knowledge of the location and the name of the desired files. FTP requires no such knowledge of platforms, because FTP server already built into the protocol itself so that the user can access the required file. It is generally use in intranet for the private networks in companies to transfer files from server to server or to access by the clients at the remote areas from the host server. The FTP has an address, user name and password which should be known by the user.

Dial-up Network

The dial-up network is a communication system through a telephone line. The internet can be accessed through a telephone line. The user should subscribe a telephone line which will be connected to the modem and the modem will be connected to the CPU of the PC. The telephone service provided will give the permission for internet connection so that the analog data in the telephone line and the digital data in the PC will be converted by the MODEM and the internet can function. Internet connection through dial-up will be connected to the exchange to the number given for internet connection. The telephone will be engaged while internet is connected through dial-up connection.

Leased Lines

A computer can be connected with leased lines permanently in addition to the MODEM and a router. The leased line can be connected to one terminal which can be shared with multiple connections through LAN. The Financial institutions, Banks, small organisations, institutions are using Leased lines from telephone service providers. The service provider charges a token amount per month. The telephone exchange establishes routers/VSAT for the leased lines at the exchange.

ISDN

Integrated Service Digital Network (ISDN) is a digital transmission over ordinary telephone wire. This technology use in ISDN adapter in the place of MODEMs and provides very fast speedup

Telenet

It is an utility needed to log on another system and user various services on that host. You can use telenet to host computer all around the world in the cost effective way. When you use telenet to a catalogue of computerised library, you can gain access to files that constitute the library records.

Baud

It is a very important term used for data transmission. The speed at which data travel over a communication Chennai is called the communication rate or the transmission speed. Thus baud defines the number of bits which are transmitted per second. The number of signalising elements transmitted per second in the baud rate. Typically the baud rate (bits per second) can communicate at 300 baud which means it can transmit or receive a maximum 300 bits or approximately 30 characters per second. Now-a-days personal computers or modern terminals typically use communication rate of 300 to 1200 baud. The baud rate between 2400 and 4800 becoming more common today. We can say bigger baud means a faster data transmission speed.

Bandwidth

The bandwidth is defined as the capacity to carry the data over a transmission media. It can be categorised as:

(a) *Narrow Band* - It is normally in the range of 50 to 300 bits per second (BPS) or up to 300 Hurtz (Hz). It is used for telegraph and telex lines where the speed of data input is governed by the typing speed of the operator.

(b) *Voice Band* - The range of the voice band is 300 to 9600 or 300 to 3000 Hurtz, generally it is used by the telephone lines.

(c) *Broad band or wide band* - It is used for speeds in the range of 64 kbps (kilo bytes per second) to 2 mbps (megabytes per second) or over 3000 Hz. It is used to group several voice grade channels into a single one.

Digital and Analog Transmission

Data is propagated from one point to another by means of electrical signals which may be in digital or analog form. There are two different ways in which the data can be transmitted over the lines.

(a) Digital transmission

(b) Analog transmission

In the digital transmission, the data is converted into binary digits or bits which has two discrete value i.e. either a digit 0 or 1. It is fixed two types of pulses only which can be represented as in figure given below. The low level of the curve indicates a 0 and the step value indicates a value as 1. This is the characteristic of a direct current. This can be used for shorter distances and are not fit for longer distances e.g. within 500 meter distance such a transmission can be used. Beyond this limit, we have to go for the analog transmission. In other hand, in an analog signal the transmitted power varies over a continuous range e.g. sound, light and radio waves.

These are no discrete values as in a digital signals. There is no such minimum and maximum limits. Thus it is very useful way to transmit signals over long distances. It is very useful way to transmit signals over long distances.

It is now being used for data transmission as well as for the computer communications. Closely observe the given figure

MODEM

It stands for MODulartor and DEModulator, a hardware device which data from digital to analog or user language to machine language and vice versa. In the digital transmission there is a such limit on the distances whereas in the case of analog transmission, there is no such limit. Thus if the terminal is to be connected to the system from far off place, we can not use a pure digital transmission. However, a computer being a digital device will accept or transmit only digital signals.

To over come this distance problem we need a hardware device on either side of the line which can convert one form to the other. This is exactly what is done by the MODEM. The technique by which a digital signal is converted to its analog form is known as MODulation. The reverse process that is the conversion of analog signal to its digital form, at a destination device, is called DEModulation. In short, we can come to a conclusion that MODulation is most often used for super imposing digital data on analog waves, there are three forms of modulation which are beyond our discussion boundary.

Communication Protocols

In a computer network, a number of computers and terminals equipment are to be connected together to form an integrated system. But, various techniques or protocols followed for actually transmitting the data over the transmission facilities is called as data communication software. In fact, the data communication software that is responsible for holding all data communications system together. It instructs to the computer system and devices how the data is to be transferred from source to target place.

These procedure or well planned discipline embedded in software are commonly termed as communication protocols. In short, a protocol is a set of rules and standards established to govern transmission between two points so that the receiver can properly interpret the bit stream transmitted by the sender. Some examples of protocols are

(a) Contention

(b) Polling

(c) Token Passing

Dumb, SMART/Intelligent Terminals

These could be many terminal connected to a single CPU in a time sharing mode. The CPU works at a fantastic speed carrying out millions of instructions per second because it serves many users working from different terminals. Concept of sharing the CPU time by a number of terminals. These terminals could be dump, smart or intelligent.

Dumb terminals are simple devices that immediately transmit each inputted data or character to the processor. In other words, it can be said that they have no local processing power. Whatever input is typed by the user, right or wrong it is just transmitted by the terminal to the CPU and the same way whatever the output the CPU is sending will displayed on the screen. These terminals thus have to disturb the CPU, more often, since the CPU has to be disturbed. It can not do work for other users, which are waiting for their turn. But, the smart terminals provide special features.

They are designed within a microprocessor chip which contains the circuits to perform arithmetic, logic and control functions, they have an internal storage capacity. So to say, they have some local processing capabilities. The input data can be carried out locally before sending it to the CPU. Some post processing can be done on the output results before displaying it on the screen. The accuracy of inputted data can be checked wherever it is possible, to have a logical checking. For instance, though they have arithmetic logic and function, they can check for the presence of a non-numeric character within a numeric data item like roll number, etc. Thus a data given as 36/10/09 can be rejected by the terminal itself. It will not disturb to the CPU by passing on these wrong data to it, as dumb terminals do. The user can correct the data and then only it is transmitted to the CPU.

Finally, we come to the conclusion that, through they can store and consolidate inputted data before sending them to the processor but smart terminals can not normally be programmed by users. Intelligent terminals combine hardware which built in microprocessor. Thus without interact with a large computer, they can process small problems because floppy disk (secondary storage device) often used to process these small tasks. Therefore, they can be programmed by users. They transmit the little difference between intelligent terminals and personal computer (PC) is that intelligent terminals built with circuits which permit them to communicate with other terminals and larger processors but in the other hand PCs have been designed generally to operate alone.

Key Points to Remember

- Computer network is a number of terminals inter-connected and share a common pathway of transmission.
- Two or more computers are inter-connected, if they will transform data from one computer to another.
- For office automation network is necessary.
- There two types of network i.e. LAN, WAN.
- The maximum distance between the various terminals/ workstations may be within 1 to 2 KMs in LAN.

- Bus topology carries the single data.
- In star topology there is a host computer.
- In a ring or circular arrangement all the nodes are connected in the form of ring.
- The combination of ring, star and point-to-point network is called as hybrid topology.
- Boud, is an important term used for data transmission.
- Boud is the speed of data traveling in a communication channel is called as communication rate/transmission speed.
- Band width is defined as the capacity to carry the data over a transmission media.
- In narrow band, 300 to 9600 or 300 to 3000 Hz. Is the range of transmission.
- In broad or wide band, generally 300 Hz is the range or 64 KBPS to 2 MBPS.
- MODEM in used in telephone exchanges and the place where data transmission made through internet.
- DUMB terminals have no local processing power.
- SMART/Intelligent terminals have local processing power.

12

Internet

Introduction

Internet is the world wide network of networks. So, it is the example of Wide Area Network (WAN). It is connection of many smaller networks. It is a global system of connected computers. It communicates data, message, voice, photos, etc. through satellite. It requires a PC, a MODEM (Modulator and Demodulator) and a telephone connection. MODEM is required the data transmission from analog (user language) to digital (machine understandable language) and vice versa. In internet applications, data transmission can be made throughout the globe. When data sending to other place, the user language (analog) will be transformed into digital (machine language) to send and the data receiving is to be transformed from digital (machine language) to analog (user understandable form) which is the function of MODEM. The MODEM is the connecting link between PC and telephone line. In the introduction of mobile technology, the telephone lines are not necessary. Through cellular phone connecting a data cable to the mobile and PC has made internet applications. By the virtue of Bluetooth technology, no cable connection is required with the Cell phone and PC. Only the PC and cell phone to be nearer to each other for internet connection. Again the cellular service providers have introduced a typical modem looking like thumb driver/pen driver MODEM which can be connected to the PC in the USB port as, when and where required the internet connection. Recently produced notebook PCs/Laptops have the facility of internet connectivity facility in built of the machine.

Merely, a three decades ago on the experiment of US Department of Defense, internet has been introduced. The network was developed by Advance Research Projects Administration (ARPA), so the network is named so as ARPAnet. This was possible by the use of unique addresses stored on a distributed database. To send a message in ARPAnet, a computer has to put data into an envelop called as Internet Protocol (IP) packet which has an address named as IP Address. ISO (International Standard Organisation) has developed ultimate standard of computer network protocol as TCP/IP (Transmission Control Protocol/ Internet Protocol), which developed the system how computers could interact each other.

Internet connection will be subscribed from the TCP/ IP services. The first TCP/IP service provider in India was VSNL (Videsh Sanchar Nigam Limited, a subsidiary company of Department of Telecommunication, Government of India). The VSNL internet connection was made possible through DSN (Domain Name System) set up with dial up to the server point telephone number given while subscribing the internet which is in the nearer Telecommunication Centre of VSNL. The modem is to be supplied by the Department which is meant for dial up and a telephone bill will be provided in local call rate for the period of the telephone line engaged for internet. To access data through an TCP/IP address, there should be a domain name which is otherwise called as web site name. The domain name can be identified its type from the name as:

Name	Type of Domain
Com	Company/Organisation having the domain are meant for commercial purposes
Co	The domain owner is a company
Edu	It is an educational institution/organisation
Ac	It is an academic institution.
Gov	It is a governmental organisation
Net	It is a networking company/network provider
Org	It is an organisation
Mil	It is a military organisation
IN	Indian organisation
UK	Organisation of United Kingdom

A domain name may be

www.ugc.ac.in

It implies, UGCis an organisation which is an academic type of organisation situated in India. Domain name, type and country specification are separated by dot (.). This domain name is an address where UGC has some data, message, communication tools for public access of their activities and requirements.

WWW/HTTP/URL

The domain name may be started from WWW (World Wide Web - which means the domain/web site can be accessed by users world wide). So, domain name should be www.UGC.ac.in. Most of the web sites are Hyper Text Type Protocols (http). So Domain names can be prefixed by 'http' as http://www.UGC.ac.in which is the Universal Resource Location (URL). So the domain name or Web Site address can be called as URL Address also. URL always starts with http://. The URL may contains many sub directories in it which can be typed separated by '/' symbol as http://www.UGC.ac.in/college.htm

It implies the web site address have many subdirectories viz. Admission, research, recruitment, administration, fellowships, etc. The admission has also subdirectories of many courses. The above address will open the information containing in the URL UGC.ac.in for information of the colleges.

Internet service providers has the applications as+

1. **email** - The most advantageous application of internet is mailing of messages, files, photos, pictures, etc. which is called as email (electronic mail). Email has an email address which is named as user defined name, service provider site/server name, extension.

   For example rajib_panigrahy@yahoo.co.in, rajib_lpanigrahy@rediffmail.com which implies 'rajib' and 'panigrahy' is the user name which is separated by underscore (_), a symbol/special character which is allowed, @ symbol is user to separate the user name and server name which identifies the server at which the email address is made, extension name as co, in, com, etc. to know the nature of the server as stated above. It is a speeder service from any kind of mailing services. Email system consists of item as inbox, outbox, sent item, etc. When mail receives, the mail will be available in inbox and the unread message will be highlighted and before opening the inbox, the unread messages will be highlighted in number in the right side of the 'inbox' in bracket. The mail sent are available in 'sent item' which can again be forwarded and the attached files can be downloaded into system when required. Outbox is the item where the mail is available till the mail is sent to the destination email address which can be identified by the user that the mail has not despatched from his machine.

2. **Browsing** - It can download the information/files/folders from a particular server by giving the address of server. The internet is the public access network, so any body can access the sites being publicised by the particular service providers. Again the user can search the unknown sites/URLs for any information by search engine in GOOGLE search which will display the sites available containing the information or any part site name. It is most advantageous application of internet for knowledge providing. In private network (intranet) the FTP service is available for service providing.
3. **Chatting** - The users are open for interact each other by the system which is called as chatting.

13

Computer Terminology

A

Abacus: The first calculating machine. The Calculation nearly beads on the ropes. It was first used in China. It was the 'first device to store the data.

Accumulator: A location with the arithmetic and logic unit that temporarily stores the result of arithmetic or logical operations. It is also called a Register.

ADA: A computer language named after Lady Ada Augusta Lovelace, friend and an Asst. of Charles Babbage(father of computer). It is developed by the request of U.S. Defence Department for the use of military applications.

Algol: It stands for ALGorithmic Language, an algorithmic and procedure oriented computer language used mainly for programming of scientific problems, developed in Europe in the year1960.

Alpha Numeric: Combination of alphabets, numbers and/or symbols.

ALU: It is the Arithmetic and Logic Unit of the computer system.

Algorithm: A step-by-step procedure of sequence of instructions to solve a given task.

ASCII: Acronym for American Standard Code for Information Interchange.

ANSI: It stands for American National Standard Institute.

Assembler: It is a programme which translates an assembly language program to its machine equivalent language.

Assembly Language: A low level language for programming a computer in which mnemonics (symbols) are used to code operations.

Application Software: It is a program or a set of programs designed for a particular application in HLL i.e. Word Processing, DBMS, etc.

Artificial Intelligency (AI): A programming language deals with computer which possess reasoning, learning, thinking power that equivalent to men.

Auxiliary Device: It is the secondary storage device, which supplements to the primary memory of the computer, having storage capacity permanently for the future use.

AND: A boolean operator having output for 1 if only input is 1.

AND Gate : An electronic logic gate whose output is logic 1 (true) only when all input logics are 1 otherwise it is 0 (false).

Application Programme: A program written for specific problem solving to procedure specific output.

Arithmetic Expression: The combination of data in arithmetic operations performed in a order.

Arithmetic Operations: The numeric calculations like addition, subtraction, multiplication, division, reminder, percentage, etc. are called Arithmetic Operations.

Arithmetic Register: A register constructed for result. of arithmetic functions.

Array: A collection of data items (fields) with each identified a subscript and arranged in such a way that a computer can retrieve data from these items associated with a particular subscript.

ASCII: It is acronym for *American Standard Code for Information Interchange* which assigns individual 7 bits codes to represent each of specific set of 128 numbers, letters and specific control.

Attribute: A data item containing information about a variable.

Automatic Carriage: A mechanism designed to feed continuous paper on a plastic forms through a printing or writing device, often using sprockets to engage holes in the paper.

Automatic Computer: A computer carry a special set of operations without human intervention.

Automation: Automatic implementation of process.

Abend: Abnormal end of task by programming or machine error.

Array: Group of two or more data names logically related identified by a single name, stored in consecutive storage location in main memory.

B

Back Up: Duplication of storage data. The duplication made by the device is called as back up device.

Band Width: The range of frequencies, available for data transmission.

Bar Code: A pattern of vertical printed lines in binary coding can be read by light band scanning.

Block: A group of related data items handled as a unit during input and output.

Batch Processing: A technique which processes a number of similar items or transactions sequentially.

Band: A measuring unit of data transmission speed.

Band Rate: Rate .of data transmission, a bit per second.

BINAC: It is Binary Automatic Computer developed by John Ickert & Mauchly in 1949.

Binary Arithmetic: A arithmetic notations with two nos. i.e. 0 and 1.

Binary Code: Any code using 2 bits 1 and 0 to represent characters, ASCII, EBCDIC, BCD are the example of binary code.

Binary Coded Decimal (BCD): A no. representation system that uses a binary code for a set of 4 digits (bits).

Binary Digit (BIT) : It is a combination of two digits 0s and 1s.

Booting: To run or Activating the computer system.

Boot Strap: Allows a large program enter into to computer memory.

Boolean Algebra: An algebra to check the logical consistency of proportions which have two probability i.e. either true or false.

Byte: A group of- bits to represent characters, 8 bits is equal to 1 byte.

Buffer: A memory area which is used for temporary storage.

Bug: An error or mistake in a program.

Bus: It is used for exchanging Information between computer components.

Cache Memory: A small high speed memory used for temporary storage. It increases processing speed of computer.

CAD: It stands for Computer Aided Design, a software used for engineering and design purposes.

CAM: It uses Computers to Automatic Manufacturing operations.

Card Punch: It is a computer output device which punches wholes in a punch card as recognising signals from the CPU.

Card Punching: The punching of holes into punched card to store data and retrieval.

Card Reader: A protective container for the storage of a real of magnetic tape.

Cassette Recorder: It is a device used cassettes to record and store data.

Cathod Ray Tube (CRT): A vacuum tube used to DISPLAY pictorial and graphical informational. i.e. Monitor or VDU which is seen TV like.

CD: Compact Disk used for more capacity of storage data.

CD-ROM: Compact Disk Read Only Memory, which uses optical lesser storage techniques.

Central Processing Unit (CPU) : It is also known as processor or computer. It consists of circuits to perform arithmetic and logic.

Chain: A set of operations that are to be performed sequentially.

Chain Printer: A high speed printer, chain embossed characters.

Character: A small collection of adjacent bits used to represent a piece of data which are addressed and handled as a unit. It corresponds a digit.- a letter or a symbol.

Character Reader/Recognition: A device which locates, Identifies, translates printed data and hand writings of a source document to machine code. It is an input device.

Character Set: A group of characters available for input or output of data on a particular computer.

Charls Babbage: The first person who invented digital computer. So he is .known as the Father of the modem computer science.

Chip: Another name is "Integrator Circuit" performing a significant no. of functions and constituting subsystem.

CIM: Computer Input for Microfilm. A system using microfilm technology rather than printing on paper.

Circuit: It connects the. electronic devices and wires used to carry certain type of function. Electric current flows through it.

Circuit Diagram: The physical representation of components and interconnection which define a specific hardware functional design.

CISCE: It stands for Complex Instruction Set Computer, a processor which has variable length instructions, variety of addressing made and many instructions.

CISC: It refers to the Customers Information Central System.

COBOL: A High Level Language acronym for COmmon Business Oriented Language. It is dedicated for Business purposes.

CLOCK: It is a kind of processor contains an electronic pulse generation.

Closed File: A file which cannot be accessed for reading or writing.

CLS: It is a DOS command used to clear the Screen.

Cluster: A group of terminals connected to large computer through controller.

CMOS: It sands for Complementary Magnetic Oxide Semi-conductor, a chip.

Computer: It is an electronic device executes program written with a set of specific instructions stored in its memory to process data fed to it and produces the useful and required output.

Communication Protocol: A common agreed rules and regulations followed to interconnect and communicate between computers.

Compiler: A program translate a HLL program to machine level language at a time.

CODASYL : A committee which has developed by US Dept. of Defence. It also adopts the standard language COBOL

CODE: A set of instructions in a computer program or A system of symbolic characters that are used to represent data.

Code-decimal: A notation where each decimal digit is separately represented in coded form by binary notation of digit.

Code Element: A basic element which construct a code. e.g. 8 bits character code having individual bits or code elements.

Command Key: The keys on the Key board used to perform specific functions.

Command Code: Operation code (O.P. code) used in assembly language.

Command Interpreter: It is a program which processes commands and other input and output from an active terminal in a time sharing system.

Command Language: It is the language of an OS through which the user of data processing system describes the requirement of their tasks to that system. It is also known as Job Control Language (JCL).

Command Line: The entry that is made when a command is to be executed by the OS.

Compact Disk (CD): It is a storage device, uses optical storage techniques and thereby provides easy handling and highly enhanced storage capacity.

Communication: It is a flow of Information from one point to another.

Communication Satellite: A satellite having facility to act as a reflectory by accepting signals to and from telecommunication signals.

Communication Server: It Is a device or terminal linking LAN.

Compatibility: It is a feature of one computer that allows programs written for computer to run an another.

Compatible: Similarity of working between different devices.

Compatible Software: A program that can run on several computers.

Compilation: The translations .of programs written In HLL into machine level language.

Completion Time: The time that compilation goes an.

COM: It stands far Computer Output Microfilm, it is an output device that records computer output on microfilm.

Computer Operator: A person who operates computer.

Computer System: The set of components connected each other to perform the program execution or to perform a certain task by this.

Computer Aided Instruction (CAI): The education procedure which is supported and assisted by computer with a sequence of instructions.

Computer Aided Diagnosis: A program used for diagnosis of disease by computer which saves the time of Doctor/Physician and assist quickly.

Computer Aided Learning (CAL): A computer based learning method.

Computer Aided Manufacturing (CAM) : The user .of computer technology in the management, control and operation of manufacturing.

Computer Awareness: Creating an understanding of what a computer and its system is, how It works, far which purpose it may be used.

Computer Animation: The use of computer in which It presents either continuously or in rapid succession, graphic representation on VDU or another devices.

Computer Architecture: Integrated logic elements to form a computer.

Computer Network: Two or mare computers integrated by communication channel.

Concentrate: To write in a sequence link together an link to a chain of two or more characters, generally strings into a single string. It is simply pinning of two strings or characters.

Computer Language: The HLL or programming languages are known as computer languages.

Computer Vendor: The organisation that manufactures.

Conditional Branching: It is also known as conditional jumping or decision making instruction e.g. IF <condition> ELSE is a conditional branching statement in some HLLs.

Configuration: Assembly of machines that are interconnected and are programmed to .operate as a system.

Configure: To Assembly a section of Hardware or Software into a system and to adjust each of the parts so that they all work together.

Conjection: An and operator.

Console: A computer unit used to control the machine manually correct errors, revise contents .of storage and provide communication in other ways between the operator and monitor.

Console Display: The visible representation of information in words, numbers, drawings, etc. on a console screen connected to a computer.

Console Type Writer: A typewriter by means of which the computer operator can monitor system and program operations. It is also called. as console printer.

Constant: Data or item which do not get changed during execution of program.

Constant Instructions: Non-executable instructions.

Control Head: Field in a data record used to identify and classify the record.

Control Register: It is a register which holds machine instructions currently being interpreted by control unit.

Control Bus: A set of wires used to transmit signals to control the operation of various unit of a computer.

Control Memory: The memory in the CU used to store instructions for internal functioning of a computer.

Control Procedure: Data link control.

Control Station: Network station that supervises control procedure.

Control Unit (CU): A sub-system of CPU that directs other parts of the CPU in the paper sequence.

Convert: To transform the representation of data.

Core Memory: The computer memory storage which composed of magnetic cores. It is otherwise known as magnetic core memory.

CRT (Cathode Ray Tube): The VDU is otherwise known as CRT.

Cursor: A movable small rectangle like spot of flashing light appears on the screen indicating the position of the user. It also indicates the text position of character on the screen.

CPU Time: The amount of time taken by CPU is execution of a program.

Cursor Control Keys: They are also called as Edit keys. The four keys help to move the cursor on the screen which are called as cursor control keys or Edit Keys.

Daisy Wheel: A print head having print elements of characters are element taking one character on the end of spokes, a central hub which forms the appearance of a daisy flower.

Daisy Wheel Printer: A daisy wheel consists of a round central as the wheel turns the spokes are impacted on a tiny hammer. This is otherwise called as letter quality printer, because It's letter are more quality than other printers.

Data: It is a collection of facts, figures, observations which can be inputted to a computer system to process by mathematics and logical operations.

Data Aggregate: It is a collection of data items in a record.

Data Bank: It is a comprehensive file a data.

Data Base: It is a set of inter-related data records in a specific structure that is designed to allow multiple applications to access data.

Data Base Management System (DBMS): The art integrated data processing system or software supporting database facilities for defining the logical and physical structure of data in a database aids in the storage, manipulation, reporting and controlling of data.

Data Bus: A bus that transfers data from one location to another location in the form of electronic signals.

Data Transmission: Movement of encoded data from one place to another.

Data Transmission Device: It is. MODEM (MOdulator and DEModulator).

Data Conversion: The conversion process of data from one machine readable form to another.

Data Communication System: A system or processor which is used to control the flow of data between machines and terminals over communication channels.

Data Dictionary: A list containing names and structures of all types of data.

Data Element: A meaningful collection of a unit character. It is also known as data items.

Data Entry: A process of putting data into computer for processing or storage. This is otherwise known as data preparation.

Data Error: Art error occurred prior to processing the data.

Data Field: Art area in the main memory of the computer where a data record is contained.

Data File: A computer file consists of records having related data items only.

Data Row: It is a transfer of data from external device.

Data Format: It refers to the structuring of representation of data, specifying type of size of each data item.

Data Items: It is otherwise known as datum, the plural form is data. It is a single member of data element.

Data Interchange: Changing of data from one storage unit to another.

Data Link: The physical connected communications path used for transmission of information from one location to the another.

Data Management: It refers to the functions performed by operating system including organising, locating, retrieving, storing and handling data.

Data Manipulation: It is the process of that allow program to store, find and retrieve records on the database filc.

Data Transfer Rate: The speed at which data is transferred from initial place to destination place.

Data Matrix: It stands to representation of information in the form of rows and columns.

Data Medium: The medium or device on which data are stored in a computer system such as magnetic disk or disks, paper tape etc.

Data Model: Logical or the physical storage representation of the inter-relationship of data.

Data Name: It is otherwise known as variable. It indicates data value as pi= 3', 14.

Data Unit: A set of one or more characters that are related in a specific way that they are treated as a whole.

Data Validation: It stands for checking of data for correctness.

Debugging: The method of finding out the bugs or errors in the program and correcting them are known as debugging.

Decision Table: It refers to the table used for representing program logic.

De Morgan's Theorem: It refers to theorem in Boolean Algebra which states to complement of Boolean expression.

Deck: The place where grouping and stocking punched cards are done.

Data Security: The precautions taken to protect the data from accidental destruction or disclosure. It is also known as file security.

Data Processing: A system that uses of a computer and its peripheral or devices and printers to manipulates data, sorting, classifying and performing other similar process at a high speed.

Data Record: Rate at which carries data from one point to another, measured in bauds (BPS).

Data Storage Device: Typically, millions of characters stored by pulses, magnetic laser or any other source with the help of a card, magnetic disks.

Data Structure: It leads to a collection of (data which are constructed in a regular and characteristic way in a computer system.

Data Sharing: The sharing method of data at several nodes from a single node by computer users.

Data Retrieval: Searching, selecting and retrieving of data from a file or data file.

Data Tracks: Typically, it refers to the information storage position on a storage devices.

Data Transfer: The technique in which data transmit from computer to storage media and vice versa.

Data Transformation: It refers to transfer of data from one computer to another or from host/central computer to data collection nodes or points.

DBMS: It stands for Data Base Management System. It is a Application Software.

Doughter Board: The board which is used to extend the capacity of a mother board.

DCE: Data Communication Equipment.

Dead Time: A period of time which is allowed between two related events to avoid overlap.

Device Cluster: It refers a set of computers connected in either of the several topologies to share the communications controller.

Desk Top Publishing (DTP): The computerised system for the use of printing or publishing to get ready documents.

Digital Computer: A computer system that works with discrete quantities such as 0s and 1s.

Digital Data Recorder: The electronic device which converts analog signals into digital values.

Digitizer: It is an input device, typically used to graphic as well as pictorial data into binary form. Graphic tablet is the best example of digitising device.

Digital Cassette: The cassette which is used for storage the digital information.

Digital Circuit: The operations like high and low voltages can be assigned by this integrated circuit.

Digital Plotter: It is an output device which is used to get hardcopy in the graphical form as signals received from digital inputted data.

Direct Memory Access (DMA): In this method where is possible{ direct transfer of data between a peripheral I/O devices without prior importance of central processor mass storage devices like floppy disk is the best example of Direct Memory Access.

DIR: It represents the directories in DOS command, generally it is used to display all the files on the monitor presented in the disk.

Diode: It is a electronic device, which is used on chips. It allows the flow of current in single direction only.

Direct Access: It means the access or the manipulation of data can be possible directly. Because it effects the location of data in the storage device, hence access time is effectively independent.

Direct Processing: It is a such a unique method, where the handling of data is possible randomly, without sorting.

Disk: It is very familiar as a direct access storage device. It is a flat in nature and circular plate and it is coated with magnetic material, so that the data can stored by the magnetised portion in the disk.

Disk Operating System (DOS) : It is an operating system, generally the computer system or routines as well as programs to run the system and also for permanent storage user disk device.

Distributed Data Processing (DDP): This is a system which is physically separated but interconnected system of computer to each other through the decentralised of computer system for the networking, typically independent computers or intelligent terminals can be used for exchange the data.

Diskette: Please see Floppy Disk.

Disk Drive: The device which is used to drive or rotate magnetic disks and access its data by the help of read/write head. Otherwise known as Disk Unit.

Disk Storage: All the components which are used for storage the data, program or software in the disk.

Display Terminal: It is the output device in which all the information appear on the screen of a Cathode Ray Tube (CRT). It is also known as DISPLAY unit or Video Display Terminal (VOT).

Document File: It is a file in word processor in which formatted with margin headers and footers.

DOE: It stands for department of electronics, A government organisation which provides Level courses such O, A, B, C.

Dot Matrix Printer: This is one kind of computer printer forms the characters using dot matrix technique with the help of 7 × 5 grid matrix formed by dots.

Double Buffering: The technique or the method is used to first store and transfer the information between peripheral devices.

Double Density: The technique which is generally used to store more information with twice the amount of Single density.

Double Sided: A magnetic disk which has recording capacity of both surface of the disk.

Down Time: The specific time during which the computer system is out of order or not operating correctly, due to mechanical failure.

Dumb Terminal: The terminal which does not have local processing power or microprocessor to control terminal tasks. It can be said that the terminal can be function when lined to the system.

Dynamic Random Access Memory (DRAM): It is Metallic oxide semiconductor memory which need periodic refreshing or recharging to retain its data. As compared to static RAM, it is higher density and speed.

EAROM : It stands for Electrically Alterable Read Only Memory, here special circuit is required to write information.

Edit: It stands for modify the format of the data in any form. Inserting and also erasing the characters are done where required.

Editor: It is one kind of software which is used to modify the text retrieve and rearrange the data stored previously in a computer file.

EBCDIC: It refers for *E*xtended *B*inary *C*oded *D*ecimal *I*nterchange *C*ode. It is 8 bits coding system developed by IBM.

Electronic Data Processing (EDP): It refers to data processing is to carried out by the electronic machines.

Eelectonic Mail: The process of sending the message by one user and receiving by the another user through the electronic service system. Every user should know the identification number.

Electronic Spreadsheet: It is an application package which is used to compute or display in the tabular form on the screen.

Elementary Data Item: The smallest unit of data item.

Element: It is member of collection of items that cannot be sub divided itself.

Emulator: It is software which enable the computer to execute program written for another system without changing the hardware.

Encoder: The device is used to produce the information machine understandable form.

End of the File (EOF): As a marker, it represents the end of a file.

ENlAC: The first digital computer developed by Mauchly and Eckert in 1946.

Environment Division: It refers to the second division of a COBOL Program.

Entity: An object or thing that has meaning for a specific application.

EPROM: It is a semiconductor memory. It can be read but not written. But the chip can be reprogrammed by using special hardware, an EPROM can be erased with ultraviolet light. After that new information can be stored on it.

Error Message: The message will be highlighted on the monitor which indicates the types of errors, that occurred during the execution of program.

Error Register: It is a special storage location where and when error condition arises.

Ethernet: It is a member of the Local Area Network (LAN) family. It carries audio, video as well as computer data from place to place.

Execution Time: The time is required to execute a program on particular computer system is known as execution time.

External Buffer: It is the place where the temporary data is stored while traversing between computer to other devices.

External Command: Especially in DOS there are some external command that run by the execution of a special program file stored on a floppy disk.

4GL: 4th Generation Language

F: It stands for 15th digit in Hexadecimal number system.

Facsimll.E (FAX): It provides electronic data transmission from place to another place including ordinary documents, pictures, graphs, maps etc. The electronics signals converted at the receiving station for creating duplicate of the original inputted image.

Feed: To input data into computer memory for the processing purpose.

Ferrous Oxide: The substance which s used for coating of recording tape and disks.

FF: It stands for Flip-Flop.

Fiber Optic Cable: This is a coaxial cable which is used for communication purposes.

Field: An individual element of an entity.

Field Length: It implies the size of the field.

FIFO: First in First Out.

Fifth Generation: In this generation Artificial Intelligence (AI) is used. Simpler programming languages are introduced in this generation. From 1985 onwards known as fifth generation.

File: It stands for a group of related data which are used for a specific task, almost always these are stored permanently in disk and tape.

File Maintenance: When data processing occurs, master file is updated on the basis of transaction files.

File Processing: It is involves with the creation, validation, comparison, sorting and merging of the files.

File Organisation: The arrangement of files in the disk.

File Structure: The term stands for the total information of fields, records, blocks and files. And in addition to that the way in which they have been organised and so on.

Fire Ware: The programs or the software stored in Read Only Memory (ROM). These are not changeable by any software, and not lost if power is turned off.

First in First Out (FIFO): This is unique processing technique by which first data gets processed first and last data gets processed last.

Floppy Disk: It is an storage device, which is also magnetised coated on one or both sides of circular plate.

Flip-Flop: It is a electronic circuit, which represents the two states (0 and 1).

Flow Chart: The pictorial representation of the algorithm.

Flow Line: The line which is connected to each or any symbol that represents an antecedent event to a successor event.

Flow Chart Symbols: These symbols are representing operation such as diamond symbol indicates decisions, rectangle stands for input/output and so on.

Format: This is a DOS command, generally used to read a floppy disk for use by dividing tracks and sectors on the surface of it on which data can be stored accordingly.

Fourth Generation: In this generation Very Large Scale Integration (VLSI) circuits are used in computers.

Fourth Generation Language (4GL): These languages are based on non procedural form i.e., Oracle, Java, etc.

Forth: This is a high level programming language, more faster than BASIC, it gives quick response.

Fortran: It is a high level programming language, it stands for Formula TRANslation, widely used in scientific fields.

Full Duplex: It refers to communication field where the receiving and sending data can be possible by the two system simultaneously.

Function Keys: On a keyboard there are some special keys, they are used to perform a particular task, e.g. Enter Key.

Full Adder: The adder, which add three binary digits.

Gamut: Pertaining all range of colours that are displayed on monitor:

Gangpunch: This is a punched card machine, which is used for reproducing information such as employee name, department number etc.

Garbage: Futile or unwanted data, which were put back into the computer memory.

Garbage in Garbage Out (GIGO): Inputting useless data or bad data and getting equally on wanted output.

Gates: This is otherwise known as logic circuits. It shows the manipulation of binary information with several inputs and one output is done by logic circuits.

Getway: It is a device used in mini or micro computer for operation and also it provides communication with other system.

General Purpose Computer: A computer which is used in general field 6ke business and as well as scientific field.

Graphic Display Terminal: The terminal which has a screen to DISPLAY graph as well as any string information.

Go Bottom: It is a DBASE command used to move the pointer to last record of the database.

Great Brass Brain: It is the first analog computer.

GRIP: It stands for GRaphics Interactive Programming language.

Graphic Tablet: It is digitising input device, used for drawing graphics.

Half Adder: It has capacity to receive two inputs for addition and give bit as a output with a carry bit (if available).

Half Duplex: In which data is transmitted in one direction but not simultaneously.

Halt: Often computer system stops processing in the middle of the program execution.

Hard Copy: It is written format on the paper, we get by the printer, in human readable form.

Hang: Due to internal error, often computer system stops execution for a while.

Hard Disk Pack: A set of removable magnetic disks used as a storage device.

Hard Disk: It is otherwise known as Winchester Disk. It has faster accessing capacity, high storage capacity. It has also multiple head and sealed one.

Hardware: The physical components of a computer system is called Hardware of the computer. e.g. CPU, printer, disk etc. We can see, touch and feel also.

Hexadecimal Number: The number which base is 16. The digit range from 0, 1, 2, 3, 4, 5, 6, 7, 8, 9, A, B, C, D, E, F.

Header Record: The record which identifies the files.

Help: In software like DOS/DBASE, generally it is used as a command to get help, how to use the program and so on.

Hertz (Hz): It is the international standard unit which measures the frequency. of the data transmission.

Hidden Files: Hidden files are the files which are stored in the disk but not disclosed by the operating system.

Hierarchical File: The file are arranged according to the rank or class is called hierarchical file such as grand father -father-son structure.

High Level Language: These languages are independent in nature with these a programmer can write the instructions in English like statement to control the whole environment as well as the data structure, which is not provided by the hardware.

High Resolution: The good quality of graphics system. e.g. VDU.

High Speed Printer: The printer which prints 600 characters per minute with great speed.

Holding Time: The time taken in communication channel for transmission of one message to another system is called holding time.

Home Computer: It is one type of personal computer with a limited memory capacity. It's monitor can be used as visual DISPLAY unit as well as Television.

Hopper: It is a device which holds punched cards and help them for data, information and other computing facilities to its connected terminals.

Hybrid Computer: The mixed of analog and digital computer is hybrid computer.

Hyper Text: This is found in word processing systems.

IC: Integrated Circuit.

IBM Model-650: It is developed in 1950, it could perform both the commercial and scientific Applications.

IBM: International Business Machine, world's largest computer manufacturer.

IBMDOS.COM: It is hidden file in DOS that help at start up..

IBMIO.COM: It is also a hidden file and gets executed at start up.

ICON: The pictorial representation of a entity, which is displayed for a user on the screen.

Identification Dimension: In COBOL the first division which indicates the purpose and other information about the program.

Idle Time: The period during which any part of the computer is not used due to lack of demand.

Impact Printer: As mane stands it strike against the paper to print the characters on the paper.

Indexed File: They have an extension name i.e. NDX OR NTX and the access of record can be done by randomly.

Index Hole: They hole represents the beginning of the track on the disk.

Indexed Sequential File: A file where records are being subjected to index sequentially.

Indonet: In 1986 CMC installed a public data network in India is called INDONET.

Information: The processed data is called information.

Information System: The total data processing system is called information system.

Inkjet Printer: It is a non-impact printer, that uses a nozzle and sprays ink at paper to form the required image.

Inkjet: This is a printing technology that .used in ink jet printer.

Input: It refers to feed the data into computer memory through input device to get output.

Input Device: A device which is used to feed the raw data into computer memory to get information for example keyboard, card reader etc.

Instruction: A command or order given to the hardware to perform a specific task. Command may to be performed arithmetic and logic functions.

Instruction Register: A register in CPU which controls a part of the program as well as stores the current instruction.

Intelligent Terminal: A terminal which has local processing power.

Inter Block Gap (IBG): The blank which separates blocks of records on magnetic tape.

Interpreter: It is translator, which translates the high level statement into machine understandable language (machine language) statement-wise.

Inter Record Gap (IRG): The gape between the record in the storage device i.e. magnetic tape.

Invisible Failure: A. failure of either hardware or software without any noticeable effect.

Item: A set of adjacent digit to convey a single unit of information.

J

Jam: While punched card machine does not receive cards.

Job: A specific task for a system.

Job Control Language (JCL.): A language which is associated with an operating system to communicate with the system.

Job Control Program: A collection of instructions to the operating system.

Joy Stick: A stick which is used to indicates direction of cursor movement on a screen.

K: It is commonly used to denote 1024 or 2 bytes.

Keyboard: It is familiar input device by which data can be entered manually into computer memory through terminal.

Key Field: A field which distinguishes one record from another.

Key Word: Initial element in a programming language statement.

Kilo Baud: One thousand bits per second.

L

Label Record: It refers a record which is used to identity a data file. It is the first record of the file.

Lan: It is a digital communication system which is inter connected to a large number of system. It covers limited geographical area up to 1 km.

Language: The language which help human to communicate with a computer. It follows syntax and vocabulary also to write the program to solve a specific task.

Laptop: This is a PC which is like folding notebook or briefcase size, portable computer, maximum 5 kg. in weight which contains all the devices of a PC that can be used any where the user move.

Large Scale Instruction (LSI): It is fabricating integrate circuits consists of maximum 20,000 transistors on a single chip.

Letency Time: It refers to the disk storage position maximum latency time can be calculate as in equals to the time taken by disk to rotate once.

Lattice: It is related to Boolean Algebra.

Least Significant BIT (LSB) : The digit in the right most position of a binary byte.

Length: It refers to the number of bits or characters presented in a word, record or data.

Letter Quality Printer: The printer produces one complete character neat and clean on a paper is called letter quality printer.

Library Functions: Some pre-written or readymade programs reside in the computer memory (ROM) are called library functions i.e. INT,COS,SQU, etc.

LIFO (Last in First Out): A technique for processing any job on a last come first served basis. Also known as a push down stack technique.

Light Pen: It is a pointing device looks like a ball point pen which is used to make interactive communication between computer user and the screen.

LILO (Last in Last Out): It is a technique for processing data and storing data in last come last served basis.

Line Protocol: In communication two ends pass their information each other sequentially in an understandable form.

Lines Per Minute (LPM): The speed measurement of a printer.

Line Printer: It prints the entire line at a time.

Link Register: It resides in ALU that acts as a extension of an accumulator during logical shift instruction.

LISP (List Processing) : It is a high level language it also follows the method for processing data in list form. The Artificial Intelligency is the one kind of organisation which lead such processing.

Load: To transfer data from auxiliary memory (mass memory/floppy disk) to primary memory (RAM) for execution.

Load Point: Initial or primary point of the magnetic tape from which reading/writing will start.

Local Area Network (LAN): Local Area Network is a network of two or more Computers in short area maximum within 2 km.

Local Storage: It is a area resides in CPU to interpret statements as well as arithmetic and logical operations.

Logic: The science which deals with reasoning proof and thinking.

Local Storage: It is a area resides in CPU to interpret statements as well as arithmetic and logical operations.

Logic: The science which deals with reasoning proof and thinking.

Logging Off: The termination of communication between the computer and the user.

Logic Operators: It refers to the logical relationship between two data items for comparing selecting, matching, sorting and so on. In addition to that Yes/No is also involved.

Logical Error: When and where is applied logic is different from the required logic.

Logic Gates: It is a electronic device which implements an elementary logic functions. it accepts one or more inputs to produce standard output e.g. AND, NOT, OR, NAND, NOR, XOR, etc. gates.

Logic Circuit: A circuit which performs logic functions or operations.

Logo: It is a programming language. It stands for Logic Oriented and Graphic Oriented Programming language, developed by Seymour Papert in 1968. It is specially designed for school going young children below 13 years in age.

Loop: A set of instructions which gets repeated for a prescribed number of time until a certain condition occurs.

Loop Stop: The series of instructions will be stop if condition is fulfilled as user wants.

Low Level Language: This is a language which computer can understand. AU the instructions are written in the terms of O's and 1's.

M

M: it refers to Mega Byte.

Machine: The processing unit otherwise known as machine.

Machine Language: A set of machine code which a computer can understand directly. In this language all the instruction are only a set of binary codes. It is otherwise known as binary language.

Machine Readable Form: The instructions which can be read by input devices connected to a computer.

Machine Oriented Language: The computer language based on the binary system so the processor or computer operators on it. It is also known as assembly language.

Magnetic Card: It is developed by IBM Corp. it has a magnetised surface i.e. coated with ferro magnetic film upon which data can be encoded and decoded or write and read.

Magnetic Disk: A storage device consist of a no. of flat circular plates coated on both surface with magnetizable materials. There are a no. of tracks on each surface to read/ write data.

Magnetic Drum: It is a storage device, consists of cylinder which is coated with magnetizable material. The cylinder Is continuously rotated with read/write head also with recording tracks on the surface of the cylinder.

Magnetic Ink Character Reader & Recognition (MICR): It is a character reader device which reads the magnetic ink characters (using MICR technique) and automatically recognise these characters to the machine.

Magnetic Tape: It is a tape or ribbon which is coated with a magnetic material on which information may be stored in the form of magnetized characters.

Mail Merge: A procedure of combining a specific text common with a rapid change of another text on the same text e.g. names and addresses, in case of printing of correspondences used in word processing softwares..

Mainframe Computer: It is a large size of computer with some terminals.

Manipulation: Changing or arranging of data, processing or retrieve at a program execution.

Mark I: It stands for Havard Mark-I, world's first electronic computer.

Mass Storage: The large capacity secondary storage system. It is also known as external storage, because it is totally external to the computer.

Master File: It is a computer file which contains relatively permanent information, generally updating periodically, specially designed for a specific task. It contains also several working files like transaction files, data files etc.

Mega Byte: 1024 kg, Mega implies million.

Memory: A storage location in the computer system for storing data or information for processing, retrieval and storage.

Memory Address: In computer there is the binary codes given to memory location.

Memory Address Register (MAR): A register used in the addressing of operands in the storage location. Each address component has been stored in a MAR while the instruction has been executed.

Memory Buffer Register (MBR): It is a special register through which every data enter and exit. Thus the register is acting as a buffer store for facilitating transfers of data to the from the memory and peripheral units.

Menu: A program generated list of options of work displayed on the screen, it indicates what to be entered anyone option to execute the desired processing for a specific and designed previously in the computer? and so on.

Micro Computer: It refers to a computer system utilising a CPU having different word length as 7 bits word, 8 bits word, 16 bits word and 32 bits and so on.

Micro Computer System: It is a complete small system, including the CPU, input and output devices like keyboard, mouse, tape, VDU, FDDs, HDDs, memory and power supply etc. They are the single user personal computers like "Desk Top" computers.

Micro Processor: It is a Large Scale Integrated (LSI) chip contains the entire CPU of a computer. The CPU mainly depends on micro processor. The micro processors are called as 8086, 80286, 80386, 80486 and Pentium processor. They are capable of 7 bits, 8 bits, 16 bits, 32 bits, 64 bits, 128 bits word length respectively.

Mini Computer: It is larger, faster and also expensive than the micro computer. It is the small system, of single user.

Mnemonic: It is a symbolic instruction code used in assembly languages.

Modem: Acronym for MODulator and DEModulator. It is a device connecting peripherals which converts digital signals into user interface and user language to digital signals. It is mainly used in telephone transmission.

Monitor: The Visual Display Unit (VDU) of the T.V. like screen is called as monitor on which the input and output can be seen.

Mother Board (MB): It is the main Printed Circuit Board (PCB) in the CPU on which the micro processor exists. It has the connection between the several devices supported to CPU Into which all the circuit boards could be plugged on it to function the applications of a computer.

Mouse: It is a manipulating device used for positioning the cursor moving by hand on a plain surface. A ball has under it which helps to move the mouse on pad along with the cursor movement can be controlled.

MS-DOS: It is an Operating System (OS) designed by Microsoft Corp. known as Microsoft Disk Operating System. It is used for PCs compatibles with multi tasking.

Multi User Operating System: It is an Operating System, it is used for multitasking and more than a user can use it. e.g. UNIX. But DOS is the Single user operating system.

MS-Windows: It Is an Operating Environment with a GUJ (Graphic User Interface) as well as multi tasking facility. It is developed by the MicroSoft Corp. Inc. (USA).

Multiplexing: It is a method on which a communication channels divided from physical shared in logical channels, so that a number of independent signals may be transmitted simultaneously on it.

Multi Processing: It is the inter connecting of computers with two or more independent CPUs that have the ability to simultaneously execution of several programs.

Multi Processor: A computer consists of two or more CPUs under a common control.

Multi Processing System: Two or more CPUs capable of driving the same applications availability in multi-processing system.

Multi Station: In communication networks where several data terminals are involved is known as multi-station.

Multi User System: In a computer system, where computers shared in terminals for different users, known as multi user system.

Mylar: A trademark of polyester films manufactured by M/S Dupont which is coated with magnetisable particles.

National Cash Register (NCR): It Is an US based firm started by John. H. Patterson to manufacturer cash register.

Nano Second: A billionth of a second (10^{-9}).

Nesting: It is repetition of a portion of program to perform a task. The loop between the another loop is called Nested loop or nesting.

Network: A series of computers inter-connected for communicating each other is known as network.

Nibble: Half of a byte i.e. 4 bits is called as a Nibble.

Node: The junction point of a network.

Non-Volatile Memory: The memory where the stored information are presented for future use when the Power is turned off.

Nor: It is a Boolean operation that gives logical value of true only or 1 when neither the inputs are true or 1.

Not: It Is a logical negation used in Boolean operations which gives negative values of 0 for 1 and 1 for 0 that means true for false and false for true.

Number Crunching: A repetition or complex arithmetic calculations made in the program execution in computer system.

Num Lock: It is a key on the keyboard of the computer system when it is ON the number pad will work for numeric operations as shift key gives upper case letters.

Numeric Pad: There Is a separate portion on a keyboard having numbers only in the right hand side Is known as the Numeric pad.

Object Oriented Programming Languages (OOP): A form of programming language that adopt a different approach to data and code.

Object Code: Output produced by a compiler or assembler in form of machine code that operates the computer system.

Object Computer: The computer used to run the object programs.

Object Language: A computer language in which converts the program directly in the machine understandable form by the help of translators (compiler or interpreter).

Object Program: A program has been translated by a compiler, assembler, interpreter, the result or the machine code instructions àre known as object program.

Object Time: The time computer takes to do a object program is known as object time.

Octal Number System: This system the base is 8. Each digit represent power of 8.

Off Line: A task is being performed by a device which is not under the control of CPU.

Off Line Device: The device which Is not under the control of the CPU.

Off Line Processing: A part of data processing system on which the device is not directly connected to the CPU.

Off Line Storage: The storage devices which are not under the directly control of the CPU.

Office Automation: The application of computers of entire office tasks.

Open: To make a file available for reading or writing. Flow chart begins with 'open'.

On Line: The operation of the system and its peripherals are under the control of CPU.

Operand: It is a variable consists of numeric value in which items, quantity, memory locations upon which a mathematical or logical operations are to be performed.

Operate Time: The phase or time of computer operation when an Instruction is being carried out.

Operation Code (OP CODE): The code of instruction specifying the operation to be performed i.e. ADD (add), SUB (subtraction), MUL (multiplication), DIV (division) etc. used In assembly. language.

Operations: The set of characters designed for specific operations. The operators are of three kinds such as *(i)* Arithmetic-operators -,+.1,*. *(ii)* The logical operators are AND, NOT, OR, NAND, NOR etc. (iii) The relational operators are <, >, -, <-, >=, #, <> etc.

Optical Character Reader (OCR): A device used for recognising optical characters, a printed document as Input and reads.

Optical Disk (Laser Disk): A storage disk which is uses optical storage technology.

Optical Fiber: It is an electronic transmission cable..

Optical Reader: It is a data entry machine which converts printer characters, pencil shaded areas into a computer input code format to execute for counting.

Or: It is a Boolean operation used in logic gates which defines output is true (1) only if either one of the input is true (1) logically compared two or more values.

Output: The computer is a processing unit, input and read data which is being processed through computer, the output will appear on the screen.

Output Devices: The device or equipment through which the output of computer programs or documents can be done. It implies the possibility of DISPLAY of output of a processing can be done through output device. The VDU is the best example' for output device.

Over Flow: A condition which is caused by an arithmetic operation, which generates a no. that is too big for the hardware or software word size limitations of the machine or any thing at the time of processing exceeds limit will give the error message "Overflow".

Over Write: A writing of a characters on an existing characters on the screen or memory.

Package: It is an application software used for user's particular problem of data or organisation.

Page: A segment of a program or data usually a fixed length defined by the system or the user as per requirement of output on the screen or on the paper.

Page Length: It is the fixed length of a computer page of a next especially defined in word processing as per the required size of paper to get output.

Paper Feed: The method whereby paper is pulled through a printer to set the paper to get ready of printing work.

Paper Tape: It is a storage medium whereby data are stored as punched hole sequence on it.

Paper Tape Code: The code that consists of a pattern of holes punched across a strip of paper tape. There are certain no. of tracks on paper tape as 5 tracks, 7 tracks and 8 tracks codes.

Paper Tape Reader: The device which can produce a copy of punched paper tape.

Parallel Computers: A set of computers connected together by a high speed communication network.

Parallel Access: The transfer of information to or from storage device where in all elements in a unit information are transferred simultaneously.

Parallel Computation: The simultaneously computation of several parts of a problem.

Parallel Processing: It refers to a computer during which two programs run concurrently which use more than one CPU.

Para Meter: It is a variable whose value is set in the main program and passed along to a subroutine and *vice versa*.

Parity Bit: A check bit appended to an array of binary digits to make the sum of all digits, including parity BIT always odd or even.

Parity Checking: It is a technique of find error that is used for checking the accuracy of computer words often data transmission and data communication. One extra parity BIT has been added to each byte to detect error.

Pascal: A high level general purpose structured programming computer language named after Blaise Pascal.

Password: A code used to access computer system or a particular program or a particular user, It is used for security purposes.

Peripherals: The various equipments like I/O devices of a computer system.

Peripheral Devices: Any unit or equipment distinct from the CPU, that may provide the system with outside communication.

Personal Computer: A small computer based microprocessor commonly abbreviated as PCs. It is used by individuals for carrying out personal jobs or for applications such as entertainment, home management and hobbies.

Pixel: It stands for PIcture Element, one of the individual dots or basic rectangular element which Is used to form a character or a graphic images on the monitor.

Pico Second: One trillionth of a second, 10×10. PLOTTER: It refers to a hardcopy output device, which Is used to produce graphical images on paper or on other materials.

Pointer: It Is used to locate some data at a particular location in the computer memory or other set of data that contains the address of a related record.

Pointing Devices: The devices which allow to the end users to give commands and alpha numeric data directly into the computer system as an alternative to the user of a keyboard. Mouse is the best example of pointing devices.

Point-to-Point Network: The network which the connections between the individual nodes Is by using point-to-point connections without host computer or central server.

PBX: It stands for Private Branch exchange.

Primary Memory: Random Access Memory (RAM) is volatile in nature because it does not retain memory capability without power. It is otherwise known as 'Main memory'. It is very expensive in comparison to the secondary or auxiliary memory.

Primary Storage: The first storage area of the computer is called primary storage (RAM).

Printer: To get a hard copy of a text or a graphic printer is used. It is a hardware devices broadly divided into impact and non-impact printer. Dot Matrix, Chain, Drum and Daisy wheel are impact printers and Ink Jet, Thermal and Laser printers are known as non-impact printers.

Print Out: Any hard copy which is produced by a printer.

Problem Solving: If follows six steps process of identifying the problem i.e. collecting and sorting, relevant information, developing and analysing, implementing the program and follow up.

Procedure: The set of instructions required to solve a problem.

Processor: It Is a hardware device which is capable of carrying out operations on data. Often it is called as central processor.

Program: A sequence of instructions that are arranged logically one after another to perform a particular task is called program.

Programmer: A person who irresponsible for designing, writing and testing the computer programs.

Programming Language: A language which is used for writing computer programs.

Programmable Read Only Memory (PROM) : It is just like ROM but can be programmed once by the user by the device called a PROM programmer or PROM blower. The contents of PROM can be erased. There programmed process are known as EPROM. If the erasing procedure Is electrically or by the use of ultra-violet rays they are called as EEPROM.

Programming Language: Generally programmers are used languages to write a computer program.

Prompt: It indicates to the user of the necessity of input or location of input on the terminal (monitor).

Protected Record or Field: It refers to a record or a field which is displayed on the terminal but cannot over written by the user.

Protocol: A set of standards for controlling the transfer or exchange of information between two devices are called protocols.

Pseudo Code: It refers to a false code by which program instructions are written.

Punched Card: A standardised stiff paper which is used for storing information through punched card.

Q

Query Language: It is a high level language. It permits a user to access information and extract data from a database.

Queue: A waiting line of items that are waiting for processing or service in a form of a queue.

Quick Format: In DOS C:\FORMAT A:/Q is used for a quick way to format a previously formatted disk or a new disk.

Quit: It permits a user to terminate the current process.

R

Radix: The base of a number system i.e. binary system radix is 2, the Radix or base of decimal system is 10 and octal is 8 etc.

Random Access Memory (RAM): This is a primary memory based on silicon chips, with access times of about 100 numbers.

Random Access: It is just like a Direct Access. This process does not required sequential search and sequential retrieval.

Raw Data: Before processed data is called raw data.

Read: The process of receiving of data either from primary or secondary memory.

Read-After-Write: The method of writing data into the disk and retrieving to ensure accuracy.

Read Only Memory (ROM): It refers to a semiconductor memory used for permanent storage. This memory circuit is put during manufacture that cannot a changed by the user or any other means.

Read Write Memory: It refers to a computer storage where in data can be stored or retrieved. Random Access Memory (RAM) is called Read/Write memory.

Read Time: This time is equals to the access time.

Real Time Processing: Processing which occurs in simultaneously at the time of data entry. The Automatic

Teller Machine(ATM) uses real time processing. Airline reservations systems are on real time processing, it is also known on line processing.

Recompile: Repetition the process or compilation of a program, due to debugging.

Record: A group of related data elements or fields.

Record Count: The total number of computer records in a file.

Reboot: To reset a computer system after hardware/ software failure. Turning the power off or on first time in the morning is called "Cold Booting" in the other hand computer is rebooted with but turning the power off or without reloading the operating system is known as "Warm Boot".

Register: Registers are the storage areas use by CPU for fast access to interpret instructions and perform arithmetic and logical operations.

Relational Database: It refers to a database in which the data is organised in rows and columns. So that the relationship between and data item, can easily be determined.

Relational Operators: The symbols used for comparisons <, >, >=, <-, =, <> etc.

Reserved Word: Some words have their special meaning to computer programming languages & they cannot be used as a variable name or data name.

Response Time: The time need to request for data and the arrival of that data.

Return Key: Enter Key is other wise known as Return Key.

RGB: It stands for Red-Green-Blue, a phrase use in cathode ray display to create colour images.

Ring Network: A topology where each machine is connected with one node. Messages between nodes have to pass through all intervening nodes in the form of ring.

ROM: It refers to Read Only Memory (ROM). This is a type of IC, usually mounted on the motherboard, it provides the basic start up routines and BIOS (Basic Input Output System) of a computer. ROM chips store firmware embedded by the manufacturer.

Root Directory: In MS-DOS root directory is usually specified by C:\>prompt, if hard disk is available.

Row: The horizontal groupings of cells in a spreadsheet and the vertical groupings of cell are known as Row and Column respectively.

RPG : It stands for Report Program Generator. This was one of the first high level language introduced in 1960 by IBM. It is dedicated for the purpose of Business as well as management tasks.

RPM : Abbreviation for Revolutions Per Minute, used to describe the rate of rotation of floppy disk and hard disk.

Run Time: The period of time or at which a computer program is run.

Run Time Error: This is an error that only happens during program execution, it may happens due to hardware failure also.

Save: To save or store permanently a program or data on a storage device like a floppy disk.

Scanner: A device that converts a printer image into digital information which is suitable for Input to a computer.

Scientific Language: A language designed for the writing of scientific or mathematical programs.

Scrolling: To move the on screen image vertically or horizontally is usually called "panning", but in other words it may be called horizontally scrolling.

Search and Replace: A word processing program to find out a specified character, word or a string in the text. And replacing with another character, word or a string.

Second Storage: It means the storing & retrieving data external to the main memory or primary memory. Floppy disk and hard disk Is- the example secondary storage media.

Secondary Memory: Non-volatile mass storage memory medium such as floppy disk, hard disk, tapes and CD-ROM etc.

Second Generation Computer: Computer developed during the period 1955-65, replacing vacuum tubes (thermionic valves) in the first generation with Transistors. Integrated Circuits (lCs) and VLSIs format in the third & fourth generation respectively.

Sector: A section or a portion of one track on a magnetic disk where data are stored- and accessed in the form of tracks and sectors.

Seek Time: The amount of time taken for the Read/ Write head to get required track position on a disk and transfer the information to the CPU.

Segment: A part of a program or a data file in memory.

Selenium: A semiconductor material, similar to silicon.

Semi-conductor: Silicon is a semiconductor and is widely used in the manufacture of electronic devices. The juncture of metals and non-metals, conductors and non-conductors under a specific electrical conditions, hence this is named as semiconductor.

Semi-conductor Secondary Storage: Typically, the primary storage of most modem computers consists micro-electronic chips, which is widely known as semi-conductor storage chips Random Access Memory (RAM) and Read Only Memory (ROM)(is the best example of semi-conductor secondary storage devices.

Sequential Access: The sequential method Is storing and retrieving data from a file sequentially but cannot randomly accessed.

Semantics Error: The wrong instruction format, in the program.

Sequential File: A file that has been organised in such a way that the records are stored or retrieved one after another sequentially.

Serial Transformation: A sequential data transmission method where each bits in a byte are handled one after another.

Silicon Chip: It Is a non-metallic semi-conducting element silicon, contains many electronic components and circuits, it Is otherwise known as Integrated Circuits (lCs).

Signal: Any electrical pulse transmitted or received via a data communications ink.

Skip: A jump to the text instruction in sequence.

Simplex: One-sided data transmission method e.g. Television.

Smart Terminal: A computer terminals that have their own limited processing capabilities. Because, they have their own microprocessor and control electronics.

Soft Copy: Any computer output which has been displayed on a visual display unit only, but does not produce a printed record. We can change such output easily.

Snobol: This is a high level language, stands for StriNg Oriented symBOlic Language.

Software (SW) : A set of instructions or programs which tells to the computer hardware, what operations are to be undertake.

Software Application: Handling of computer programs.

Software Package: If refers to a readymade computer programs supplied by vendors or computer manufacturers to satisfy specific applications.

Software Piracy: The process of copying any commercial software without written permission of the creator.

Sort: Arrangement of data Items of an array into ascending or descending order.

Source Program: A program, which is written in a high Ieve1language.

Special Purpose Computer: A computer system which is specially designed to solve a specific types of problems.

Spell Check: A specific feature of most word processors which provides spell check facilities.

Spoollng: It is for Simultaneous Peripheral Operation On One Temporarily saving input/output data by means of storage device for future use.

Spread Sheet: Spread sheet are widely used in the field of accounting, scientific & business purposes. It provides rows and columns.

Static RAM (SRAM) : This is Random Access Memory storage, it doesn't lose Its data storage capabilities, If power is turned off.

Star Work: In star topology, each work station is connected to host computer or central server through a dedicated point-to-point communication links.

String: A set of characters or a word.

Structured Programming: A systematic method of program design, easy to understanding and handling.

Structured Query Language (SQL): A QUERY language which is used in advanced database management system packages.

Sub Program: Sub program is a program In a large program which carry out a specific library functions when needed.

Sub Routines: Subroutines are like a functions. They reside outside the main program and they can be called repeatedly by the main program.

Subscripted Variable: The individual or particular element with in an array is known subscripted variable.

Super Computer: A special kind of large mainframe computer system.

Superscript: This is the opposite of subscript.

Syntax: A group of grammatical rules and regulations, that must be followed while coding program statements.

Syntax Error: When programmer violates the rules of grammar, the message "Syntax Error" will display on the monitor.

Synthesizer: This is a device which produce sound by converting digital instructions.

System Analysis: Analyzing in detail on the components and the environment of the computer system.

System Disk: A disk that is used to boot a system.

System Software: It controls the total environment of the system, generally system software supplied by the hardware manufacturer. Operating system is the best example of system software.

TB: Terabyte.

Tape: It is used for recording data e.g. Magnetic tape.

Tabulator: The machine which can automatically able to feed punched cards.

TCP/IP: It stands for Transmission Control Procedure/ Internet Protocol, widely used in commercial purposes.

Tele Communication: The transmission of signals or information through phone lines, cables and T. V. etc.

Tele Printer: Resembles to a typewriter, widely used in telecommunications for receiving and transmitting data from and to a very distance points. TERA BYTE : One million byte (2).

Text Editor: An application used by the programmers to edit a source program. If also facilitates to the user to change or modify text files e.g. Note pad in Windows, edition MS-DOS etc.

Terminal: A device through which data can either enter or leave. Visual Display Unit (VDU) is generally known as terminal.

Third Generation Computer: The period between 1965-80 is known as third generation, using Large Scale Integration Circuits (LSI).

Time of Day Count: An electronic device presents in the BIOS area which constantly increases the time in hours, minutes and seconds to calculate the time of a particular day.

Timer: An electronic automatic timing device which refreshes clock signals within central processor.

Time Sharing: One central processor can serve more than one user simultaneously.

Touch Terminal: Instead of using input devices the user can input his/her choice by touching the screen.

Track: One of the concentric circles on a disk for recording data on it.

Track Ball: A roller ball device which is used to control the movement of the cursor on the screen.

Track Pitch: The separation of two adjacent tracks in a disk.

Trailer: The last data item in the record.

Transistor: The terms transistor is the combination of two words i.e. transfer-resistor. The main task of it, is to control the flow of current.

Translator: It is used to convert high level language to machine level language which is computer can understand.

Truth Table: Mathematical table which represents the input-output relationship of the binary variables.

Truncation: The important process to ignore the least significant digit of a given number.

Two Dimensional Arrays: An array consists of variable having two subscripts (row and columns) is called two dimensional array.

UART: An Integrated circuit, stands for Universal Asynchronous Receiver Transmitter.

ULSI: It refers to Ultra Large Scale Integrated Circuits, ULSI. Intel 486 is the best example of VLSI.

User's Defined Function: This function is different from library function because the user can develop a function for himself/herself to use it like a library function.

Undelete: In DOS this command is used to restore or call back deleted files.

Unix: An multi user operating system that supports time sharing. It is widely used on mainframe computers. It developed by Bell Laboratories during the early 1970's, for mini computers but now being used for PCS.

Update: The latest amendments deletion or additions of the data file.

User Friendly: A user can handle the system without great deal or specialised knowledge or training on it. Because the user friendly packages are provide very relevant and polite messages when and where the user makes any mistakes.

Uaser Printer: It is a non-impact printer which uses a laser beam or electro-photographic techniques to create printed output approximately 13,000 lines per minute.

Utility Program: Utility programs are provided by any computer centre or any vendor to perform specific jobs.

Validation: The act of manually checking.

Vacuum Tube: An electronics device, also known as Valves, were used about mid 19605. After words they were replaced by transistors.

Variable: The variable also known data name. It indicates the data type (String or Numeric).

Versatile: Computer can performs any task any movement as user needs.

Video Adopter: An circuit which controls the signals for DISPLAY on the screen.

Virus: A program that effects the operating system as well as data file.

Very Large Scale Integration (VLSI): An integrated circuit having thousands of electronic circuits on a silicon chip.

Video Display Unit (VDU): An unit consists of a Cathode Ray Tube (CRT).

Von Neumann: A famous mathematician, who developed concept of stored program in 1947.

Volatile Memory: A memory that doesn't contains the previous inputted data or information if the power supply is turned off.

W

Wan: It is a data communication network, it stands for Wide Area Network, it covers a large geographic area, a district, state, country or globe. It may be through Internet (public network) or Intranet (private network).

Warm Boot: Where the computer is re-booted without turning the power off.

Wild Card: A single character or a group of character (String) which is used in retrieving items or deleting files (in DOS) when the user need.

Winchester Disk: A non-removable magnetic oxide coated disk internal to computer system. It is also known as hard disk. Initially it was developed by IBM in 1973. It has greater data storage capacity.

Windows: A great contribution of Microsoft, it provides enhanced file handling features. Because the user can open/ load more than one program or data file at once. It is also known as Graphic User Interface (GUI) operating environment.

Word: A word is the basic unit of information stored in a computer, It may consists of a 8 to 16 or 32 bits, its depends on the processor of a particular computer system.

Word Processor: It refers to a software package which is used for writing, editing, revising, deleting and printing the text or manuscripts etc.

Word Wrap: This is a significant feature of word processors that automatic replacement of the word in the next (new) line if that word is not fit at the end of the line according to the margin taken by the user.

Work Sheet: Otherwise known as Spreadsheet (in LOTUS 123/MS-EXCEl.)

Write: An work processor application software available in Windows software.

Write Protect Notch: Write protect notch on a floppy disk which prevents over writing on the previously stored information.

Xenix: It is a multi user operating system, with. the generic name UNIX was developed by AT & T. XOR ; eXclusive OR Logic operation), in which has an output of 1 if any input is 1.

XT: eXtended Technology it was developed by IBM. These computers use an 8 bits microprocessor.

ZIP: To compress a file on floppy disk using PKZIP.EXE and UNZIP is used to decompress the file using UNZIP.EXE.

14

Computer Abbreviations

ABC – American Association for the Advancement of Science

AADB – Aircraft Accident Data Base

ABC – Atanasoff-Berry Computer, Automatic Bond Width Control

ABEND – Abnormal End

ABS – Absolute

ACC – Accumulator

ACE – Automatic Computer Engine

ACIA – Asychronous Communication Interface Adapter

AD – Analog to Digital

ADC – Analog to Digital Conversion, Analog to Digital Computer

ADPS – Automatic Data Processing System

ADS – Application Development System

AGNET – Agricultural Network

AI – Artificial Intelligency

AIDS	–	Accident/Incident Database System, Artificially Intelligent Draftsman for Schematics
ALGOL	–	Algorithmic Language
ALU	–	Arithmetic Logic Unit
AM	–	Amplitude Modulation
ANSCII	–	American National Standard Code for Information Interchange
ANSI	–	American National Standard Institute
APL	–	A Programming Language
ARP	–	Address Resolution Protocol
ASCC	–	Automatic Sequence Controlled Calculator
ASCII	–	American Standard Code for Information Interchange
ASIC	–	Application-Specific Integrator Circuit Design
ASK	–	Amplitude Shift Key
ASR	–	Automatic Send and Receive
ATL	–	Automated Take Library
ATM	–	Automatic Teller Machine/Asynchronous Transfer Mode
ATN	–	Augmented Transition Network
AUX	–	Auxiliary input on an amplifier
BASIC	–	Beginners All Purpose Symbolic Instructions Code
BBC	–	British Broadcasting Corporation
BBS	–	Bulletin Board System
BCD	–	Binary Coded Decimal

BER – Bit Error Ration

BICAS – Business International Country Assessment Service

BIOS – Basic Input-Output System

BIT – Binary digit

BLT – Basic Language Transistor

BLU – Binary Logic Unit

BN – Binary Number

BOP – Bit Oriented Protocol

BOT – Beginning of the Top

BPI – Bytes Per Inch register

BPM – Batch Processing Monitor

BSC – Binary Synchronous Communication

BSN – Business Subscriber Network

BOF – Beginning of File

C-DAC – Centre for Development of Advance Computing

CAD – Computer Aided Design

CADD – Computer Aided Designing & Drafting

CAE – Computer Aided Education

CAFS – Contents Addressable File Store

CAI – Computer Aided Instruction

CAAL – Computer Aided and Augmented Learning

CALL – Computer Aided Learning Language

CAM – Computer Aided Manufacturing

CAPS – Capital letters

CAST – Computerized Accounting System of Treasury

CAT – Computer Assisted Training, Computerised Axial Tomography/Computer Addressed Training

CAV – Contain Analog Velocity

CBIS – Computer Based Information System

CBL – Computer Based Learning

CBT – Computer Based Training

CBX – Computerised Branch exchange

CCD – Change Couple Device

CCITT – Consultative Committee on International Telegraph and Telephone Compact Disk

CD – Compact Disk Erasable

CDR – Compact Disk Readable system

CD ROM – Compact Disk Read Only Memory

CDL – Computer Description Language

CGA – Colour Graphic Adapter

CGI – Common Gatetway Interface

CICS – Customer Information Control System

CIM – Computer Input Microfilm

CIMS – Computer Integrated Manufacturing System

CIR – Control Instruction Register

CISC – Complex Instruction Set Computers

CKT – Circuit

CLASS – Computer Literacy And Studies in Schools

CLI – Command Line Interface

CLS – Clear the Screen

CLV – Constant Linear Velocity

CMOS – Complementary Magnetic Oxide Semiconductor

COBOL – Common Business Oriented Language

CODASYL – Conference of Data System Language

COMAL – Common Algorithmic Language

CORAL – Class Oriented Ring Associated Language

CP/M – Control Programming for Microprocessors

CPS – Characters Per Second

CPU – Central Processing Unit

CRC – Cyclic Redundancy Check

CRT – Cathode Ray Tube

CSI – Computer Society of India

CSLIP – Compressed Serial Line Internet Protocol

CSMA – Carrier Sense Multiple Access

CSMA/CD – Carrier Sense Multiple Access with Collision Detection

CTRL – Control

CU – Control Unit

CUE – Computer Using Educators

DAA – Data Access Arrangement

DAN – Distributed Area Network

DARPA – Defence Advanced Research Project Agency

DART – Drawing Art

DASD – Direct Access Storage Device

DAT – Digital Audio Tape/Dynamic Address Translation

DATACOM – DATA COMmunication

DBASE	–	Data Base
DBMS	–	Data Base Management System
DD	–	Double Density
DDP	–	Distributed Data Processing
DEP	–	Digital Equipment Corporation
DECNET	–	DEC Network
DIM	–	Dimension
DIP	–	Dual Inline Package
DIPB	–	Distributed Information Processing Board
DIPS	–	Data Information Processing System
DMAL	–	Direct Memory Access Logic
DMP	–	Dot Matrix Printer/Direct Memory Access
DNA	–	Digital Network Architecture
DOS	–	Disk Operating System
DPI	–	Dots Per Inch
DPU	–	Display Processing Unit
DRAM	–	Dynamic Random Access Memory
DSDD	–	Double Sided Double Density
DSP	–	Digital Signal Processing
DSS	–	Decision Support System
DSSD	–	Double Sided Single Density
DTP	–	Desk Top Publishing
DDPS	–	Distributed Data Processing System
DTR	–	Data Transfer Rate
DVST	–	Direct View Storage Tube Display
EAPROM	–	Electrically Alterable PROM

EBCDIC	–	Extended Binary Coded Decimal Interchange Code
ECIL	–	Electronics Corporation of India Ltd.
ECMA	–	European Computer Manufacturing Association
EDP	–	Electronic Data Processing
EDSAC	–	Electronic Delay Storage Automatic Calculator
EEPROM	–	Electrical Erasable Programmable Read Only Memory
EFT	–	Electronic Fund Transfer
EGA	–	Enhanced Graphics Adapter
EISA	–	Extended Industry Standard Architecture
EMAIL	–	Electronic Mail
EMMS	–	Electronic Mail/Message System
ENIAC	–	Electronic Numerical Integrator And Calculator
EOF	–	End of File
XOR	–	Exclusive OR
EOT	–	End of Tape/End-of-Transmission
EPBAX	–	Electronic Private Branch Automatic Exchange
EPROM	–	Erasable PROM
ERN	–	Education and Research Network
EXP	–	Exponention
FAX	–	FAscimile Transmission
FDD	–	Floppy Disk Drive
FDDI	–	Fibre Distributed. Data Interface

FDHD – Floppy Disk with High Density

FDM – Frequency Division Multiplexing

FEP – Front End Processing

FF – Flip-Flop

FIFO – First In, First Out

FLOP – Floating Point

FM – Frequency Modulation

FNP – Front-end Network Processor

FORTRAN – Formula Translation

FSK – Frequency Shift Keying

FTP – File Transfer Protocol

GB – Giga Byte (1 GB = 1024 MB)

GIGO – Garbage in Garbage out (Garbage are unwanted data)

GPSS – General Purpose System Simulation

GT – Greater Than

GUI – Graphical User/Graphics Utility Interface

HCI – Human Computer Interface

HDD – Hard Disk Drive

HEX – Hexadecimal

HGC – Herculous Graphics Card

HIPO – Highly Input Programmable Output Hierarchy Plus Input Output

HLL – High Level Language

HOMES – Home Office Major Enquiry System

HP – Hawlett Packard Inc. (popularly known as HCL)

HRG	–	High Resolution Graphics
HSLN	–	High Speed Local Network
HTML	–	Hyper Text Markup Language
HTTP (http://)	–	Hyper Text Transfer Protocol
HTTPD	–	Hyper Text Transfer Protocol Daemon
HYPCOM	–	HYPothetical Computer
I/O	–	Input and Output
IAS	–	Intermediate Access Storage
IBG	–	Inter Block Gap
IBM	–	International Business Machine Corporation
IC	–	Integrated Circuit
ICIM	–	International Computer India Manufacturing
INT	–	Integer
ICS	–	Input/Output Control System
IP	–	Internet Protocol
IPL	–	Initial Programming Load
IPO	–	Internet Processing Output
IPX	–	Internet Work Packed exchange
IR	–	Instruction Register
IRG	–	Inter Record Gap
IRL	–	Interrupt Request Level
ISA	–	Industry Standard Architecture
ISAM	–	Index Sequential Access Method
ISCII	–	Indian Standard Code for Information Interchange

ISDN	–	Integrated Services Digital Network
ISO	–	International Standard Organisation
ISR	–	Information Storage & Retrieval
IT	–	Information Technology
ITS	–	Information Through Speech
JCL	–	Job Control Language
JUGHFAD	–	Jonzy's Universal Gopher Hierarchy Excavation and Display
K	–	Kilo Byte (lK= 1024 Byte)
KB	–	Kilo Byte, Key Board
KHz	–	Kilo Hartz
KIPS	–	Knowledge Information Processing System
KWIC	–	Key Word In Control
LAN	–	Local Area Network
LBT	–	Listen Before Talk
LCD	–	Liquid Crystal Display
LDDI	–	Local Distributed Data Interface
LED	–	Light Emitting Diode
LEN	–	Length
LHN	–	Long Haul Network
LIFO	–	Last In First Out
LILO	–	Last In Last Out
LIPS	–	Logic Information Processing System
LISP	–	List Processing
LIC	–	Logical Link Control
LOG	–	Logarithm

LOGO – Logic Oriented Language

LPM – Lines Per Minute

LSI – Large Scale Integrator

M – Mega Byte (1 M = 2024 K)

MB – Mega Byte, Mother Board

MAN – Metropolitan Area Network

MAR – Memory Address Register

MBM – Magnetic Bubble Memory

MBPS – Mega Byte Per Second

MBR – Memory Buffer Register

MCA – Micro Channel Architecture/Master of Computer Application

MCI – Media Control Interface

MDR – Memory Data Register

MFLOPS – Million of FLOating Points Per Second

MHz – Mega Hertz

MICR – Magnetic Ink Character Reader

MIDI – Musical Instrument Digital Interface

MIPS – Million Instructions Per Second

MIS – Management Information System

MME – Multi Media Extensions

MOD – Modulation

MODEM – MOdulator and Demodulator

MOS – Metal Oxide Semiconductor

MOSFET – Metal Oxide Semiconductor Field Effect Transistor

MPC	–	Multimedia PC
MS	–	Micro Soft Inc.
MSI	–	Medium Scale Integration
MUX	–	Multiplexer
NAL	–	NAtional Automatical
NAND	–	Not And
NBS	–	National Bureau of Standards
NCC	–	Network Control Centre/National Computer Centre (UK)
NCR	–	National Case Register
NIC	–	Network Interface Centre, National Informatic Centre, Network Interface Card
NIR	–	Network Information Retrieval
NLQ	–	Near Letter Quality
NOR	–	Not Or
NOS	–	Network Operating System
NS	–	Nano Second
NTP	–	Network Transfer Protocol
NCR	–	Optical Character Reader
AOCR	–	American OCR
EOCR	–	European OCR
OLE	–	Object Linking & Embedding
OMR	–	Object Mark Reading and Recognition
OS	–	Operating System
OSI	–	Open System Interconnection
PBX	–	Private Branch exchange

PC – Personal Computer, Program Control

PCAT – Personal Computer-Advanced Technology

PCDOS – Personal Computer-Disk Operating System

PCXT – Personal Computer-extended Technology

PCB – Print Circuit Board

PCM – Pulse Code Modulation

PCM – Punched Card Machine/Plug Compatible Mainframes

PDL – Program Design Language/Page Description Language/Program Design Language PDN - Public Data Network

PDP – Programmable Data Processor

PXRL – Practical Extension & Report Language

PER – Program Evolution & Review

PIA – Peripheral Interface Adapter

PIF – Program Information File

PIN – Personal Identification Number

PIPO – Parallel In Parallel Out

PISO – Parallel In Serial Out

PLI – Programming Language-I

POS – Point of Sale

PPU – Peripheral Processing Unit

PRIMENET – Prime Computers Network

PROLOG – Programming in Logic

PROM – Programmable Read Only Memory

PSTN – Public Switching Telephone Network

QAM – Quardrature Amplitude Modulation
QBE – Query By Example
QD – Quard Density
QL – Query Language
QSAM – Queed Sequential Access Method
RD – Research & Development
RAD – Random Access Disk
RAM – Random Access Memory
RDBMS – Relational Data Base Management System
RGB – Red Green Blue (Monitor)
RJC – Remote Job Control
ROM – Read Only Memory
RPG – Report Program Generation
RW – Read Write
SROM – Static Read Only Memory
SW – Software
SAD – System Analysis and Design
SCL – Semi Conductor Limited
SCSI – Small Computer System Interface
SD – Single Density/Soft Disk
SDLC – Synchronous Data Link Control
SIMLA – SIMulation LAnguage
SLIP – Serial Line Internet Protocol
SMT – Surface Mounted Technology
SMTP – Simple Mail Transfer Protocol
SNA – Systems Network Architecture

SNOBOL	–	String Oriented Symbolic Language
SQL	–	Structured Query Language
SQR	–	Square
SSDD	–	Single Sided Double Density
SGML	–	Standard Graphics Markup Language
SSSD	–	Single Sided Single Density
SVGA	–	Structured Visual Graphics Adapter
SYS	–	System
SO	–	Silicon Oxide
TAB	–	Table handling
TBE	–	Transmitter Buffer Empty
TCP	–	Transaction Control Protocol/Internet Protocol
TDM	–	Time Division Multiplexing
TIFF	–	Togged Image File Format
TIPTOP	–	Tape InPut Tape OutPut
TMC	–	Tabulation Machine Company
TOP	–	Technical and Office Protocol
TPI	–	Tracks Per Inch
TPS	–	Transaction Processing System
TTL	–	Transistor-Transistor Logic
TTS	–	Transaction Tracking System
TTY	–	Tele Typewriter
UART	–	Universal Asynchronous Receiver Transmitted
ULA	–	Unconditional/Uncommitted Logic Array
ULSI	–	Ultra Large Scale Integration

UNIVAC – Universal Automatic Computer
UPC – Universal Product Code
UPROM – Ultraviolet PROM
UPS – Un-interrupt Power Supply
USENET – User's Network
VAN – Value Added Network
VDE – Voice Data Entry
VDT – Video Display Terminal (VDU)
VDU – Visual Display Unit/Video Display Unit
VESA – Video Electronics Standard Association
VGA – Visual Graphics Adapter/Video Graphics Adapter
VLB – Vesa Local Bus
VLSI – Very Large Scale Integration
VSAT – Very Small Aperture Terminal
VT – Vacuum Tube/Voltage Transformer
WAIS – Wide Area Information Server
WAN – Wide Area Network
WATS – Wide Area Telephone Service
WCE – World Conference on Computer in Education
WFL – Work Flow Language
WIMP – Windows, lcons, Mouse, Pointer
WISS – Workstation Independent Segment Storage
WORM – Write Ones Read Many
WP – Word Processing

WPM – Words Per Minute

WWW – World Wide Web

WWWW – World Wide Web Worn

WYSIWYG – What You See is What You Get

X – Exchange/Exclusive

XGA – Extended Graphics Adapter

XNS – Xerox Network Service

XOR – Exclusively or

XT – Extended Technology

YACC – Yet Another Computer's Compiler

ZBTSI – Zero Byte Time Slot Interchange

ZCS – Zero-Code Suppression

ZD – Zero Defect

Bibliography

Agrawala, M.D., *Beginners Guide to the Internet*, TFY Publications. Delhi (1996).

Agarwal, V.B., A *Complete Course in Certificate Computer Studies*, Pitambar, New Delhi.

Balguruswami, G., *BASIC for Beginners*, Frank Bros. & Co, New Delhi.

Balmawali, Savita, *Introduction to Computer Science*, Vikas Publishing House, New Delhi.

Chakravatrty, U.C., Dastidar, L.D.G., *Software & Systems an Introductory*, Wheelers Publishing Co. Ltd., New Delhi.

Donald, H. Sanders, *Computer Today*, McGraw-Hill International, 1988.

Donovan, John.J., *System Programming*, McGraw-Hill Publishers, New Delhi.

Duncan, Neil, *Basic Computing for Schools*, Hem Kunt Press, New Delhi.

Introduction to Computer Science, ITEL Educational Solutions Ltd, Pearsons Education, New Delhi (2006).

Jaico Dictionary of Computers, Jaico Publishing House, New Delhi.

Jain, V.K., *Fundamentals of Computer*, BPB Publications, New Delhi.

Jain, R.K., *Insight into Flowcharting*, S.Chand & Co, New Delhi.

Jain, V.K., *Computer with Smile*, Holy Faith International, New Delhi.

Jain, V.K., *Information Technology (0 Level)*, BPB Publishers, New Delhi.

Kapoor, V.K., *Introduction to Computer Data Processing & System Analysis*, Sultan Chand & Sons, New Delhi.

Mehta, Subash, *Computer Formula*, Academic Publishers, New Delhi.

Mitra, Laila, *SAD and Data Management*, International Institute of Management Science, Cal.

Mukharjee, R.N., *Computer Studies*, Kalyani Publishers, Ludhiana.

Nayak, S.R, Panigrahy, R.L., *ICSE Computer Science* (Vol. 1 & Vol. 2), Allied Publishers India (P) Ltd., Calcutta. (2000).

Panigrahy, R.L., *Business Computing*, Commonwealth Publishers, New Delhi.

Patri, Digambar, *Computer Application for Beginners*, Kalyani Publishers, Ludhiana.

Rajaraman, V., *Fundamentals of Computer*, Prentice-Hall of India Pvt. Ltd., 2nd Edition, 1996.

Rajaraman, V., *Computer Programming in PASCAL*, Prentice-Hall of India Pvt. Ltd, New Delhi.

Rajaraman, V. and Rajaraman, D., *Computer Premier*, Prentice-Hall of India Pvt. Ltd, New Delhi.

Sarada, N.L, *Micro Computers*, Pitambar Publishing House, New Delhi.

Sharma, R.K., Gupta, S.K., Nayar, S., *Office Management*, Kalyani Publishers, Ludhiana.

Sinha, P.K, *Computer Fundamentals*, BPB Publications, New Delhi, 2nd Edition, 1992.

Saxsena, Sanjay, *Computer Basics & Internet*, Vikas Publishing House, New Delhi (2009).

Thomas, Robert M., *DOS 6 & 6.22 Instance Reference*, BPB Publications, New Delhi.

Wikipedia Encyclopedia.

Index

R

S

T

U

V

W